Tokyo

Japan

KNOPF
CITY GUIDES

THIS IS A BORZOI BOOK PUBLISHED BY ALFRED A. KNOPF

Published in the United States by Alfred A. Knopf, a division of Random House, Inc., New York, and simultaneously in Canada by Random House of Canada Limited, Toronto. Distributed by Random House, Inc., New York.

www.aaknopf.com

Knopf, Borzoi Books, and the colophon are registered trademarks of Random House, Inc.

Tokyo:
ISBN 0-375-70963-0
First American Edition

Originally published in France by Nouveaux Loisirs, a subsidiary of Gallimard, Paris 2000, and in Italy by Touring Editore, Srl., Milano 2000.

SERIES EDITORS: Anne-Josyane Magniant & Marisa Bassi
TOKYO EDITION:
Sophie Lenormand with Isabelle Dubois-Dumée
GRAPHICS:
Élizabeth Cohat, Yann Le Duc
LAYOUT:
Olivier Lauga, Yann Le Duc
MAPS: Édigraphie
STREET MAPS: Touring Club Italiano
PRODUCTION:
Catherine Bourrabier

Translated by Susan Liddington
Edited and typeset by First Edition Translations Ltd, Cambridge, UK

Printed in Italy by Editoriale Lloyd

Authors

Getting there: Yann Perreau (1)
A research student in philosophy and mad about travel, Yann Perreau spent five years on the move between Africa and Asia. His two-year stay in Tokyo gave him the key to understanding the Japanese capital and to decoding the customs of daily life in Japan.

Where to stay:
Angela Jeffs-Ueda (2)
A weekly columnist for *The Japan Times*, A. Jeffs-Ueda has been a freelance journalist in Tokyo since 1986. Formerly a London-based editorial consultant, she has a real passion for travel, and so a knowledge of hotels worldwide. This enables her to affirm that 'Japanese hospitality is unequaled anywhere and totally unique'.

Where to eat:
Matsuhiro Yamamoto (3)
The food critic M. Yamamoto produces the annual *Dible Tōkyō*, a guide to restaurants in Tokyo. His editorial collaboration on numerous guides and culinary articles has enabled him to become well acquainted with Japanese restaurateurs.

After dark: Stephen Comee (4)
Career journalist and nō actor, S. Comee is a regular writer of articles on Japan and the East for Tokyo magazines. An *aficionado* of Asian cuisine, wines and saké, his zest for having a good time has been reinforced by the Japanese custom of going out with colleagues after work.

What to see and **Further afield:** Stephen Mansfield (5)
An English journalist and photographer living in the Japanese capital, S. Mansfield regularly covers major stories on Asia and Japan for over 80 magazines throughout the world. The author of several travel guides, he is a specialist on Laos, a country on which he has already written four books.

Where to shop: Takeshi Matsuyama (6)
A lover of the traditional Japanese arts, M. Matsuyama is the author of works on the Japanese way of life: *Appreciating China Tea*, *The Pleasure of Travel in Japan*, *The Way of Life in Kyōtō*. Since 1970, he has worked on Japanese magazines such as *Men's Ex*.

Key

- telephone number
- fax number
- price of price range
- opening hours
- credit cards accepted
- credit cards not accepted
- toll-free number
- e-mail/web site address
- ★ tips and recommendation

Access

- subway
- bus
- private parking
- parking attendant
- no facilities for the disabled
- train
- car
- boat

Hotels

- telephone in room
- fax in room on request
- mini-bar in room
- television in room
- air conditioning in room
- 24 hours room service
- caretaker
- babysitting
- meeting room(s)
- no pets
- breakfast
- open for tea/coffee
- restaurant
- live music
- disco
- garden, patio or terrace
- gym, fitness club
- swimming pool, sauna

Restaurants

- vegetarian food
- view
- formal dress required
- smoking area
- bar

Sightseeing

- on-site store(s)
- guided tours
- café

Stores

- branches, outlets

The Insider's Guide is made up of **8 sections** indicated by a different color.

Things you need to know (mauve);
Where to stay (blue);
Where to eat (red);
After dark (pink);
What to see (green);
Further afield (orange
Where to shop (yellow
Finding your way (pur

Ningyōchō Sushi ●●●
In the heart of old Tokyo

Practical information is given for each particular establishment: opening times, prices, ways of paying, different services available.

"Bargain"
This star marks good value hotels and restaurants.

How to use this guide

In the area

➔ **Where to stay:** ➥ 20 ➥ 2

➔ **After dark:** ➥ 68

➔ **What to see:** ➥ 86 ➥ 88

➔ **Where to shop:** ➥ 126 ➥

The section **"In the area"** refers you (➥00) to other establishments that are covered in a different section of the guide but found in the same area of the city.

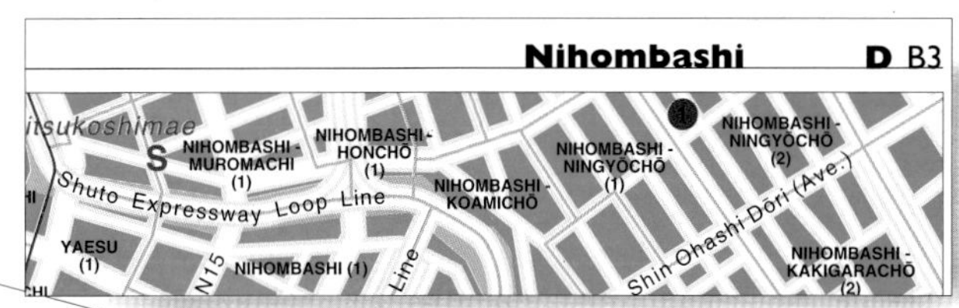

The small map shows all the establishments mentioned and others described elsewhere but found "in the area" by the color of the section.

The name of the district is given above the map. A grid reference (**A** B-C 2) enables you to find it in the section on Maps at the end of the book.

Not forgetting

■ 伊勢廣 **Isehiro (5)** 1-5-4 Kyōba

A small, traditional building in an alleyw

The section "Not forgetting" lists other useful addresses in the same area.

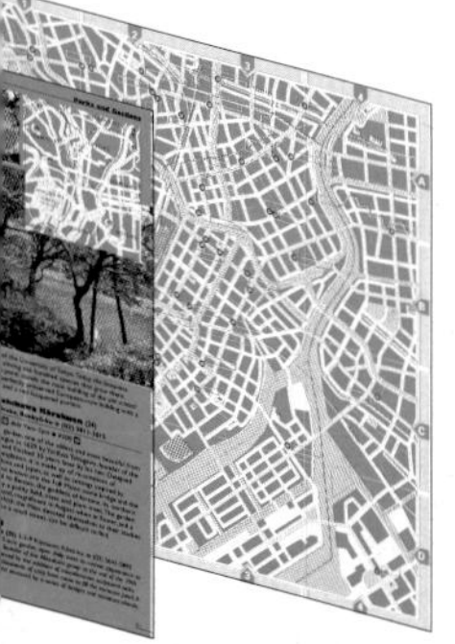

The opening page to each section contains an index ordered alphabetically (Getting there), by subject or by district (After dark) as well as useful addresses and advice.

The section "Things you need to know" covers information on getting to Tokyo and day-to-day life in the city.

Theme pages introduce a selection of establishments on a given topic.

The "Maps" section of this guide contains 7 street plans of Tokyo followed by a detailed index.

Formalities

No visa is required by tourists for stays of less than 90 days, but passports must be valid for six months after the date of return. For longer periods, or visits for business purposes, inquire at the Embassy in the UK: *101 Piccadilly, London W1V ☎ 020 7465 6500;* in the US: *2520 Massachusetts Avenue NW, Washington DC 20008 ☎ 202 238 6700*

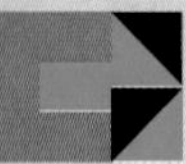

Getting there

Cash

Plan to take a small amount of Japanese currency in cash before departure. This will be necessary to pay for connecting transport services.

Electrical current

Operates at 110 volts and 50 Hz in Tokyo (60 Hz in the west of Japan). You may therefore need an adapter and a transformer to use electrical appliances made in other countries. Some hotels are equipped with 220-volt sockets.

Driver's licenses

You can rent a car on arriving in Japan if you have an international driver's license, which you should be able to procure locally before you leave. If your license is not in Japanese, consult the Japanese Automobile Federation. 🕓 Mon.–Fri. 9am–4.30pm • ¥3,000; allow 1–2 days ***JAF*** *Masonic 39 Mori Bldg 1F, 2-4-5 Azabudai, Minato-ku ☎ (03) 3578-4910 ➟ (03) 3578-4911*

Time difference

When it is 8pm in Tokyo, it is noon in London and 7am in New York.

Japan National Tourist Organization
One Rockefeller Plaza, Suite 1250, New York, NY 10020 ☎ 212 757 5640
➡ 212 307-6754
Heathcoat House, 20 Savile Row, London, W1X 1AE ☎ 020 7734 9638
➡ 020 7734 4290
The Tourist Organization has a great deal of useful information to help you prepare for your trip (accommodation, transport services, itineraries, museums). **www.jnto.go.jp**

41 Things you need to Know

Websites:
www.bento.com
www.japan-guide.com
www.tokyoclassified.com

To call Tokyo
From the US:
011 81 3 + number
From the UK:
00 81 3 + number

Public holidays

If a public holiday falls on a Sunday, the following Monday becomes a holiday. Public services and museums are closed from December 28 to January 3.

January 1 *Shōgatsu* (New Year's Day)
January 5 *Seijin no hi* (Adults' Day)
February 1 *Kenkoku Kinen no hi* (National Foundation Day)
March 21 *Shunbun no hi* (Spring Equinox Day)
April 29 *Midori no hi* (Green Day)
May 3 *Kenpo Kinenbi* (Constitution Day, 1947)
May 5 *Kodomo no hi* (Children's Day)
July 20 *Umi no hi* (Marine Day)
September 15 *Keiro no hi* (Respect-for-the-Aged Day)
September 23 *Shūnbun no hi* (Fall Equinox Day)
October 10 *Taīku no hi* (Health and Sports Day)
November 3 *Bunka no hi* (Culture Day)
November 23 *Kinro Kansha no hi* (Labor Thanksgiving Day)
December 23 *Tennō Tanjō Bi* (Emperor Akihito's Birthday)

INDEX (A-Z)

Basic facts

The Land of the Rising Sun is about twelve hours' flying time from Europe or the west coast of the US. All international flights, apart from those of China Airlines, land at Narita, located about 44 miles to the northeast of Tokyo. National flights land at Haneda airport, which is much closer.

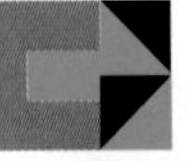

Getting there

Airports

Narita (1)
International flights land at both Narita terminals, depending on the company, while national flights land at Terminal 2.

Flight info
☎ *(0476) 34-5000*

Tourist Information Center (TIC)
These information booths will give you details of tourist sites and available accommodation depending on your budget. They are to be found on the ground floor of each terminal.
☎ *(0476) 34-6251*
⌚ *9am–8pm*

Exchange
If you forgot to change money before leaving home, you are advised to do so at the airport, as all forms of transport into Tokyo have to be paid for in cash.
⌚ *daily 7am–10pm*

Lost & Found
Go to the Airport Information Center.
☎ *(0476) 32-2105*
Terminal 2
☎ *(0476) 34-5220*

Hotels
Some flights arrive very late at night. Choose a room in one of the 16 hotels nearby. Hotel shuttles will take you there.

Hotel Nikko
☎ *(0476) 32-0032*
● *¥17,000*

Holiday Inn Tobu
☎ *(0476) 32-1234*
● *¥16,000* ☕ *inc.*

Narita Airport Rest House
☎ *(0476) 32-1212*
● *¥13,200*

Marroad International Hotel Narita
☎ *(0476) 30-2222*
● *¥13,000*

Day-rooms & shower-rooms
A compromise solution is to rent a room by the hour in the airport, or pay for a shower to freshen up.
⌚ *7am–9pm*
● *single ¥600/hr; double ¥900/hr; shower ¥350/ 30 mins*

Terminal 1
2nd floor
☎ *(0476) 32-4734*

Terminal 2
2nd floor
☎ *(0476) 34-8537*

Rest room

Terminal 2
3rd floor
☎ *(0476) 34-8537*
⌚ *daily 5–10pm*

Haneda (2)
This airport, located about 12½ miles to the south of Tokyo, only accommodates national carriers and China Airlines. Services are more limited than at Narita. There is no TIC but the airport's information booth provides maps of Tokyo.

Information
☎ *(03) 5757-8111*

Airport connections

Narita-Tokyo

Bus
Serves all the major city hotels, Tokyo City Air Terminal (T-CAT) to Chūo-ku, Tokyo station and Shinjuku station. Tickets available at the counters in the arrival lobby.

Airport Limousine
☎ *(03) 3665-7220*

every 20 mins; journey time 1–2hrs
● *one-way ¥2,700–3,600*

Train
Two railroad companies provide a connection with the city.

JR Line
The Narita Express, the fastest connecting service, links the airport to Tokyo's main train stations. Reservations essential.
☎ *(03) 3423-0111*
7.43am–9.42pm, every 30 mins; journey time 1hr–1hr 30 mins
● *one-way ¥3,000–4,200*

Keisei Line
The cheaper Skyliner takes you to Ueno.
☎ *(0476) 32-8512*
7.50am–9.58pm; every 20 mins; journey time 1 hr
● *one-way approx. ¥2,000*

Taxi
Extremely expensive.
● *¥30,000 minimum*

Haneda-Tokyo

Monorail
Links the airport to Hamamatsu-chō station, Yamanote line
➡ 150 in 20 mins.
5.20am–11.15pm
● one-way approx. ¥500

Narita-Haneda

Bus
Only direct means of transport.

Airport Limousine
☎ *(03) 3665-7220*
every 15 mins; journey time 1–2 hrs
● *one-way ¥2,700*

Train (3)

The railroad is still the cheapest means of transport, also revealing the magnificent wild countryside.

Shinkansen
This bullet train is one of the technological symbols of modern-day Japan. It covers over 1,125 miles at an average speed of 131mph.
Osaka-Tōkyō in 3 hrs; departures every hour
● *one-way approx. ¥13,500.*

Japan Rail Pass
This pass allows unlimited travel in Japan ➡ 10.

Trans-Siberian
A unique experience if rather long (15 days). The journey takes you from Moscow to Nakhodka (north of Vladivostok); then by boat to the port of Yokohama. You can take the train as far as Beijing, then reach Japan by airplane. Visas essential.

Boat (4)

As a result of the damaging effect of the airplane on maritime traffic, there are only three ways of reaching Japan by sea. All start in neighboring countries.
● *one-way ¥16,000–25,000*

Nakhodka (CEI)-Yokohama
The last stage of the Trans-Siberian rail journey.

Pusan (Korea)-Osaka
4 times/week; 24 hrs

Taiwan-Okinawa
Okinawa Thu. or Fri.; Taiwan Mon.

Basic facts

The city of Tokyo is multi-centered, with the Imperial Palace ➡ 86 at its heart. Encircled by the major Yamanote railroad line, 11 of the 23 districts *(ku)* of greater Tokyo contain most of the economic activity of the city, as well as the historic and cultural sites.

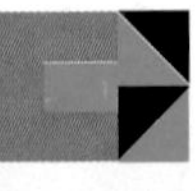

Getting around

Addresses

The city is divided into *ku* (administrative districts), which are themselves divided into numbered *chome* or *banchi* (quarters). These consist of blocks of streets that are also numbered. So, to find an address in Tokyo, all you need to know is that the first figure corresponds to the *chome*, the second to the block and the third to the building. For example, Sunaba restaurant ➡ 48, whose address is 6-3-5 Akasaka, Minato-ku, is in the Minato district in the 6th quarter of Akasaka in block No 3 at No 5. Wherever you are going it is advised to have your destination written in Japanese on a piece of paper, with the name of a nearby landmark.

Signposting
Blue signs on street corners or on telegraph poles show the *ku*, the *chome* and their numbers, as well as that of the block.

Floors
Some addresses specify the name of the building as well as the floor. The Japanese use the American system, in which 1F is the ground floor, 2F the next floor up, etc.

Koban
There are over 1,250 mini-police stations at major crossroads to help both the locals and tourists to find their way.

On foot

Tokyo is a city where many people walk. Respect the traffic signals, as do the Japanese. Never cross the street outside the crosswalk or when cars have the green signal.

Transport

Given the size of the city, public transport has a major role to play. There is a wide choice from the JR to private railroads, subways, buses, taxis and the monorail.

Information
☎ *(03) 3834-5577*

Timetables
🕔 *5am–midnight*
Some stations close at the weekend and on public holidays.

Signposting
Every line has its own color and name.

JR trains
The 22½-mile long, circular JR Yamanote Line (see map) links up the main quarters.

Information (in English)
☎ *(03) 3423-0111*
All the subway lines connect up at one point or another with the Yamanote Line.

Subway ➡ 150
(chikatetsu)
Clean and safe, the subway is also the fastest means of transport. Directions are indicated by the name of the terminus, interchanges by circles in the color of each line and exits by yellow signs marked 'Exit'. Eight of the 12 lines are operated by the TRTA (Teito Rapid Transit Authority), and the four others, called TOEI, by the city. The latter are slightly more expensive.

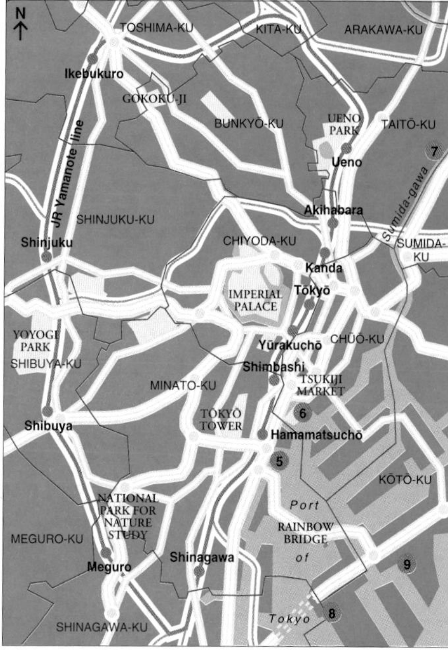

Information
Ask for the English brochure *Subways in Tokyo* at TRTA ticket offices. This is a useful guide to how they work.
☎ *(0476) 34-8537*
🕑 *9am–6pm*

Tickets
Every network has its own type of ticket. They can be bought from the machines at each station. Some give information in English, but if you aren't sure of your destination – prices depend on distance – buy the cheapest ticket. You can pay the difference to the *Seisancho* (ticket collector) or at the 'Fare adjustment' machines at the exit.

Tickets
● *JR ¥130 minimum; subway ¥160–190*

Cards
A more advantageous way to travel about freely. The amount due for the journey is automatically deducted at the exit point. Subway cards can be used on the TRTA and TOEI lines. Buy them at the subway ticket machines, except for JR cards, which are obtained at a special machine.

SF Card (subway)
● *¥1,000, ¥2,000, ¥3,000*

Orange Card (JR)
● *¥1,000, ¥3,000, ¥5,000, ¥10,000*

Japan Rail Pass
Lets you travel at very reduced prices over the whole national JR network and on the *shinkansen*. Only valid for stays of less than 90 days. Buy it before you leave home from a travel agent specializing in Japanese vacations.

Buses *(basu)*

Currently, taking the bus is a bit of an adventure… but you should try it if you want to see the city cheaply. Apart from some lines, the signs are in Japanese. A single tariff, whatever the distance. Have ¥100 coins ready to pay the exact fare. ● *¥200*

Taxi *(takushī)*

Only to be used for short distances. One trip can quickly add up to ¥2,000–3000. A free taxi can be recognized by the red light located in the front (green if occupied). Do not attempt to get in before the driver opens the doors.
● Minimum fare ¥660 for 1 1/4 miles, then ¥181.25/mile; 30% higher at night.

Waterbus

A trip on the Sumida-gawa to Asakusa ➡ 104 or Odaiba Island ➡ 108.

Tōkyō Cruise Ship
☎ *(03) 3841-9178*
● *¥350-660*

Car

Driving around Tokyo is not recommended. You must keep to the left, signs are in Japanese, streets are overcrowded and parking spaces very hard to find. If you still want to try, bring your international driver's license.

Location
● *¥7,000-9,000/day*

Dollar Rent-a-car
☎ *(03) 3485-7196*

Hertz
☎ *(0120) 489-882*

Toyota
☎ *(03) 3264-0100*

Basic facts

Aware of the problems posed by their language, Tokyo residents try to find ways of simplifying the day-to-day life of visitors: *Koban* (local mini-police stations) to give you information; bilingual signs, even in the case of *jishin* (earthquake); special telephone numbers in English…

Getting by

Tourism

TIC - Tourist Information Center (10)
Tōkyō International Forum Bldg B1F, 3-5-1 Marunouchi, Chiyoda-Ku
☎ *(03) 3201-3331*
Mon.–Fri. 9am–5pm; Sat. 9am–noon; closed public holidays
M *Ginza, Yurakucho*
Multilingual staff, literature, maps and books on the Japanese way of life. Hotel reservation office on site:
Welcome Inn
9.15am–noon, 1–5.15pm (Last reservation 30 mins before closing)

Guides
For a guided tour of Tokyo, call on the services of a guide-interpreter.
Japanese Guides Association
Shin Kokusai Bldg, 3-4-1 Marunouchi, Chiyoda-ku
☎ *(03) 3212-2706*

Embassies

British Embassy
Ichibancho, Chiyoda-ku, http://www.uknow.or.jp/be/index_e.html
☎ *(03) 5211-1100*
US Embassy
1-10-5 Akasaka, Minato-ku, http://usembassy.state.gov/posts/ja1/wwwhmain.html
☎ *(03) 3224-5000*

Money

The Japanese use cash for almost all their purchases. As a result, few establishments apart from those with a more international outlook accept credit cards. Don't be afraid to carry a lot of money, as Tokyo is a very safe city.

Coins/notes
The monetary unit is the yen (¥)
Coins: ¥1, 5, 10, 50, 100, 500
Notes: ¥1,000, 5,000, 10,000

Banks
Tokyo isn't short of banks. However, they don't all carry out exchange transactions, or provide 'cash in advance'. The most efficient are Sumitomo, Fuji, Mitsubishi and Citibank.
Mon.–Fri. 9am–3pm

Exchange
¥106=$1, 160=£1, correct at the time of printing.

Traveler's checks
Change them in banks with the sign '*Authorized Foreign Exchange Bank*'. Outside opening hours, inquire at major hotels or *depato* (department stores ➡ 126).

Credit cards
Be warned, few automatic cashpoints take foreign cards. Try those at Citibank, open 24hrs.
Info Citibank
(0120) 504 189

Tips
Under no circumstances.

Media

National press
In English or bilingual
Dailies
Available in kiosks in stations and the major hotels.
Japan Times; Asahi Evening News; Daily Yomiuri; Mainichi
Weeklies
Time; Newsweek
Monthlies
Hiragana Times; Tōkyō Journal; Japan Select Magazine

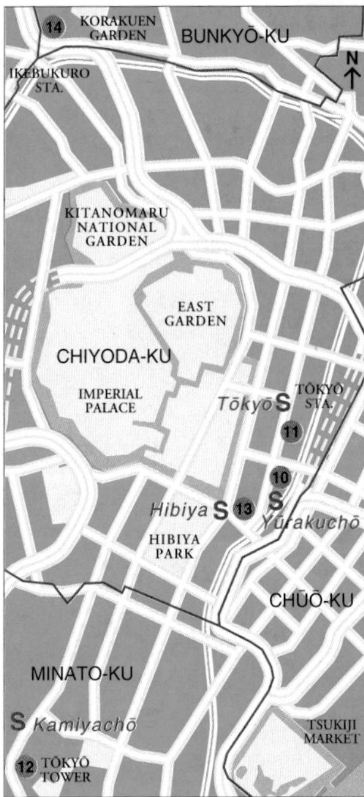

International press

Magazine House
3-13-10 Ginza, Chūō-ku
☎ *(03) 3545-7227*
🕒 *Mon.–Fri. 10am–7pm*

Mail *(Yūbinkyoku)*

Red mail boxes for national mail and blue for international.

Central post office (11)
2-7 Marunouchi, Chiyoda-ku
☎ *(03) 5472-5852*
🕒 *Mon.–Fri. 9am–5pm; Sat. 9am–3pm*
● *postcard ¥70; letter ¥110*

Telephone

Local telephone service run by NTT, international by ITJ and KDD

Information
Local
(0120) 36-4463
🕒 *Mon.–Fri. 9am–5pm (in English)*

International
Telephone Number System Dialing codes
☎ *0057*

Telephone number system

Dialing codes
0476 Narita;
03 Tokyo;
045 Yokohama

International

Tokyo–UK–US
Dial the code of one of the companies, 001 (KDD), 0041 (ITJ), 0061 (IDC), followed by 00 44 for UK, 00 1 for US then the number (without the 0).

UK–US–Tokyo
Dial 010 81 from the US or 00 81 from the UK then the code (without the 0) and the number.

Public telephones

Local calls
● *¥10 for each 3 mins*

Cards
Available in machines near to or inside appointed shops. NTT cards are not valid for overseas calls.
● *¥1,000*

International calls
Only gray call boxes displaying the sign 'International' or 'ISDN' can be used.

Cards
● *¥1 000-5 000*

Health

Tokyo Medical Clinic (12)
Doctors speaking English; pharmacy on the ground floor.
32 Mori Bldg, 3-4-30 Shiba-Kōen, Minato-ku
☎ *(03) 3436-3028*
🕒 *Mon.–Fri. 9am–5pm; Sat. 9am–1pm*

Emergencies
🕒 *daily 24 hrs*

American Pharmacy (13)
1-8-1 Yūrakuchō, Chiyoda-ku
☎ *(03) 3271-4034*
🕒 *Mon.–Sat. 9.30am–7.30pm; Sun. 10am–6.30pm*

Lost & found *(Wasuremono)*

Nothing gets lost in Tokyo. Most articles are taken to one of these offices.

General (14)
Metropolitan police
1-9-11 Koraku, Bunkyō-ku
☎ *(03) 3814-4151*

JR Train
☎ *(03) 3423-0111*

TRTA subway
☎ *(03) 3834-5577*

Heidan subway
☎ *(03) 3834-5577*

Taxis
☎ *(03) 3648-0300*

Emergencies

Police ☎ *110*
☎ *(03) 5472-5851 (in English)*

Fire service
☎ *119*

For Westerners, almost every detail of Japanese life seems very foreign. Certainly, the difficulty of the language does not help, but armed with a bit of curiosity and a few clues, the gates to eternal Japan, a country which was closed in on itself for many years, will open up to you.

Getting by

Ablutions

The Japanese toilet ritual in no way resembles our own. As a rule, you must wash and rinse yourself completely using the equipment provided (stool, basin and ladle) before entering the high, square bath to relax. You can dispense with these rules in your hotel bathroom, but you will have to apply them in the *ryokan* ➡ 18, *sento* and *onsen*.

Sento *(15)* *(public baths)*
Frequenting public baths is still customary in Japan. Each district has at least one. When you go, take soap, shampoo, towel and a basin. Put your clothes in a locker in the changing rooms provided, and wash in the communal room. Then immerse yourself in the hot or very hot baths.

Onsen *(hot springs)*
The volcanic mountains around Tokyo abound in hot springs ➡ 112, 122.

Traditional arts

Westerners call them hobbies, but in Japan they are considered an art, even a Zen spiritual quest. *Chadō*, *shodō* and *kadō*, in which *dō* means 'the way of', are ways of creating harmony between nature and man and attaining serenity by respecting the rules. Information from the TIC ➡ 10.

***Chadō (tea ceremony)* (16)**
This ceremony goes back to the Nara period (710–784) when it was performed by the monks to keep themselves alert while meditating. It follows a very strict ritual needing a mental discipline formerly required of samurais ➡ 80.

Kadō (ikebana)
The aim of this 15th-century art is to create a floral composition that represents the balance between heaven, earth and humanity.

Shodō (calligraphy)
In the Heian period (794–1192), fine writing was a sign of learning. Priests, samurais and the nobility cultivated this highly regarded art, which is still taught in schools.

Courtesy

The Japanese don't expect Westerners to understand all the rules of behaviour; but they appreciate it if you make an effort. Try adding 'san' at the end of a person's name, so that 'Mrs Aoki' becomes 'Mrs Aokisan'. Even if you know no Japanese but want to thank someone or apologize, do so in English; the Japanese are sensitive to intonation and will understand the intention.

Gifts
Japan is a country of gifts. You must never arrive empty handed. Gifts are never opened in the giver's presence, to avoid embarrassment. If you

18

16

receive one, you should give one of the same value in return.

Appointments
Telephone to confirm and always arrive five minutes early.

Greetings
The Japanese dislike all physical contact. They will now shake hands, but don't grip too firmly. Too much eye contact can offend, and they like to keep personal space around themselves. The one exception is the rush hour, when everyone is tightly packed on the subway. The *ojigi* (Japanese bow of greeting) is famous worldwide. It is used to say *ohayō* (good morning), *konnichiwa* (hello), *konbawa* (good evening), *sayōnara* (goodbye), *arigatō* (thank you) or even *sumimasen* (sorry). The depth of the bow depends on the relationship.

Meishi ***(visiting cards)***
If you speak to a Japanese for more than two minutes, it is customary to exchange visiting cards, in English and Japanese, of course.

Avoid...
...blowing your nose in public. This gesture is considered vulgar, although it is quite in order to clear your throat and eat your *ramen* (noodles) noisily. Pointing with the index finger is thought rude; point with the whole hand, palm up.

Religion

Even if the Japanese say they are non-practicing, many of their ritual gestures and remarks show that religion has merged in them with thought and action.

Shintoism
The ancestral religion of Japan. This form of animism is based on the cult of multiple divinities, *kami*, the most famous of which is the Emperor, deified until 1945.

Buddhism *(17)*
Imported from Korea in the 6th century, there are now numerous schools, including Zen. They have in common the avoidance of philosophical complications while addressing themselves to the practical, to the heart rather than reason.

Confucianism
Confucius taught the principle of a naturally ordered and hierarchic society. This ethical code is seen in Japan in the obedience and respect displayed by the people to their leaders, the child to the father, the employee to the employer...

Seasons *(18)*

The seasons regulate the daily actions of the Japanese. The choice of color or motif for a kimono, of ingredients for a meal ➥40, of the dishes in which it is served, or even of the interior décor... is a response to natural laws dictated by the seasons.

Last trains

When you make your reservations, remember that all trains stop at midnight. If you're a night owl, go for a lively area such as Roppongi, Shinjuku or Ikebukuro in order to avoid expensive taxi rides after midnight.

Where to stay

Ryokan

Staying in a Japanese guesthouse will give you a better understanding of the Japanese mentality. Very modest in capacity but offering a warm and friendly welcome, rooms in the *ryokan* are sparsely furnished: a low table at which to eat and a cupboard for the futon, which is laid straight onto the *tatamis* at night.

Love hotels

Given the cramped nature of Japanese apartments, 'love hotels' are designed for parents (or children) looking for a touch of intimacy, as well as devotees of the afternoon tryst. Recognizable by their crazy architecture, tinted windows and pink or mauve neon signs.

Capsule hotels

Located in the vicinity of train stations, these substitute hotels are recommended for those who have missed the last train. Cubicle-coffins equipped with an alarm clock and a television. To be avoided by claustro-phobics and tall people.

Prices

Prices are for one night in a standard double room for two people. Taxes are not included (5%, plus 10% service). Be warned, if the total price for one night's stay is over ¥15,000, a local tax of 3% will be added.

55

Hotels

THE INSIDER'S FAVORITES

Reservations

It becomes difficult to find a room in Tokyo during national holiday periods linked to festivals ➡80, and at the end of February when the city fills up with the thousands of students who come to sit their university entrance exams.

Japanese National Tourism Office: *☎ (03) 3211-4201 ➡ (03) 3211-9009*
Japan Ryokan Association*: ☎ (03) 3231-5310 ➡ (03) 3201-5797*
Japan Hotel Association*: ☎ (03) 3279-2706 ➡ (03) 3274-5375*
Japanese Inn Group*: ☎ (03) 3843-2345 ➡ 03) 3483-2348*

INDEX BY PRICE

5 PRICE CATEGORIES FOR HOTELS
● less than ¥10,000
●● ¥10,000 – 20,000
●●● ¥ 20,000 – 30,000
●●●● ¥ 30,000 – 40,000
●●●●● ¥ 40,000 and over

Staying in a traditional guesthouse is the best way to discover the atmosphere of eternal Japan. You will sleep on futons laid out on *tatami* mats. They are put away during the day, and only made up at night. Be aware that as most of the *ryokan* are run by families, you will have to be back before 11pm. Check when you make your reservations.

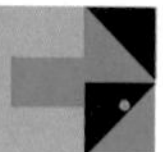

Where to stay

Kimi Ryokan (1)

2-10-34 Ikebukuro, Toshima-ku ☎ (03) 3971-3766 ➟ (03) 3987-1326

M *JR Ikebukuro* ***42 rooms*** ●

This small family-run guesthouse, clean and bright, is well liked by its regular visitors. The rooms are simple and pleasant, and the communal bathrooms immaculate. No meals are served, but on the other hand, you can watch television and drink tea in the lobby. English spoken.

Suzuki Ryokan (2)

7-15-23 Yanaka, Taitō-ku ☎ (03) 3821-4944

M *JR Nippori* ***10 rooms*** ●

Lovers of the real Japan will be enchanted by this guesthouse, located near the entrance to the Yanaka cemetery ➥ 106 and bursting with charm. Even if the members of staff are sometimes a trifle sullen, this does no more than contribute to its unpretentious authenticity.

Suigetsu Hotel / Ryokan Ogai-so (3)

3-3-21 Ikenohata, Taitō-ku ☎ (03) 3828-3181 ➟ (03) 3823-4340

M *Nezu* ***123 rooms*** ●● *Shara-no-ki* *Katsura*

This pair of hotels, the only ones of their type, share a block in the old quarter of Nezu. The staff only have a smattering of English at best, but this doesn't stop them being very pleasant and helpful. If sleeping Japanese-style doesn't suit you, just ask for a Western-style room.

Sukeroku no Yado Sadachiyo (4)

2-20-1 Asakusa, Taitō-ku ☎ (03) 3842-6431 ➟ (03) 3842-6433

M *Tawaramachi* ***20 rooms*** ●● @ *front@sadachiyo.co.jp*

Willows and lanterns lead you to this very select *ryokan*, which prides itself on having kept up the ancestral Edo traditions. The kimono-clad staff, brimming with goodwill, speak only a little English. The rooms are all different sizes, the smallest only five *tatamis* wide (about 86 sq ft). Ask about special rates for long stays.

Ryokan Asakusa Shigetsu (5)

1–31-11 Asakusa, Taitō-ku ☎ (03) 3843-2345 ➟ (03) 3843-2348

M *Asakusa* ***23 rooms*** ●● @ *info@shigetsu.com*

Run by the same family for years, this *ryokan* welcomes an enthusiastic foreign clientele. The rooms, with bathroom, are of various dimensions and styles. However, don't be afraid to share the Japanese-style baths on the top floor, from which you can take in all the old quarter of Asakusa ➥ 104. English spoken.

Not forgetting

■ **Ryokan Ryumeikan Honten (6)** 3–4 Kanda-Surugadai, Chiyoda-ku ☎ (03) 3251-1135 ➟ (03) 3251-0270 ●● *A place worth searching out despite the lack of signs in roman script and the look of the area. The Hamada family has been running this establishment for over a century and a dozen very pretty Japanese-style rooms are on offer, accompanied by wholly traditional service.*

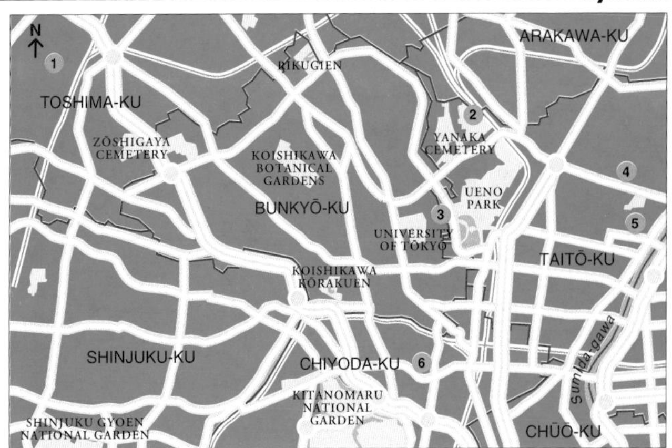

Ryokan customs:
Take your shoes off at the door and use the *surippa* (slippers) supplied to walk in the communal areas; take them off before entering your room.
Avoid putting your luggage away behind the *shoji* (screen) and the *tokonoma* (alcove) which are purely decorative and ceremonial.
When you walk around the *ryokan*, wear the *yukata* (dressing gown), ensuring that you cross the left side over the right.
Observe the custom of ablutions in the communal baths ➥ 14.

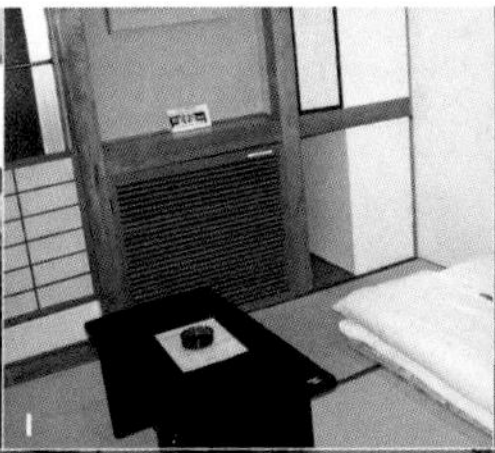

In the area

Where to eat: 42 ➡ 44 ➡ 46
After dark: ➡ 68
What to see: 84 ➡ 88 ➡ 110
Where to shop: 126 ➡ 128

Where to stay

Palace Hotel (7)

1-1 Marunouchi, Chiyoda-ku ☎ (03) 3211-5211 ➡ (03) 3211-6987

M *Otemachi* ***389 rooms*** *(of which 3 suites)* ●●●●● *Crown* *Crown Lounge, Royal Bar* *Humming*

The prestigious location of this hotel, opposite the Imperial Palace, attracts the international business elite. Some rooms are literally regal and two floors are reserved for non-smokers. The décor, luxurious and devoid of ornament, exudes a relaxed and refined atmosphere, and occasionally you will see ladies in sumptuous kimonos gracefully passing each other in the lobby. The vast drawing-room terrace, used in summer, gives directly onto the moat. Swans gliding across the water add a touch of serenity to the view.

Kokusai Kankō Hotel (8)

1-8-3 Marunouchi, Chiyoda-ku ☎ (03) 3215-3281 ➡ (03) 3215-1140

M *JR Tōkyō* ***94 rooms*** *(of which 2 suites)* ●●● *Fontaine, Kokusai Hanten, Kitamachi* *Avon* *Lila*

Visitors are welcomed in the European manner in the gloss-painted green and cream-white lobby, where you will see a very pretty painting, depicting barges in Amsterdam (Kokusai means 'international'), by the contemporary artist Shigehiko Ishikawa. The rooms are simply furnished. The whole ensemble gives an impression of luxury, but western visitors will have to do without the small comforts they are used to. You will get some idea of the clientele at the Lila, the café on the first floor. Those who survive its smoky soirées manage to keep smiling as they are handed their checks, which are somewhat steep but justified by the ideal location of the establishment.

Tōkyō Station Hotel (9)

1-9-1 Marunouchi, Chiyoda-ku ☎ (03) 3231-2511 ➡ (03) 3231-3513

M *JR Tōkyō* P ***59 rooms*** ●●● *Camellia, Oak Bar* *Garnette*

This hotel, housed in a wing of Tokyo Station ➡ 88, is redolent of the past. The red carpet leads to the lobby on the first floor, where the dark wood and the period fitments accentuate its faded charm. The rooms sport drapes with pompons at the windows, but manage to avoid descending into kitsch thanks to their sunny colors. Business and political leaders appreciate the traditional atmosphere of the establishment's bars and restaurants. Coffee is served in a delightful snug little lounge at the back.

Yaesu Fujiya Hotel (10)

2-9-1 Yaesu, Chūō-ku ☎ (03) 3273-2111 ➡ (03) 3273-2180

M *JR Tōkyō* P ***377 rooms*** ●● *Wisteria, Vent Vert* *Oak House* *L'Avenue*

This high-class, comfortable establishment dates from 1985. It targets the Japanese businessman with its resolutely male atmosphere. The neighboring sports store is further proof of that if proof were needed. The tiled mural in the lobby has the four seasons as its theme, and there is a majestic staircase with a brass banister. The pot plants seem to show off, and the flowers themselves look unbending. There is a fine panoramic view from the upper stories.

The Tõkyõ railway station is a reminder of the Meiji era, and is considered a historic monument. Built opposite the Imperial Palace, it serves the financial areas of Marunouchi and Otemachi to the west and the business district of Nihombashi to the east.

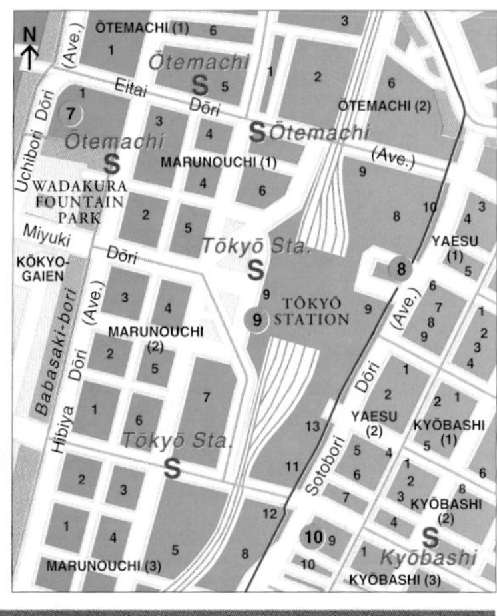

8

9

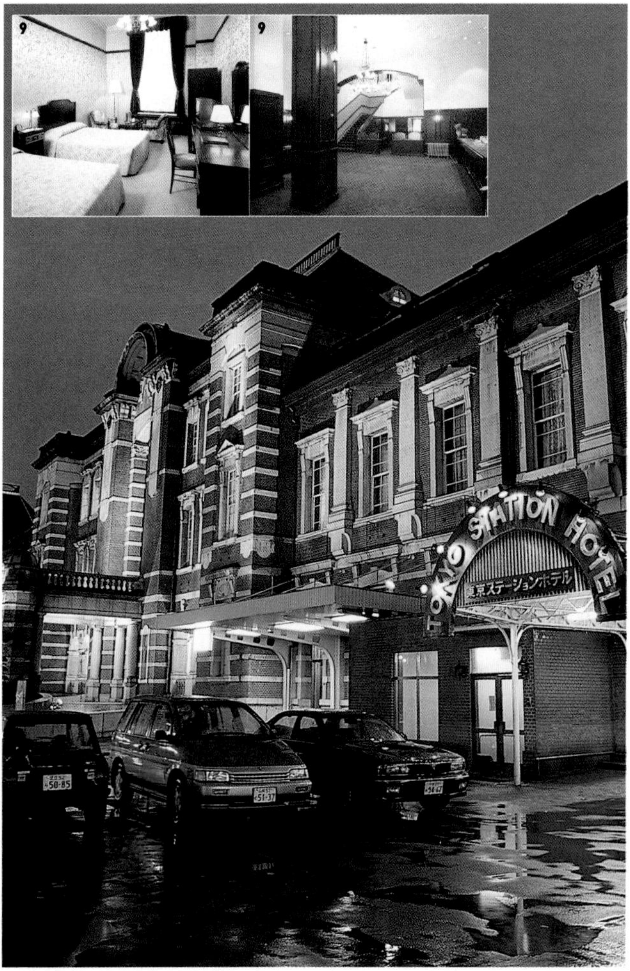

9 9

In the area
Where to eat: ➡ 42
After dark: ➡ 68
What to see: ➡ 86 ➡ 88 ➡ 103 ➡ 110
Where to shop: ➡ 126 ➡ 128 ➡ 144

Where to stay

Hotel Kazusaya (11)

4-7-15 Nihombashi-Honchō, Chūō-ku
☎ (03) 3241-1045 ➡ (03) 3241-1077

M *Shin-Nihombashi* P ***71 rooms*** ●● *Nireinu* *Nireinu*
@ *kazusaya@takarabune.or.jp*

The chic façade of this business hotel, in gilded imitation stone, and its international restaurant, the Nireinu, stand out conspicuously in this traditional small street, still packed with button sellers' and barbers' stalls. Resolutely utilitarian but hospitable nonetheless, the establishment offers special rates for long stays. English spoken.

Tōkyō City Hotel (12)

1-5-4 Nihombashi-Honchō, Chūō-ku
☎ (03) 3270-7671 ➡ (03) 3270-8930

M *Mitsukoshimae* P ***260 rooms*** ●● *California Club, Nagitei*

Located in an area offering multiple possibilities – you will find everything here, from Armani suits to clippers for trimming Bonsai trees – this unpretentious hotel is more interesting than it appears at first glance. Forget the big soft toy dressed as a waiter posted at the entrance to draw passers-by into the Californian bar-restaurant in the basement, and pass straight into the small lobby, which sets the mood with its natural colors, light wood, white blinds, blue chairs and coffee corner. Small, clean rooms with mosquito nets at the windows and ultra-soft coverlets. Friendly service. Extremely pleasant.

Sumisho Hotel (13)

9-14 Nihombashi-Kobunachō, Chūō-ku
☎ (03) 3661-4603 ➡ (03) 3661-4639

M *Ningyōchō, Mitsukoshimae* ***63 rooms*** *(of which 10 Japanese style)* ●● *Sumisho* @ *sumisho@po.teleway.ne.jp*

An air of the traditional *ryokan* is exuded by this seven-story hotel that offers a choice of Western- or Japanese-style rooms. Delightful details, such as the exquisite mini Zen garden with its stone lanterns and small grassed areas glimpsed here and there, are particularly appealing.

Royal Park Hotel (14)

2-1-1 Nihombashi, Kakigarachō, Chūō-ku
☎ (03) 3667-1111 ➡ (03) 3667-1115

M *Suitengū-mae* P ***450 rooms*** *(of which 9 suites)* ●●●● *Sumid, Hamada, Genjkoh, Palazzo* *Royal Scots, Orpheus* *Symphony* *Fontaine* @ *rphfront@pluto.dti.ne.jp*

Resolutely international hotel with a spacious lobby where oriental pottery and pictures of Kimono fabric are found side by side, a European-style décor that combines simple and elegant contemporary furniture with a wealth of sumptuous fabrics, and vast, pleasantly decorated rooms. A formidable-looking chandelier called the Milky Way is suspended above a gilded abstract sculpture. You can relax by using the pool or the gym in the Royal Fitness Club, or by sipping a cocktail while enjoying the panoramic view from Orpheus, the bar on the 19th floor.

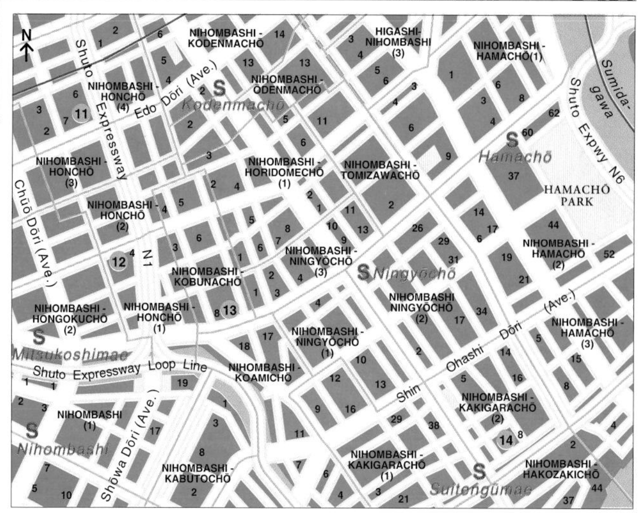

From the Edo period, all land and sea distances were measured from the famous Nihombashi bridge. Unfortunately, the bridge is partially hidden today by the expressway that passes a few feet above it.

13

14

In the area

- Where to eat: ➥ 42 ➥ 44 ➥ 46
- After dark: ➥ 68
- What to see: ➥ 86 ➥ 88 ➥ 90 ➥ 102 ➥ 110
- Where to shop: ➥ 126 ➥ 128

Where to stay

Hotel Seiyo Ginza (15)

1-11-2 Ginza, Chūō-ku ☎ (03) 3535-1111 ➟ (03) 3535-1110

M *Suitengū-mae* P **80 rooms** ●●●●● *Attore, Kitcho* ➥ *44, Pastorale* *Bar GI* *Prelude*

Tucked away in an unobtrusive white building, this luxurious oasis welcomes, among others, Hollywood stars visiting Tokyo, reassured by its watchwords: total discretion and personal service. Once you're through the discreet entrance, the tone is set immediately by the Harry Winston jewelry boutique. The spacious and delightfully decorated rooms marry a contemporary style with very beautiful antiques. As for the bathrooms, they are among the largest in the capital, and for your bed you can choose from seven different types of pillow.

Imperial Hotel (16)

1-1-1 Uchi-Saiwaichō, Chiyoda-ku ☎ (03) 3504-1111 ➟ (03) 3504-1258

M *Yūrakuchō, Hibiya* P ***1059 rooms** (of which 66 suites)* ●●●● *Les Saisons, La Brasserie, Cicerone, Euroka* *Old Imperial Bar, Rainbow Lounge* @ *miyazaki@imperialhotel.co.jp*

The dimensions of the Imperial are impressive, and its history never ceases to fascinate. Financed by the Imperial family, since 1890 this establishment has been a well-loved meeting place for its regular visitors, who appreciate the unique character of each room and the scent of roses which hangs heavy in the elevators. The Old Imperial Bar, designed by Frank Lloyd Wright, retains traces of its Art-Deco décor, but pride of place in the hotel goes to the music room, where visiting virtuosi practise.

Ginza Daiei Hotel (17)

3-12-2 Ginza, Chūō-ku ☎ (03) 3545-1111 ➟ (03) 3545-1177

M *Higashi-Ginza* P ***107 rooms*** ●● *Actors* @ *g-daiei@oregan.ne.jp*

A modest-sized business hotel, whose ever-smiling staff speak fluent English. The rooms, small but well laid out, offer every possible comfort to the customer on a business trip. The name of the restaurant, Actors, is a veiled reference to the neighboring kabuki theater, the Kabuki-za ➥ 68.

Not forgetting

■ **Mitsui Urban Hotel Ginza (18)** 8-6-15 Ginza, Chūō-ku ☎ (03) 3572-4131 ➟ (03) 3572-4254 ●●● *Combining steel, glass and tile, this hotel revolutionizes the concept of the business hotel by its charm and elegance. The spacious and restful lobby snakes alongside a patio garden, and the small rooms aspire to refinement. The hotel achieves the difficult task of combining solid tradition with a resolutely contemporary image.* ■ **Hotel Alcyone (19)** 4-14-3 Ginza, Chūō-ku ☎ (03) 3541-3621 ➟ (03) 3541-3263 ●● *The Western- or Japanese-style rooms of this old ryokan are very simple, but their light colors give a feeling of space. Unusually, pets are allowed. Highly recommended.* ■ **Dai-ichi Hotel Tokyo (20)** 1-2-6 Shimbashi, Minato-ku ☎ (03) 3501-4411 ➟ (03) 3595-2634 ●●●● *European elegance and Japanese hospitality. All the rooms prove to be unforgettable, with their high ceilings and their cleverly matched colors. On the 18th and 19th floors, very beautiful suites with panoramic views. The hotel isn't called Dai-ichi (Number One) for nothing!*

In 1872, passengers arriving from Yokohama by train gazed at the sea, geisha houses and other picturesque sights. Ginza is now a business center, located a stone's throw from the prestigious shopping mall.

16 15 16

In the area

Where to eat: ➥ 48 ➥ 50 ➥ 52
After dark: ➥ 68 ➥ 70 ➥ 72 ➥ 76 ➥ 78
What to see: ➥ 84 ➥ 86
Where to shop: ➥ 130

Where to stay

Akasaka Prince Hotel (21)

1 Kioichō, Chiyoda-ku ☎ (03) 3234-1111 ➠ (03) 3262-5163

M *Akasakamitsuke* P ***761 rooms*** *(of which 23 Japanese style and 101 suites)* ●●●● *Blue Gardenia* *Top of Akasaka* *Fountain Terrace* *Potomac*

Designed by Kenzo Tange in 1984, the futuristic lines of this hotel still manage to surprise. The sparkling whiteness of its façade, together with that of its interior, is highly appreciated by its jet-setting clientele. Despite an uncompromising décor, the Western- or Japanese-style rooms are enormous and comfortable, and the wall-to-wall picture windows give an exceptional view.

Capitol Tokyū Hotel (22)

2-10-30 Nagatachō, Chiyoda-ku ☎ (03) 3581-4511 ➠ (03) 3581-5822

M *Kokkai-gijidōmae* P ***459 rooms*** *(of which 19 suites)* ●●●● *Keyaki Grill, Genti* *Misao, Lipo* *Garden Café*

Rising up from among spacious gardens, this lovely hotel is the result of a sophisticated marriage between Asia and the West. The lobby is renowned for its *ikebana* floral arrangements, and the Garden Café offers a soothing view over the water garden. The décor ranges from sumptuous to minimalist, and the rooms, with their *shoji* at the windows, come in harmonized cool colors. A haven of quiet in the heart of the metropolis.

Ōkura Hotel (23)

2-10-14 Toranomon, Minato-ku ☎ (03) 3582-0111 ➠ (03) 3582-3707

M *Kamiyachō* P ***857 rooms*** *(of which 51 suites)* ●●●●● *Yamazato, Sazanka, Toh-Ka-Lin* *Orchid, Highlander* ***Musée Ōkura Shûkokan*** *Tue.–Sun. 10am–4.30pm* ● *¥300*

Founded by Baron Kishichiro Okura and the hotelier Iwakiro Noda, this haven of tranquility was opened for the Olympic Games in 1962. At the center of a Japanese garden featuring a *koi* pond and a shrine overlooking a waterfall, it remains for its regular visitors the one and only hotel in Tokyo. The interior, brimming with traditional motifs and symbols, was renovated in the 1980s by Sir David Hicks. The small museum houses Japanese antiques, including one national treasure, and contemporary art.

Not forgetting

■ **New Ōtani Hotel (24)** 4-1 Kioichō, Chiyoda-ku ☎ (03) 3265-1111 ➠ (03) 3221-2619 ●●●● *Built on the fortifications of the old Edo castle and a 400-year-old garden, this hotel keeps one foot in the past and sets the other in the future, taking pride in its position at the forefront of hotel comfort. Lovely view over the State Guest House and Tokyo Tower.* ■ **ANA Hotel Tōkyō (25)** 1-12-3 Akasaka, Minato-ku ☎ (03) 3505-1111 ➠ (03) 3505-1155 ●●●● *A hotel where a warm, cozy atmosphere reigns, both in the communal areas and in the rooms, tastefully decorated in shades of coffee and cream. On a clear day, Mount Fuji is discernible in the distance, and at night you can observe the glittering city from the Sky Bar on the 36th floor.* ■ **Roppongi Prince Hotel (26)** 3-2-7 Roppongi, Minato-ku ☎ (03) 3587-1111 ➠ (03) 3587-0770 ●●● *This 'city resort' coils around an extraordinary atrium. Its quirky and minimalist style is reflected in the uncompromising refinement of the rooms. These open out onto the voluptuous curves of the swimming pool.*

Tokyo's expatriates band together on the periphery of Roppongi, which has become a true bastion of the west. In contrast, the center is a meeting place for the young people of Tokyo, drawn there by its discos, clubs and restaurants, while the elitist Akasaka is so discreet that one wonders if it still exists.

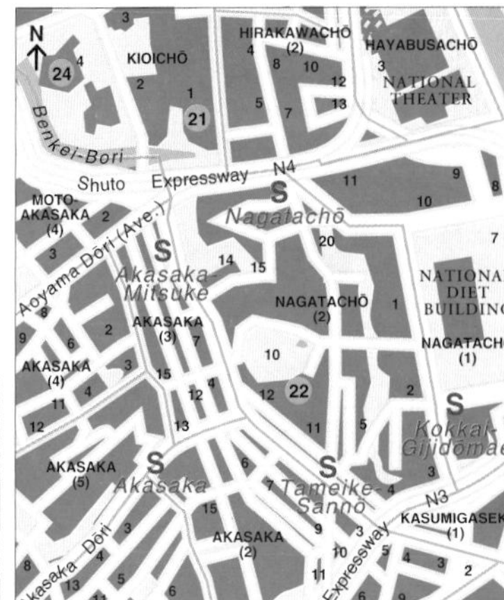

23

25

25

22

23

In the area

Where to eat: ➡ 58
After dark: ➡ 74
What to see: ➡ 94 ➡ 102
Where to shop: ➡ 126 ➡ 140 ➡ 142

Where to stay

Green Plaza Capsule Hotel (27)

1-29-2 Kabukichō, Shinjuku-ku ☎ (03) 5457-0109

M *JR Shinjuku* ***600 capsules*** ● *Potomac*

More often than not the clientele at capsule hotels is made up of people who have missed their trains. With its ultra-kitsch lobby, you could be forgiven for thinking that you were in a 'love hotel'. To get there, go down to the basement and take the elevator to the third floor. The capsules are lined up from there like coffins, although rather more comfortable!

Tōkyō Hilton International Hotel (28)

6-6-2 Nishi-Shinjuku, Shinjuku-ku ☎ (03) 3344-5111 ➡ (03) 3344-5575

M *Shinjuku* P ***806 rooms*** *(of which 50 suites)* ●●●●● *Checkers, Twenty One, Musashino, Ocho / Dynasty* ➡ *58, Teppon Grill* *St. George's Bar* *Marble Lounge* @ *info@tokyo.hilton.com*

This hotel, with its sensuous curves, is in every way a worthy member of the Hilton empire. Its staff are welcoming, friendly and obliging, and the place is very lively. The rooms combine western comfort with Japanese touches, such as the *shoji*. There are two tennis courts on the roof!

Park Hyatt Hotel (29)

3-7-1 Nishi-Shinjuku, Shinjuku-ku ☎ (03) 3349-0111 ➡ (03) 0344-5575

M *Shinjuku* P ***178 rooms*** *(of which 23 suites)* ●●●●● *New Grill* ➡ *50, Kozue, Girandole, The Peak Lounge* *The New York Sky Bar, The Peak Bar* @ *mil@tyoph.co.jp*

Beloved of the media and the financial jet set, the Park Hyatt has unerring appeal because of its superb décor, designed by John Morford. From the lobby to the Peak Lounge, the style is of Zen-like simplicity: noble materials, natural colors, original works of art, and vast, soft divans.
A wealth of little luxury items, such as Molton Brown products, grace the rooms, the most spacious in all Tokyo. Occupying the top 14 floors of the tower designed by Kenzo Tange, the views over Kanto plain are breathtaking, even from the sports hall, where you will feel yourself sprouting wings. The less active can always enjoy it from the Sky Bar.

Not forgetting

■ **Century Southern Tower Hotel (30)** 2-2-1 Yoyogi, Shibuya-ku ☎ (03) 5354-0111 ➡ (03) 5354-0100 ●●● *An ultra-civilized atmosphere and subtly sophisticated rooms. The hotel provides a 24-hour help service for business visitors. Exceptional panoramic views.* ■ **The Century Hyatt (31)** 2-7-2 Nishi-Shinjuku, Shinjuku-ku ☎ (03) 3349-0111 ➡ (03) 3344-5575 ●●●● *The elevators running up and down the façade set the tone: this is Las Vegas. Nevertheless, the rooms have a contemporary European flavor. Ask for a room overlooking Shinjuku Central Park.* ■ **Keiō Plaza Inter-Continental Hotel (32)** 2-2-1 Nishi-Shinjuku, Shinjuku-ku ☎ (03) 3344-0111 ➡ (01) 3345-8269 ●●●● *A spectacular décor, with superb* ikebana *floral arrangements and a peerless choice of service: economical rooms, overly refined Japanese-style suites, or Western suites in soft pastel shades.* ■ **Shinjuku Washington Hotel (33)** 3-2-9 Nishi-Shinjuku, Shinjuku-ku ☎ (03) 3343-3111 ➡ (03) 3342-2575 ●●● *This is more than a business hotel, with ergonomic suites making the most of limited space.*

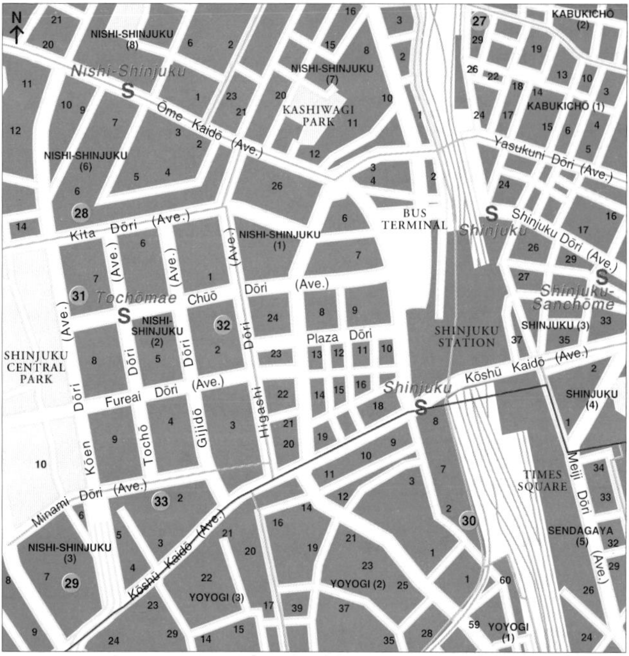

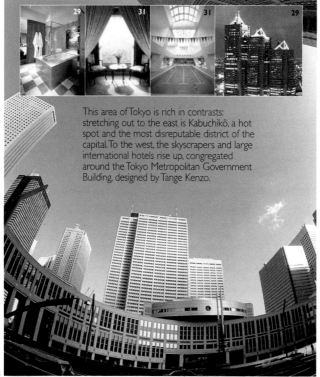

This area of Tokyo is rich in contrasts: stretching out to the east is Kabuchikō, a hot spot and the most disreputable district of the capital. To the west, the skyscrapers and large international hotels rise up, congregated around the Tokyo Metropolitan Government Building, designed by Tange Kenzo.

In the area

- **Where to eat:** ➥ 60
- **After dark:** ➥ 68 ➥ 78
- **After dark:** ➥ 96 ➥ 98 ➥ 102
- **Where to shop:** ➥ 126 ➥ 138 ➥ 142

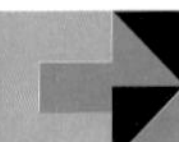

Where to stay

Arimax Hotel Shibuya (34)

11-15 Kamiyamachō, Shibuya-ku ☎ (03) 5454-1122 ➠ (03) 3460-6513

M *JR Shibuya, Shibuya* P ***23 rooms*** ●●●● *Polyantha* *The Bar* *Rosemarin*

Silks, brocades, stylish furniture and subtle lighting give this hotel its intimate and chic character. Its façade, which combines marble, granite, bronze and frosted glass, contrasts with the warm and elegant European-style interior. The room-suites, with their small bathrooms, range from English Regency to neoclassical in style. The reception area and a minute coffee lounge vie for space in the small lobby, which leads to the Polyantha, a highly regarded French restaurant.

Shibuya Tōbu Hotel (35)

3-1 Udagawachō, Shibuya-ku ☎ (03) 3476-0111 ➠ (03) 3476-0903

M *JR Shibuya, Shibuya* P ***198 rooms*** *(of which 4 suites)* ●● *Verdure* *Raffine* @ *tobu-sby@mbf.sphere.ne.jp*

A cascade of greenery prettily adorns the red-brick façade of this establishment, tucked away in a back street in the center of Shibuya. Its practicality and comfort make it an ideal place to stay for suburbanites who have come in to plunder the shops. The pleasant rooms, with their lovingly coordinated soft colors, make a complete contrast with the bridal suite, abandoned to an orgy of sequins and flounces. Similarly, the coffee shop is almost too intimate for comfort, while the Raffine bar cultivates a rather raffish image.

Shibuya City Hotel (36)

1-1 Maruyamachō, Shibuya-ku ☎ (03) 5489-1010 ➠ (03) 5489-1030

M *Shibuya* ***57 rooms*** ●● *Raiz*

A small, beguiling hotel, located in a fold of Shibuya hill. Large modern rooms with very comfortable beds and restful colors. An establishment much superior to the neighboring 'love hotels', but less distracting!

Excel Hotel Tōbu (37)

1-12-2 Dōgenzaka, Shibuya-ku ☎ (03) 5457-0109 ➠ (03) 5457-0309

M *Shibuya* P ***408 rooms*** *(of which 1 suite)* ●●●

This hotel gives a certain buzz to the district, renamed Bitter Valley (the literal translation of Shibuya). It occupies the upper floors of a gleaming tower rising into the sky above Mark City. The minimalist décor of the communal areas and the rooms – picture windows from floor to ceiling, fluted columns of steel and furniture with pure lines – is emphasized by the association of black and white with beige and brown tones. Austere and functional elegance.

Not forgetting

■ **Shibuya Business Hotel (38)** 1-12-5 Shibuya, Shibuya-ku ☎ (03) 3409-9300 ➠ (03) 3409-9378 ●● *A modestly priced hotel, secluded in a quiet little street, with rooms that are small, informal but fully equipped. The staff show the expected level of efficiency, tempered with a friendly attitude, and a slightly monastic atmosphere reigns: visitors are forbidden in the rooms, and the front door closes at 2am.*

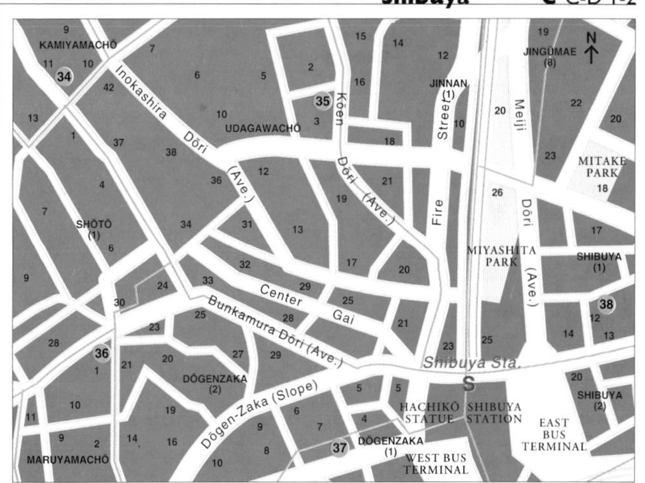

If the boutiques of Harajuku draw the teenagers, those of Shibuya are a paradise for people in their twenties and thirties. However, the multicultural Bunkamura complex ➡ 98 restores the age balance, especially at night. On the other side of the road, 'love hotels', cafés, bars and live-music venues jostle for attention.

35

34

34

34

In the area

Where to eat: ➡ 62
After dark: ➡ 72 ➡ 78
What to see: ➡ 84 ➡ 100
Where to shop: ➡ 142

Where to stay

Takanawa Prince Hotel Sakura Tower (39)

3-13-1 Takanawa, Minato-ku ☎ (03) 5798-1111 ➡ (03) 5798-1122

JR Shinagawa ***309 rooms*** *(of which 11 suites)* ●●●● *Shichikenjaya* *Silk Hat, Vendange*

This hotel, built in 1998, attracts families and women travelers. Blue tiles with a floral motif run across one side of the building, which is pale pink (*Sakura* means cherry blossom). The pastel-colored rooms are simple and elegant, decorated with matching prints and equipped with bathrooms with whirlpools. All give onto the garden, but the most popular are the corner rooms, for their outlook.

Takanawa Prince Hotel (40)

3-13-1 Takanawa, Minato-ku ☎ (03) 3447-1111 ➡ (03) 3446-0849

JR Shinagawa ***414 rooms*** *(of which 16 Japanese style and 30 suites)* ●●● *Le Trianon, Katsura* *Prince Royal*

Dating from the 1970s, the communal areas, dark and somewhat gloomy, contrast with the spacious and welcoming rooms, with their soft, sunny colors. This hotel's charm lies in the 218 acres of garden that belonged to the Imperial family and where the Japanese-style annex is located, housing a business center and exceptionally high-quality, traditional suites. An oasis of discretion and tranquility.

Pacific Meridien Tōkyō Hotel (41)

3-13-3 Takanawa, Minato-ku ☎ (03) 3445-6711 ➡ (03) 3445-5137

JR Shinagawa ***954 rooms*** *(of which 41 suites)* ●● *Piccolo Mondo*

This hotel stands at the center of traditional gardens. Its curved façade is enchanting in certain lights as it shimmers like pearl. The rooms, in nicely coordinated hues, benefit from unrestricted views and promise comfort and tranquility. The top two floors comprise luxurious suites much appreciated by Westerners. The Blue Pacific lounge is worth a visit for its panoramic view and its Star Dust show.

Not forgetting

■ **Keihin Hotel (42)** 4-10-20 Takanawa, Minato-ku ☎ (03) 3449-5711 ➡ (03) 3441-7230 ●● *A sign at the entrance announces that the hotel was founded in 1871. Framed floral fabrics adorn the stairwell leading to the lobby, creating a cozy and rather old-fashioned atmosphere. Beautiful Japanese- or Western-style rooms.* ■ **Tōyoko Inn (43)** 4-23-2 Takanawa, Minato-ku ☎ (03) 3280-1045 ➡ (03) 3280-1046 ● *This well-kept business hotel, opened in 1999, offers small but carefully planned rooms. Those facing the sea are light and airy.* ■ **New Takanawa Prince Hotel (44)** 3-13-1 Takanawa, Minato-ku ☎ (03) 3442-1111 ➡ (03) 3444-1234 ●●● *Designed by Togo Murano, this city resort brings to mind an enormous wedding cake mislaid among the greenery. The rooms are in tones of sweet pea and lemon. The exquisite teahouse also serves* kaiseki ryori *dinners* ➡ *40.* ■ **Shinagawa Prince Hotel (45)** 4-10-30 Takanawa, Minato-ku ☎ (03) 3440-1111 ➡ (03) 3441-7092 ●● *This business and leisure complex is a great favorite. Among the services provided are: a bowling alley, tennis courts, a golf course, 28 karaoke machines and a panoramic restaurant... The vast lobby features a stained-glass window by Jean-Pierre Cassigneu, whose lithographs adorn the 1,736 rooms. The whole is quintessentially Japanese.*

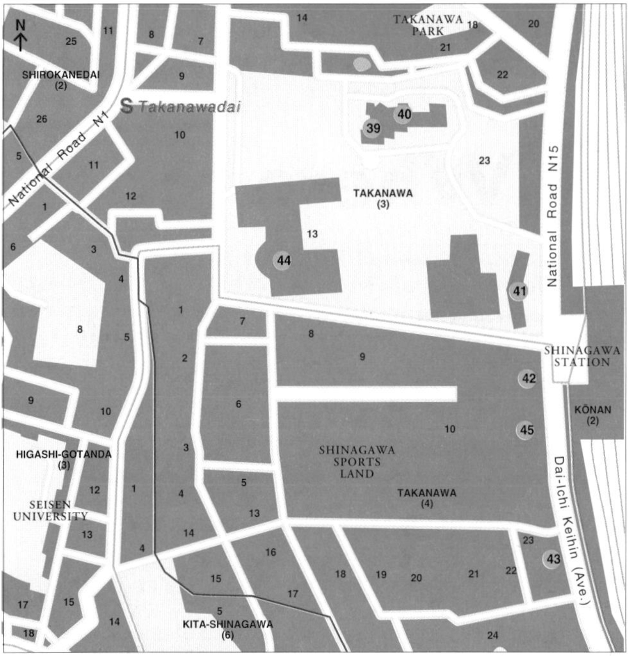

N
SHIROKANEDAI (2)
S Takanawadai
National Road N1
TAKANAWA PARK
TAKANAWA (3)
National Road N15
39
40
41
42
43
44
45
SHINAGAWA STATION
KŌNAN (2)
SHINAGAWA SPORTS LAND
TAKANAWA (4)
HIGASHI-GOTANDA (3)
SEISEN UNIVERSITY
KITA-SHINAGAWA (6)
Dai-Ichi Keihin (Ave.)

40

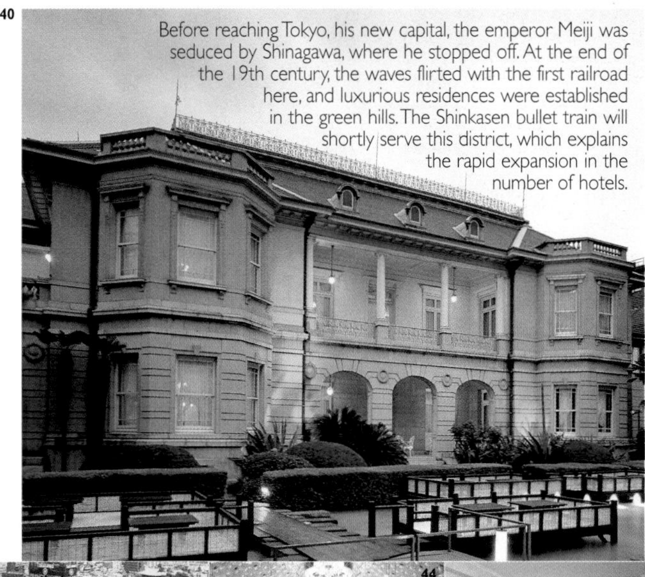

Before reaching Tokyo, his new capital, the emperor Meiji was seduced by Shinagawa, where he stopped off. At the end of the 19th century, the waves flirted with the first railroad here, and luxurious residences were established in the green hills. The Shinkasen bullet train will shortly serve this district, which explains the rapid expansion in the number of hotels.

40

44

39

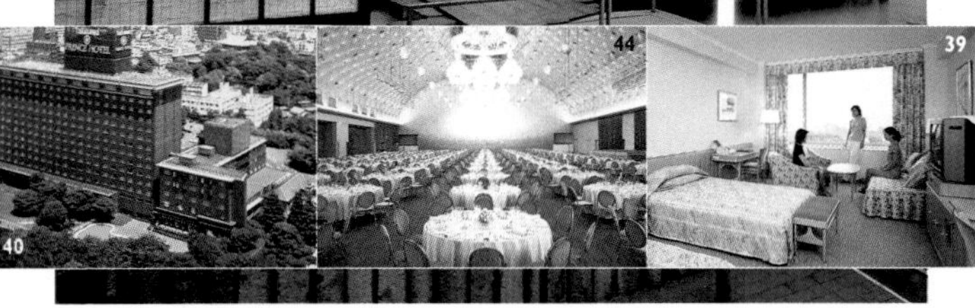

In the area

- Where to eat: ➡ 42
- After dark: ➡ 69
- What to see: ➡ 84 ➡ 86 ➡ 88
- Where to shop: ➡ 126 ➡ 144

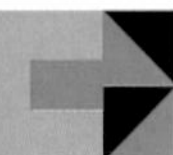

Where to stay

Hotel Edmont (46)

3-10-8 Iidabashi, Chiyoda-ku ☎ (03) 3237-1111 ➡ (03) 3234-4371

Iidabashi **450 rooms** *(of which 2 Japanese style)* ●●● *Four grains, Hirakawa, Umihiko, Yamihiko* *Carousal* *Beltempo*

Designed for professionals on business trips, the rooms at the Edmont are real office-bedrooms. Advantages for the Westerner: the beds are bigger, the baths longer and wider. As for the Japanese-style rooms, they adjoin a small inner garden.

Tōkyō International Youth Hostel (47)

18F Central Plaza, 1-1 Kaguragashi, Shinjuku-ku
☎ (03) 3235-1107 ➡ (03) 3267-4000

Iidabashi **33 rooms** *(of which 2 Japanese-style)* ●

An unexpected location for a youth hostel, only a stone's throw from the former moat of the Imperial Palace ➡ 86. As well as dormitories, this glass and brick tower sports two Japanese-style rooms housing six people, and communal baths with a beautiful view. Note that the doors close at 10.30pm. Non-members are accepted, and breakfast and dinner are attractively priced (¥400 and ¥800 respectively).

Hill Top Hotel (48)

1-1 Kanda-Surugadai, Chiyoda-ku ☎ (03) 3293-2311 ➡ (03) 3233-4567

Ochanomizu, Jinbōchō **75 rooms** *(of which 2 suites)* ●●● *La Vie, À Bientôt, Garden, Yamano-ue* *Non-Non* *Hill Top*

Opened in 1954 under the name Kama no Ue, 'hill top', this hotel soon became a refuge for writers yearning for peace, including Yukio Mishima, who was one of its regular guests. The picturesque, quaint main building, more comfortable than elegant, is a real gem. It retains numerous original features, such as its wooden paneling and copper pipes, which emit ionized air, according to the wishes of its eccentric founder. Romantics come here for the ambience and for the view over Mount Fuji and the Chichibu mountain range.

Not forgetting

■ **Fairmont Hotel (49)** 2-1-17 Kudan-Minami, Chiyoda-ku ☎ (03) 3264-1151 ➡ (03) 3264-2476 ●●● *Hidden away in a lovely peaceful corner, the Fairmont is reached by a shady avenue that winds alongside the inner canal. The rooms have a very European simplicity and elegance, while the suites reflect the Japanese spirit. The members of staff are helpful and touchingly gauche! No airs and graces here, just charm and kindness.* ■ **Kudan Kaikan Hotel (50)** 1-6-5 Kudan-Minami, Chiyoda-ku ☎ (03) 3261-5521 ➡ (03) 3221-7238 ●● *Just two words describe this magnificent building: classic and comfortable. From your room you can contemplate the Budōkan ➡ 110 on the other side of the canals, as well as the lush, steep hillside, planted here and there with cherry trees. The setting combines traditional and modern materials, a marriage of two worlds.* ■ **Tokyo YMCA (51)** 7-1 Kanda-Mitoshirochō, Chiyoda-ku ☎ (03) 3293-1911 ➡ (03) 3293-1926 ●●● *Present in Japan since 1880, the Young Men's Christian Association largely caters for a clientele of businessmen. This explains the official rather than graceful atmosphere of the lobby. The comfortable rooms are decorated in warm colors, and a rock garden has been laid out on the 7th floor.*

46

47

48

49

51

With its student atmosphere and its wealth of second-hand booksellers, Kanda is often compared to the Latin Quarter in Paris. But it is also the place for bargains: guitars and sports equipment, not forgetting the cut-price electronics of Akihabara Electric Town ➥ 144. Kudanshita and the surrounding area with their many historical sites promise more unworldly pleasures.

In the area
Where to eat: ➥ 24
After dark: ➥ 73
What to see: ➥ 90 ➥ 109
Where to shop: ➥ 126 ➥ 128

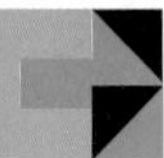

Where to stay

Dai-ichi Tokyo Sea Fort (52)

2-3-15 Higashi-Shinagawa, Shinagawa-ku
☎ (03) 5460-4411 ➠ (03) 5460-4401

M *Tōkyō monorail Tennōzu Isle* P ***123 rooms*** *(of which 9 suites)* ●●●● *Grand Café, Tennoz* *Sea Fort Club* *Grand Café* @ *seafort@daiichi-hotel.co.jp*

Nicknamed 'The Great Escape', this hotel makes the most of its major asset: its distance from the bustle of the city. The rooms, small enough for you to feel at home, or large enough to relax in, display a traditional, simple décor. At night, the view over the bay from the Sea Fort Club bar on the 21st floor is simply spectacular. When it comes to gigantic proportions, however, nothing beats the Grand Café, where the vast picture windows, on three levels, offer panoramic views of the activities in the harbor. Treat yourself in the evening with a candlelit dinner.

Hotel Nikkō Tōkyō (53)

1-9-1 Daiba, Minato-ku ☎ (03) 5500-5500 ➠ (03) 5500-2520

M *Akasaka-mitsuke* P ***453 rooms*** *(of which 18 suites)* ●●●● *Terrace on the Bay* *Captain's Bar, Veranda* *Marco Polo* @ *info@hnt.co.jp*

Opened in 1996 under the 'Tokyo Balcony' banner, this part-city, part-beach resort is sited on the waterfront. The rooms and suites all boast balconies so you can enjoy the view over the harbor. As for the suites, they each have a *rotenburo* (outdoor bath). Designed by a Californian studio, the public spaces display a nautical theme, combining characteristics of both East and West. The ensemble is impressive without being overpowering, and is totally contemporary. A highly sought-after place to escape for the weekend.

Meridien Grand Pacific Tōkyō (54)

2-6-1 Daiba, Minato-ku ☎ (03) 5500-6711 ➠ (03) 5500-4507

M *Yurikamome Daiba* P ***884 rooms*** *(of which 24 suites)* ●●●● *9 restaurants* *Ruy Lopez, Caprice* *Lobby Lounge*

The décor and the furniture, of French inspiration, set the tone in this luxury hotel built in 1998. The Meridien Grand Pacific is near Daiba park, the last vestige of the old Edo, the Tokyo Joypolis leisure park ➥ 108 and the restaurants of Sunset Beach. It goes without saying that the views over the harbor are fantastic.

Tōkyō Bay Ariake Washington Hotel (55)

3-1 Ariake, Kōtō-ku ☎ (03) 5564-0111 ➠ (03) 5564-0525

M *Yurikamome Kokusai-tenjijō Seimon* P ***761 rooms*** ●● *Beer Hall*

This enormous 20-story, ship-like hotel is better suited to congresses and exhibitions than romantic weekends. The rooms, with their well-stocked refrigerators, hair dryers and pants pressers, facilitate the task of the guests, who are supposed to do without the help of the staff. Those who want to have a meal worthy of the name should go to the first floor, where they will be able to choose from a whole host of varied restaurants.

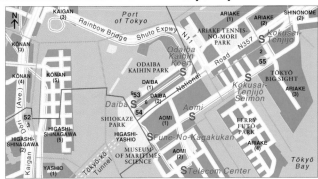

Between Hamamatsuchō and Shinagawa, the waterfront is currently undergoing massive change with the expansion of Haneda airport and the latest great project, Tokyo Teleport Town. These coastal areas, and those reclaimed from the sea, are rapidly being overrun by the major hotel chains eager to stake out their territory.

Tips
Under no circumstances.

Where to eat

Taxes
A supplementary tax of 3% is added to the check if it comes to over ¥7,500 per person.

Open or closed?
The *nōren*, a sort of short divided curtain, is placed over the entrance showing that the restaurant is open. On closing, it is removed.

Snacks
Generally located near stations, in parks (Ueno ➡ 106), *yatai* (itinerant food sellers) offer simple, tasty snacks: *oden*, *tōfu*, *yaki-imo* (sweet potato) that you can eat with saké.

Shomben Yokochō
Next to Shinjuku train station there is a block of old buildings with two narrow alleyways running across it. These are lined with *yakitori-ya*, *rāmen-ya*, *izakaya* and other very inexpensive restaurants. This is the Shomben Yokochō quarter, Piss Alley, so called because the establishments share the same toilet facilities.

64 Restaurants

THE INSIDER'S FAVORITES

Note: Do not wait too late to have dinner as some places (ramen-ya, sushi-ya) close very early because of the last subway.

INDEX BY TYPE

PRICE CATEGORY
● less than ¥ 3 000
●● ¥ 3 000 – 5 000
●●● ¥ 5 000 – 10 000
●●●● ¥ 10 000 – 15 000
●●●●● more than ¥ 15 000

Japan is without a doubt the restaurant capital of the world, boasting more than 80,000 establishments. Most visitors know sushi, *tempura* and the legendary *fugu* (pufferfish) at least by name, but they will be astonished and delighted to discover the richness of Japanese cuisine. It is possible to eat every day without ever having the same dish twice.

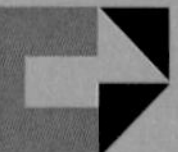

Where to eat

Restaurants

The Japanese are real gourmets and great connoisseurs of the culinary arts. Therefore, in any establishment, you can be sure of the freshness of the produce.

Reservations
Apart from the major restaurants, it is not customary to book.

Limited time
You may find that a restaurant bills you for twice the price of the meal. This isn't a way of cheating you, it is simply that the time allotted to each customer (about one hour) has been exceeded. So, once you've taken your last sip of *cha* or saké, don't hang around!

Etiquette

When you eat with *hashi* (chopsticks), avoid sticking them upright in the food, especially in the rice, and don't use them to pass food around. These actions are linked to the rites of the death ceremony. Don't sprinkle the food with sauce, but dip it in. However, sucking noodles into your mouth noisily and drinking the *miso* soup straight from the bowl are considered good manners.

Cuisines

Japanese chefs don't specialize in just one cuisine (gourmet, regional, etc.), but in a single type of produce, such as *unagi*, or a cooking method, such as *yaki* (grilling). As a result, it is not uncommon to visit two or three restaurants in one evening.

Kaiseki-ryori
Originally these were dishes served at the tea ceremony. Now the menus are set, and reflect the seasonal tastes of the Japanese.

Noodles

Soba (*1*)
Home-made buckwheat noodles are still highly appreciated in Tokyo, eaten in hot or cold soup, depending on the season – *kake* (with leek), *komo-nanban* (with chicken); or cold – *seiro* (plain, served in a bamboo dish which gives it its name), or *tenzaru* (with a *tempura* of *ebi* and vegetables). Order the *tamagoyaki* (2) (grilled omelet) too.

Udon
Thicker wheat noodles, eaten in the same way as *soba*.

Ramen
Of Chinese origin, these noodles are served in a soup based on chicken, *kombu* (seaweed), pork bones, and accompanied by various dishes such as *chōshu* (grilled pork) or *naruto* (fish paté).

Oden
A stew made up of various types of seasonal produce, such as *gammodoki* (fried

tōfu), *konnyaku* (arum root jelly) and *hampen* (fish pâté) simmering in a *kombu*-based stock.

Robatayaki *(3)*
In a rustic farm setting (*robata* means hearth) with a family atmosphere, simple dishes such as *zakana* (fish) or *onigiri* (rice balls) prepared and grilled at your table. Very popular in Tokyo.

Sashimi and sushi *(4)*
Sashimi or *otsukuri*, thin slices of seafood, are eaten as an appetizer with saké. They are followed by *nigirizushi* (rice pâtés topped with *sashimi*) and *makizushi* (sushi rolled in a piece of seaweed) or which you dip in *shōyu* (soy sauce) and *wasabi* (green radish).

Shabu-shabu and sukiyaki *(5)*
Sukiyaki, a dish made up of beef, vegetables, *shungiku* (chrysanthemum leaves), *shiritaki* (noodles), *negi* (leeks) and *tōfu*. This is cooked in stock, *warishita*, and eaten dipped in raw egg. *Shabu-shabu* is similar. It consists of slivers of beef and vegetables dipped in stock and flavored with *ponzu* (vinegar) and *gomodare* (sesame) sauces. *Kani-shabu* is a crab-based version.

Tempura *(6)*
Seafood and vegetable fritters. They are eaten hot, dipped in *oroshi-shōga* (with ginger) or *daikon-oroshi* (with white radish).

Tonkatsu *(7)*
Breaded pork fillet fried and served with a cabbage salad or in *katsudon* (soup). Very popular with 'salarymen'.

Unagi *(8)*
Eel has a reputation for promoting health, and is eaten grilled, plain (*kabayaki*) or on a bed of rice (*unajū*). It should be seasoned with *sanchō*, a special pepper.

Yakitori *(9)*
Skewers of chicken (*tori*), grilled, salted and sprinkled in soy sauce. You can also have skewers made of vegetables.

Yōshoku
This cuisine encompasses all the dishes imported from Europe in the Meiji period, but adapted to be served with rice.

- don
A general term to designate rice-based dishes served in a *domburimono* (china bowl). The most common are *ten-don* (shrimp and vegetables), *age-don* (various types of fried fish), *okako-don* (10) (chicken, chervil, vegetables and egg).

In the area

- Where to stay: ➡ 20 ➡ 22 ➡ 34
- After dark: ➡ 68
- What to see: ➡ 86 ➡ 88 ➡ 02 ➡ 110
- Where to shop: ➡ 126 ➡ 128

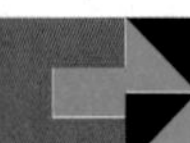

Where to eat

㐂寿司 Kizushi (1)

2-7-13 Nihombashi-Ningyōchō, Chūō-ku ☎ (03) 3666-1682

M *Ningyōchō* ***Sushi*** ●●●● *Mon.–Sat. 11.45am–2.30pm, 5–9.30pm*

In the heart of old Tokyo, this *sushi-ya* has succeeded in retaining the atmosphere of days gone by. Sit at the bar or at the one and only table, and order *nigirizushi* or *makizushi*. These dishes consist of six items per person. The *neta* (toppings), depending on the season, are made up of *maguro* (red tuna), *ika* (boiled squid), *ebi* (prawn), *akagei* (ark shell), *awabi* (abalone)… All these delights will be served Tokyo fashion, of course!

たいめいけん Taimeiken (2)

1-12-10 Nihombashi, Chūō-ku ☎ (03) 3271-2464

M *Nihombashi* ***Yōshoku*** ● *Mon.–Sat. 11am–11pm*

Very popular with 'salarymen' and shoppers, this canteen-like establishment serves real *yōshoku*. On the ground floor the clientele is always busy and in a rush; on the first the atmosphere is more relaxed. Apart from traditional dishes, the *omu-raisu* (rice omelet), the *kare-raisu* (Japanese rice curry) and the *kaki* (oyster) fritters in winter, there is a wide choice of *ramen*, but the best bargain is still coleslaw or borsch. It will only cost you ¥50 a dish! A derisory price, set by the first owner in his will.

みかわ Mikawa (3)

3-4-7 Nihombashi-Kayabachō, Chūō-ku ☎ (03) 3664-9843

M *Kayabachō* ***Tempura*** ●●● *Mon.–Tue., Thu.–Sun. 11.30am–1.30pm, 5–9pm*

Here's a restaurant it's always good to visit. The cuisine, based on seafood, bears no resemblance to 'fish and chips'. You will be spoilt for choice with the differing flavors of shrimp's head, whitebait in the spring, tender *aori-ika* (raw squid) in the summer, intensely flavored conger eel and the remarkable fried oyster.

吉野鮨本店 Yoshino-sushi (4)

3-8-11 Nihombashi, Chūō-ku ☎ (03) 3274-3001

M *Nihombashi* ***Sushi*** ●●● *Mon.–Fri., Sun. 11am–2.30pm, 4.30–9pm; Sat. 11am–2.30pm*

On this very spot, for seven generations, the art of Tokyo-style sushi preparation has been passed down from father to son. The style is classic but the *chirashizushi* and *nigirizushi* are extremely fresh. The lunchtime menu at ¥1,500 is excellent value for money.

Not forgetting

■ 伊勢廣 **Isehiro (5)** 1-5-4 Kyōbashi, Chūō-ku ☎ (03) 3281-5864 ●●●
A small, traditional building in an alleyway houses this yakitori-ya, highly regarded for its set menus, with appetizer and dessert included. In the downstairs room a good-natured ambience reigns around the table d'hôte while skewers of chicken are grilled behind the bar, and upstairs the guests eat in a Japanese-style dining room. Be warned, you will have to wait in line, especially at lunchtime. Closed on Sundays.

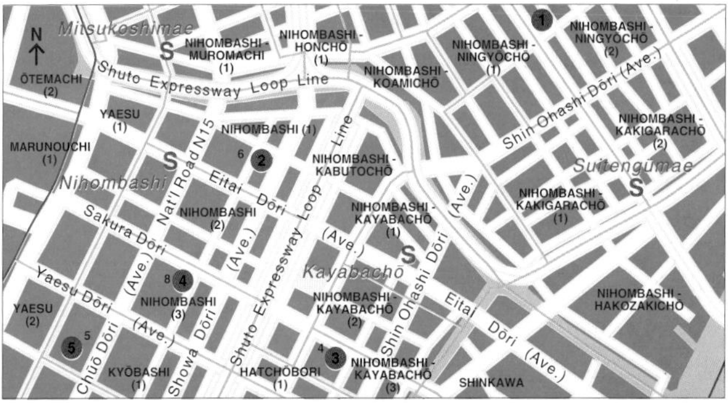
N
Mitsukoshimae
NIHOMBASHI - MUROMACHI (1)
NIHOMBASHI - HONCHŌ (1)
NIHOMBASHI - NINGYŌCHŌ (1)
NIHOMBASHI - NINGYŌCHŌ (2)
ŌTEMACHI (2)
Shuto Expressway Loop Line
NIHOMBASHI - KOAMICHŌ
Shin Ohashi Dōri (Ave.)
YAESU (1)
NIHOMBASHI (1)
NIHOMBASHI - KAKIGARACHŌ (2)
MARUNOUCHI (1)
NIHOMBASHI - KABUTOCHŌ
Suitengūmae
Nihombashi
Eitai Dōri
Nat'l Road N15 (Ave.)
NIHOMBASHI - KAYABACHŌ (1)
NIHOMBASHI - KAKIGARACHŌ (1)
Sakura Dōri
NIHOMBASHI (2)
(Ave.)
Shin Ohashi Dōri (Ave.)
Kayabachō
Yaesu Dōri (Ave.)
NIHOMBASHI (3)
Shuto Expressway Loop Line
NIHOMBASHI - KAYABACHŌ (2)
Eitai Dōri (Ave.)
NIHOMBASHI - HAKOZAKICHŌ
YAESU (2)
Chūō Dōri (Ave.)
Showa Dōri
KYŌBASHI (1)
HATCHŌBORI (1)
NIHOMBASHI - KAYABACHŌ (3)
SHINKAWA

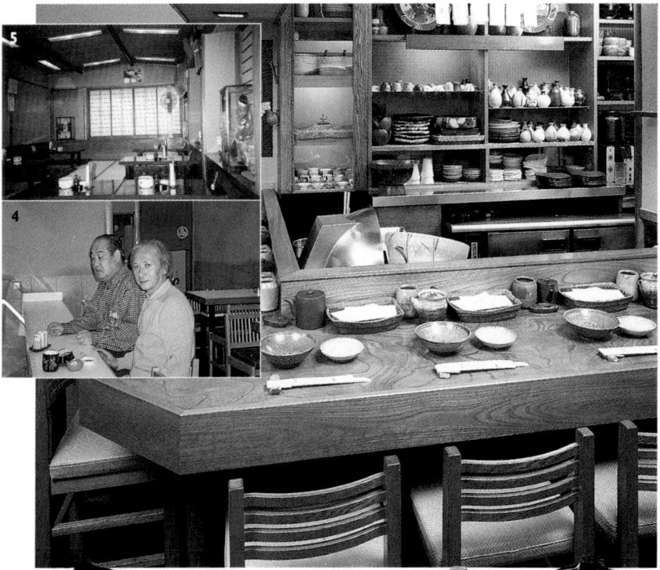
5
4

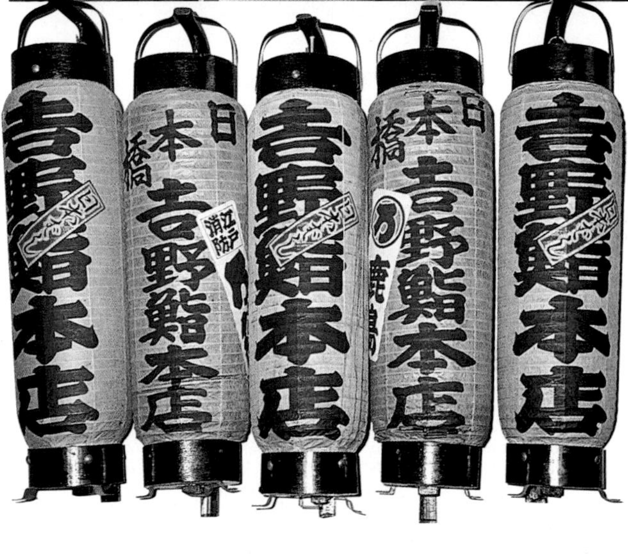
吉野鮨本店
日本橋
吉野鮨本店
吉野鮨本店
日本橋
吉野鮨本店
吉野鮨本店

In the area

Where to stay: ➥ 20 ➥ 22 ➥ 24
After dark: ➥ 68
What to see: ➥ 86 ➥ 88 ➥ 90 ➥ 102 ➥ 110
Where to shop: ➥ 126 ➥ 128

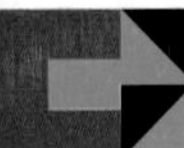

Where to eat

吉兆 Kicchō (6)

Hôtel Seiyo B1, 1-11-2 Ginza, Chūō-ku ☎ (03) 3535-1177

M *Kyobashi* ***Kaiseki-ryori*** ●●●●● *daily 11.30am–2.30pm, 5–9.30pm*

Characteristic of Kicchō is the simple, modern cuisine, inspired by the *kaiseki* repertoire, served in private dining rooms. The seasonal produce from both land and sea is terrific. The dishes are prepared and cooked in the traditional manner and served in wooden bowls. Try a selection with the chef's own *mini-kaiseki* served at a Western-style table. Saké (warm or cold) and a very respectable wine list.

次郎 Jiro (7)

B1, 4-2-15 Ginza, Chūō-ku ☎ (03) 3535-3600

M *Ginza* ***Sushi*** ●●●●● *Mon.–Fri. 11.30am–2pm, 5pm–8.30pm; Sat. 11.30am–2pm; closed public holidays*

Well away from the crowds flooding into the metro, this tiny restaurant serves extremely fresh Edomae sushi. Indeed, apart from raw fish, the *neta* (toppings on vinegared rice) include shad and other boiled fish, seasoned and surrounded by *nori* (seaweed). The *maguro* is delicious throughout the year, but in December the flesh, whether lean or more fatty, is unbeatable. At other times you will appreciate the unrivalled flavor of the abalone, prawns, eel, conger, sardines or mackerel. Reservations essential.

煉瓦亭 Renga-tei (8)

3-5-16 Ginza, Chūō-ku ☎ (03) 3561-3882

M *Ginza* ***Yōshoku*** ● *Mon.–Sat. 11.15am–2pm, 4.40–8pm*

Japan has adopted those European dishes that go well with rice under the name *yōshoku*. The establishment has been serving this type of cuisine for over a century; as well as Viennese escalopes and shrimp fritters, fried oyster fritters are the winter classics.

しゃぶせん Shabusen (9)

Ginza Coae F2 & B1, 5-8-20 Ginza, Chūō-ku ☎ (03) 3572-3806

M *Ginza* ***Shabu-shabu*** ●● *daily 11am–9.30pm*

The main dining room has a wide oval bar on which copper cooking pots for *shabu-shabu* sit imposingly. Although it is nicer to enjoy this dish in a group, the convivial eating arrangements allow the solitary customer to feel at home too. On the same principle as a fondue, the *shabu-shabu* is made up of thin slivers of beef and vegetables dunked briefly with chopsticks into a steaming broth, seasoned with various ingredients.

Not forgetting

■ **Aux Amis des Vins (10)** 2-5-6 Ginza, Chūō-ku ☎ (03) 3567-4120 ●●● *For those who miss Western cuisine, this bistro offers a French menu and very good French wine list. A delicious leg of lamb is served on Fridays. Make reservations.* ■ グラナーダ銀座店 **Granata Ginza (11)** 4-6-1 Ginza, Chūō-ku ☎ (03) 3535-6334 ●●● *Italian cuisine at a reasonable price, for Ginza. A tip: try the risotto with squid ink.* ■ 新富寿し **Shintomizushi (12)** 5-9-17 Ginza, Chūō-ku ☎ (03) 3571-3456 ●●●● *Edomae sushi specialties. The tuna, horse mackerel and conger eel are highly flavorful. Never closed.*

KYŌBASHI (3)
YAESU (2)
GINZA (1)
Ginza-Itchōme
Sotobori Dōri (Ave.)
Tōkyō Expressway
GINZA (2)
GINZA (3)
Dōri
Chūō
GINZA (4)
Ginza
Harumi Dōri (Ave.)
SONY BLDG
GINZA (5)
NIHONSHU CENTER
お昼のサービス定食
お手頃すき焼定食
豚ロースしゃぶしゃぶ定食
牛ロースしゃぶしゃぶ定食

9

6

10

In the area
Where to stay: ➡ 20 ➡ 22 ➡ 24
After dark: ➡ 69
What to seee: ➡ 86 ➡ 88 ➡ 90 ➡ 110
Where to shop: ➡ 126 ➡ 128

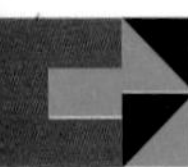

Where to eat

とん㐂 Tonki (13)

B1F, 6-5-15 Ginza, Chūō-ku ☎ (03) 3572-0702

M *Ginza* ***Tonkatsu*** ● *Mon.–Sat. 11.30am–3.30pm, 5–9.30pm*

In view of the hordes of 'salarymen' who crowd in here at lunchtime, you should definitely come here to sample the *katsudon* and *teishoku tonkatsu*.

アショカ Ashoka (14)

2F, 7-9-18 Ginza, Chūō-ku ☎ (03) 3572-2377

M *Ginza* ***Indian cuisine*** ●● *daily 11.30am–9.30pm*

A décor worthy of a maharajah's palace. Discreet, attentive waiters in traditional costumes serve moderately hot dishes from northern India. Vast choice, from the tandoori chicken and the lamb curry, to the *thali* (a selection of curries) or other specialties.

福臨門酒家 Fook Lam Moon (15)

6-13-16 Ginza, Chūō-ku ☎ (03) 3543-1989

M *Ginza* ***Chinese cuisine*** ●●●●● *Mon.–Sat. 11.30am–3pm, 5–10pm; Sun., public holidays 11.30am–4pm, 5.30–9pm*

To enjoy a real *fukahire* (shark's fin) soup, head for this place. This restaurant serves Cantonese specialties in a subdued setting with well spaced-out tables. You will be treated to simple, authentic dishes such as Peking duck, preparation of which is completed before your eyes, and stir-fried *tōmyao* (a Chinese vegetable). An ideal place to discover some very good Chinese wines. Menu in English. Remember to make reservations.

哥利歐 Gorio (16)

8-18-3 Ginza, Chūō-ku ☎ (03) 3543-7214

M *Shinbashi, Higashi-Ginza* ***Meat specialties*** ●●●●● *daily noon–10pm; closed 2nd Sun. of the month*

To be avoided by vegetarians. This is the best place to go for a steak cut from a piece of top-quality Kobé beef. Cooked over a wood fire, it is served on an iron platter lightly sprinkled with rough salt to extract all the flavor. A meal fit for a king. The house recommends the sirloin steak, but the bottom round isn't bad either. Whatever you choose, your pocket will feel it: expect to pay between ¥15,000 and ¥38,000 apiece. But can one put a price to an unforgettable experience?

Not forgetting

■ ロオジエ **L'Osier (17)** 7-5-5 Ginza, Chūō-ku ☎ (03) 3571-6050 ●●●●● *Jacques Borie, the chef, serves up a contemporary, sophisticated French cuisine. You are strongly advised to make reservations.*

■ 天亭 **Tentei (18)** 8-6-3 Ginza, Chūō-ku ☎ (03) 3571-8524 ●●● *) Your host will fry a really fresh, top-quality fish right in front of you. The tendon (a bowl of rice covered with tempura) at lunchtime is worth the trip.*

■ 大島ラーメン **Ōshima Ramen (19)** 8-10-16 Ginza, Chūō-ku ☎ (03) 3571-3460 ● *The bowl of ramen (noodles), topped with katsu (grilled pork) and a generous portion of vegetables, has acquired a high reputation among 'salarymen'. To be eaten at the bar at any time, as the restaurant closes at 4am. No credit cards.*

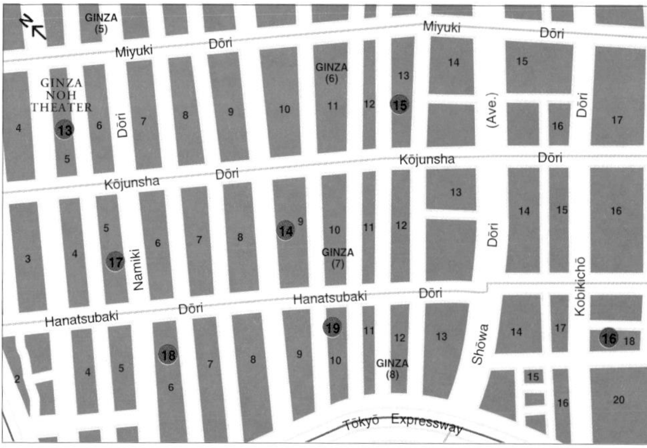

GINZA (5)
Miyuki Dōri
GINZA NOH THEATER
Kōjunsha Dōri
Namiki Dōri
GINZA (6)
GINZA (7)
GINZA (8)
Hanatsubaki Dōri
Shōwa Dōri (Ave.)
Kobikichō Dōri
Tōkyō Expressway

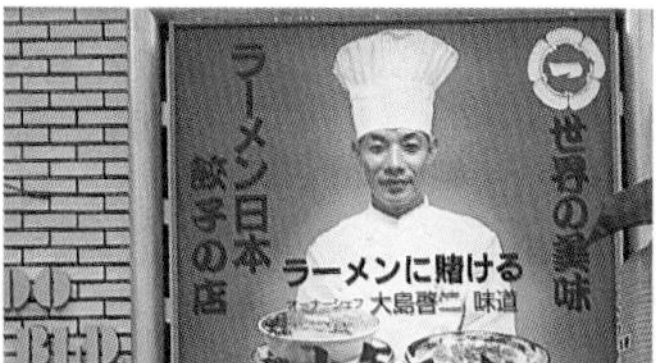

16

13

TONKATSU TO

19

ラーメン日本
餃子の店
ラーメンに賭ける
大島啓二 味道
秘伝 大島ラーメン
世界の美味
KEIJI OHSHIMA'S ORIGINAL TASTE
大島ラーメン
お米から生まれたスープ
RICE SOUP

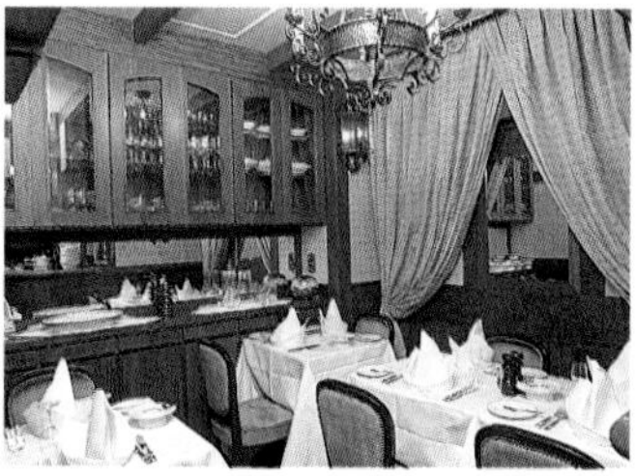

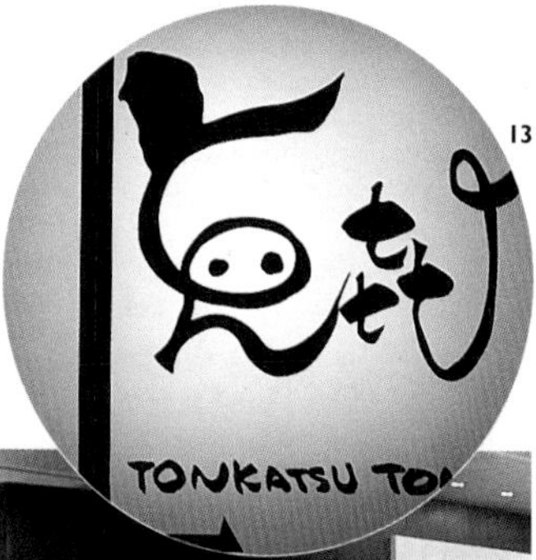

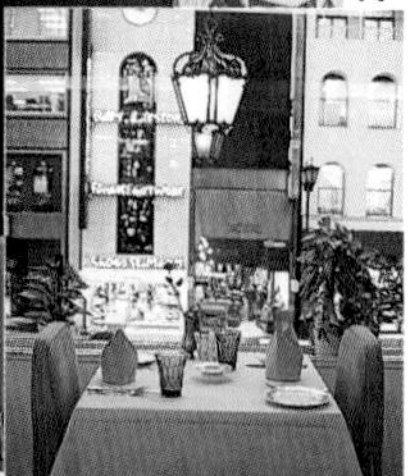

14

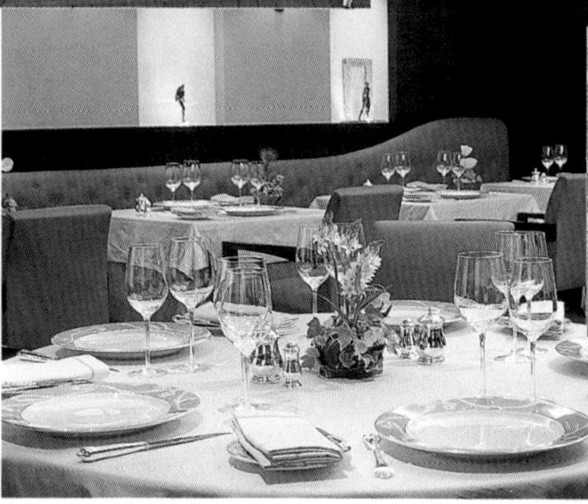

17

In the area

- Where to stay: ➥ 26
- After dark: ➥ 68 ➥ 70 ➥ 72 ➥ 74 ➥ 76
- What to see: ➥ 84 ➥ 86 ➥ 102
- Where to shop: ➥ 130 ➥ 132 ➥ 142

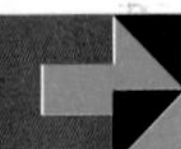

Where to eat

ジュンバタン・メラ **Jembatan Merah** (20)

Nichijuukin-Akasaka Bldg B1, 3-20-6, Akasaka, Minato-ku
☎ (03) 3588-0794

M *Akasakamitsuke* ***Indonesian cuisine*** ● *daily 11am–3pm, 5–10pm*
3F, 1-3 Maruyamachō, Shibuya-ku ; B1, 6-5-1 Nishi-Shinjuku, Shinjuku-ku

There's no way you'll miss this restaurant's brightly painted entrance. Go down the few steps and suddenly you're right in the heart of Indonesia. A quaint little store adjoins the entrance, then you make your way into the large dining room decorated with dark wood and enlivened by numerous icons, plants and various objects. Soup made from sheep's hooves, *ayamagorendabudabu* (spicy chicken) and *rendandagin* (boiled beef with spices) will defy your taste buds! Vegetarians are not forgotten with the *tempeh* (soya pâté with a touch of hazelnut) or *gado gado* salad. Menu in English.

ビストロ・サンノー **Bistrot Sanno** (21)

1F, 3-5-2 Akasaka, Minato-ku ☎ (03) 3582-7740

M *Akasaka* ***French cuisine*** ●●● *Mon.–Sat. noon–2pm, 6–10pm*

The chef–owner, Sunayama, was trained in Paris at top restaurants Lasserre and the Grand Véfour. He now prepares the great French classics for you, such as smoked rainbow trout, lobster bisque or leg of lamb. After that, let yourself be tempted by the *tarte tatin* or *crêpe Othello*. Of course, French is spoken, but so is English. The place is small, so don't forget to make reservations. The wines come from all over the world.

赤坂璃宮 **Akasaka Rikyū** (22)

Plaza Mikado B1F, 2-14-6 Akasaka, Minato-ku ☎ (03) 5570-9323

M *Akasaka* ***Chinese cuisine*** ●●● *daily 11.30am–3pm, 5.30–10pm*

The ideal place to sample food from Hong Kong in Tokyo. In contrast with the other Chinese restaurants, this one specializes in serving roast goose in place of the traditional roast duck, and truth be told the goose fat has a matchless taste. At lunchtime, you will appreciate the uncomplicated flavor of the *ramen* soup. Indeed, you won't be disappointed by the many dishes on the menu: soups, fried fish or fish stews. Reserve your table.

砂場 **Sunaba** (23)

6-3-5 Akasaka, Minato-ku ☎ (03) 3583-7670

M *Akasaka* ***Soba*** ● *Mon.–Fri. 11am–7.30pm; Sat. 11am–7pm; closed 3rd Sat. of the month*

Everything about this restaurant illustrates the discreet charm of the *soba-ya* of yesteryear, highly regarded by the people of Tokyo. Once installed with a good saké at a sturdy rustic wooden table or on a *tatami* mat, you will be served with *itawasa* (a sort of quenelle) and *yakitori* (skewers of meat). But you really should order the *soba* here.

Not forgetting

■ 赤坂四川飯店 **Akasaka Sisenhanten (24)** Zenkoku Ryokan Kaikan 5-6F, 2-5-5 Hirakawachō, Chiyoda-ku ☎ (03) 3263-9371 ●●● *You will experience one of the four great Chinese cuisines here, that of Sichuan, with its spicy flavors. The place is especially suitable for groups if reservations are made ahead. Open daily.*

Akasaka takes the time to live by the rhythm of the seasons. Wandering through its back streets gives you the chance to discover this residential district, harboring the famous *ryotei*, exclusive restaurants with only a discreet little sign to denote them. These establishments, which are not for common mortals (whether visitor or Japanese), play host to the movers and shakers of the political and financial worlds.

In the area

- Where to stay: ➥ 26
- After dark: ➥ 68 ➥ 70 ➥ 72 ➥ 74 ➥ 76 ➥ 78
- What to see: ➥ 86 ➥ 88 ➥ 102
- Where to shop: ➥ 130 ➥ 132 ➥ 142

Where to eat

二丁目魚新 **Nichōme-Uoshin** (25)
2-8-13 Akasaka, Minato-ku ☎ (03) 5570-4885

Akasaka ***Kaiseki-ryori*** ●●● *Mon.–Fri. 11.30am–2pm, 5–11pm; Sat. reservations only; closed public holidays, five days in mid-Aug.* *1-34 Akasaka, Minato-ku*

The chef is a professional fish merchant, retrained as a restaurateur. He will delight you with his unique menus – on maritime themes, of course. Best quality produce but at reasonable prices: expect to pay between ¥1,200 and ¥2,000 for the lunchtime menus. No doubt this is one of the reasons why there is such a crush at the gate.

トラットリア・バルダルノ **Trattoria Valdarno** (26)
Ark-Mori Bldg 1F, 1-12-32 Akasaka, Minato-ku ☎ (03) 5575-3315

Tameike-Sannō ***Italian cuisine*** ● *daily 7.30am–11pm*

At Valdarno's the pizza is excellent, but the real reason to visit the place is for its Tuscan cuisine. The *bistecca alla fiorentina*, sirloin steak and beef fillet on the bone are the specialties of the house and attract hordes of customers. The immense dining room is decorated in an Art-Deco style, which is not devoid of charm. The lunch at ¥1,200 has won such a reputation that the restaurant is always full.

フィッシュ **Fish** (27)
Ark-Mori Bldg 3F, 1-12-32 Akasaka, Minato-ku ☎ (03) 5562-4305

Tameike-Sannō ***Yōshoku*** ● *daily 11am–10pm*

Ground meat, vegetables and a serving of rice are the basis of *kare-raisu* (curries), with their marvelous spicy aroma particularly appreciated by visitors to Tokyo. Once seated at the bar, let yourself be tempted by the white-meat fish curry, accompanied by a nice white wine from the Languedoc or by an excellent tomato or mango juice.

Basara (28)
Ark-Mori Bldg 2F, 1-12-32 Akasaka, Minato-ku ☎ (03) 5549-7518

Tameike-Sannō ***Kaiseki-ryori*** ●●● *daily 11.30am–2pm, 5.30–10pm*
Aoyagi *1-22-1 Toranomon, Minato-ku ☎ (03) 3580-3456* ●●●●●

This restaurant, with its emphatically modern Zen décor, brings together pleasant rooms, either traditional or Western style, and a massive sushi bar, separated by wooden grilles and rough concrete partitions. At lunchtime, order one of the many *don*, dishes based on rice that simmers away in a pot in traditional fashion. *Oyako-don* (with chicken and egg), *anago-don* (with conger eel), *gyūnikushikure-don* (with beef) or others will not fail to delight you. In the evening, opt for a Japanese meal.

Not forgetting

■ 八屋 **Hachiya (29)** 9777 Ark-Mori Bldg 3F, 1-12-32 Akaksaka, Minato-ku ☎ (03) 3586-6088 ● *The ramen served with* shōyu *(soy sauce) are a real treat. If you are really hungry, accompany them with* gyōza *(vegetable and meat fritters), called* mizu-gyōza, *and which are one of the specialties worth making a note of. In summer, you must try the chilled soup with ramen. No credit cards.*

HACHIYA
ラーメン
の
八屋
OPEN

29

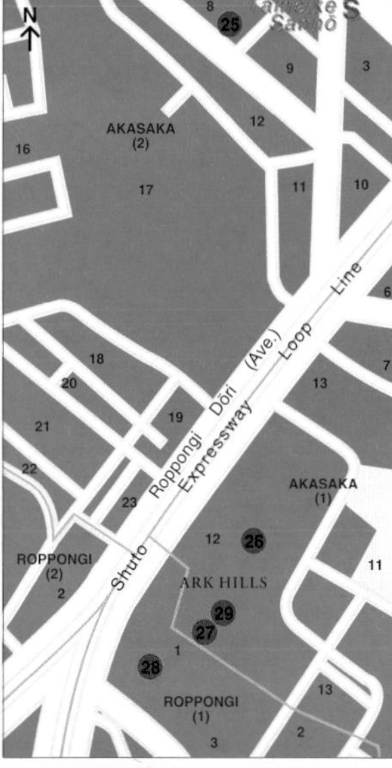
N
Tameike Sannō
AKASAKA (2)
Shuto Expressway Loop Line
Roppongi Dōri (Ave.)
AKASAKA (1)
ROPPONGI (2)
ARK HILLS
ROPPONGI (1)
25
26
27
28
29

25

26

26

In the area
Where to stay: ➥ 26
After dark: ➥ 68 ➥ 70 ➥ 72 ➥ 74 ➥ 76 ➥ 78
What to see: ➥ 84 ➥ 102
Where to shop: ➥ 130 ➥ 132 ➥ 142

Where to eat

奈可久 **Nakahisa** (30)
B1F, 7-8-4 Roppongi, Minato-ku ☎ (03) 3475-0252

M *Roppongi* ***Sushi, seafood*** ●●● *Mon.–Sat. 11.30am–2pm, 5–10pm; closed public holidays, Jan. 1, Aug. 15*

This luxury restaurant still serves Edomae *nigirizushi*, which will surprise you by the subtle combination of vinegared rice and different *neta* (toppings). But it is highly recommended to try the sea bream or the turbot with *konbu* (seaweed) first. If you are short of time, sit at the bar and try the superbly flavored *kaiten-zushi* (sushi on a conveyer belt).

本むら庵 **Honmuran-an** (31)
1F, 7-14-18 Roppongi, Minato-ku ☎ (03)3401-0844

M *Roppongi* ***Soba*** ● *Mon., Wed.–Fri. 11am–3pm, 5–9pm; Sat., Sun. 11am–9pm; closed 3rd Mon. of the month*

Some Western-style tables, a room with *tatami* mats and a small kitchen occupy this minimal and friendly space. At the back of the restaurant, behind a plate-glass window, is the *soba* workshop where the *soba-shokunin* lays out the dough and cuts it into long, fine threads. The recipe for buckwheat noodles varies from family to family, but it is undoubtably here in this renowned *soba-ya* that they are at their purest and most delicate. Those with big appetites can always order a *kamonanban* (soup with *soba*, duck and chives) to allay their hunger. An ideal place to stop off in the afternoon and sip a saké served with *tsumami* (a selection of tapas).

天ぷら魚新 **Tempura Uoshin** (32)
B1F, 5-5-8 Roppongi, Minato-ku ☎ (03) 3403-1051

M *Roppongi* ***Tempura*** ●●● *Mon.–Sat. 11.30am–2pm*

Behind the bar you at which you sit, watch the dexterity with which the cook fries the pieces of *tempura* in his large cooking pot. For your meal you will be served *kuruma-ebi* (prawns) as an appetizer, then you will be offered the fish of the season. At lunchtime you will enjoy the simple flavor of *tendon*, *agedon* or *teishoku*, which would seem to be the best value for money. For an evening among friends, reserve the little *tatami* alcove with its own bar and personal cook.

野田岩 **Nodaiwa** (33)
1-5-4 Higashi-Azabu, Minato-ku ☎ (03) 3583-7852

M *Kamiyachō* ***Unagi*** ●●● *Mon.–Sat. 11am–1.30pm, 5–8pm*

This restaurant, which has an established reputation for *unagi* (eel), is located in a corner building lavishly decorated with old beams and other salvaged materials. There are two seasons a year for enjoying eel: from mid-April through end June and from October through mid-December. Don't miss your chance. Each season has its own pleasures: the eels are fine and delicate tasting in the spring, while the meat is more melt-in-the-mouth and robustly flavored in the fall. You'll have the choice of two methods of preparation: *kabayaki*, which consists of grilling the whole eel on a skewer, or *unajū*, served on a bed of rice. On the upper floors there are small, individual *tatami* rooms that you really need to reserve. You are served more quickly, though, if you sit at a table. Be warned! It is very crowded at the start of every sitting.

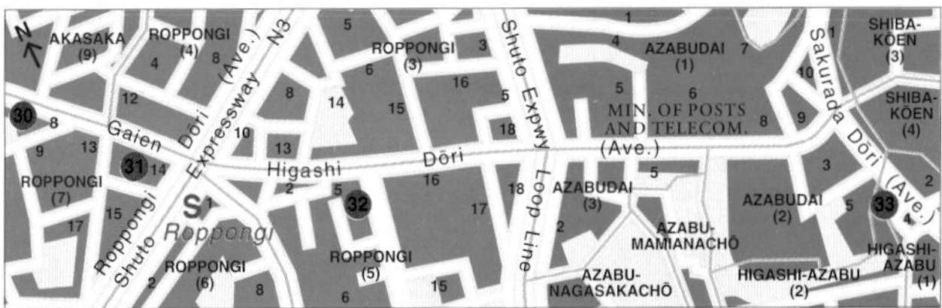

Roppongi is the fief of 'expats' and the heart of Tokyo nightlife. *Nomiya*, those bars where you drink and eat *tsumami*, proliferate, but it is equally true that some of the best specialist restaurants are also to be found here.

33

32

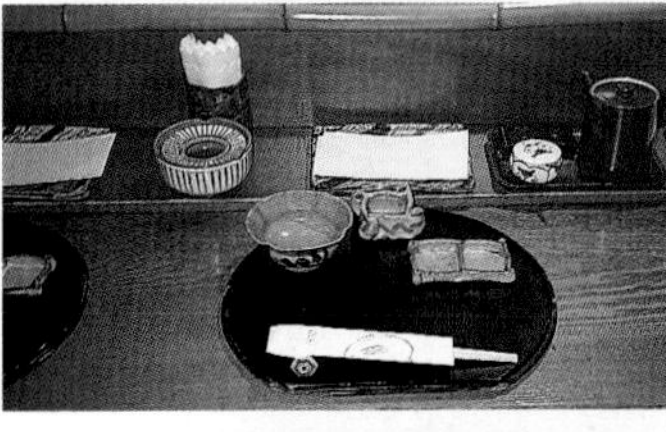

31

33

In the area
- Where to stay: ➥ 26
- After dark: ➥ 68 ➥ 70 ➥ 72 ➥ 74 ➥ 76 ➥ 78
- What to see: ➥ 84 ➥ 102
- Where to shop: ➥ 130 ➥ 132 ➥ 142

Where to eat

中国飯店 Tyūgoku Hanten (34)
1-1-5 Nishi-Azabu, Minato-ku ☎ (03) 3478-3828

M *Roppongi* **Chinese cuisine** ●●● *daily 11.30am–3pm, 5pm–4am*

Come here in search of the provinces of China. From Peking duck to the stir-fries of Sichuan, not forgetting steamed crab from Shanghai – its short season is from October to end November – the menu is strangely reminiscent of the travel diary of some famous gourmet. In winter, try the house specialty, grilled *taro* with chives, as an appetizer.

Têtês (35)
2-13-12 Nishi-Azabu, Minato-ku ☎ (03) 5468-5505

M *Roppongi* **Vietnamese and Thai cuisine** ●● *daily 11am–4am*

Its trendy New York-style décor and its large picture windows opening onto the street attract a younger, more dynamic clientele, who crowd in there after leaving the disco. Têtês happily combines the aromatic herbs and subtle spices of Vietnamese and Thai cuisine, which go admirably with the wines of Bordeaux.

千利庵 Senri-an (36)
2-25-19 Nishi-Azabu, Minato-ku ☎ (03) 3400-1782

M *Roppongi* **Soba** ●● *Mon., Tue., Thu.–Sun. 11.30am–2.30pm, 5–9pm*

On the other side of the window, like a goldfish in a bowl, the *soba-shokunin* dexterously slices up the noodles that you are about to eat. Besides the *tamago-togi* (with an egg) and *kamo-nanban* (with chicken and leek), in summer you must take time to enjoy the delicious chilled *udon*, served in unlimited quantities with steaming duck soup. As an appetizer, try their *tsumami* with the house saké.

麻布食堂 Azabu-shokudō (37)
4-2-9 Nishi-azabu, Minato-ku ☎ (03) 3409-4767

M *Roppongi* **Yōshoku** ● *Mon.–Sat. 11.30am–2pm, 5.30–9pm*

The *omeraisu* (rice omelet), *hayashiraisu* (slivers of beef, vegetables, tomato sauce, rice), *menchikatsu* (fried meatballs) or *kani-koroke* (crab croquettes), even the sirloin will help you to appreciate the *yōshoku*, those European recipes that have been adapted in the Japanese fashion. A bar and two small tables vie for space in this Parisian-style bistro where wine is on offer with the evening meal.

Not forgetting

■ 分とく山 **Waketokuyama (38)** 3F, Yawata Bldg 3F, 4-12-13 Nishi-Azabu, Minato-ku ☎ (03) 3400-2968 ●●●● *This meeting place for aficionados of* kaiseki ryōki *is on the second floor of a small building. Place your confidence in the chef, Hiromisu Nozaki, for your meal; everything is suffused with a very Japanese spirit. Dinner only from 5pm; closed on Sat., Sun. and public holidays.* ■ **Bistrot de la Cité (39)** 4-2-10 Nishi-Azabu, Minato-ku ☎ (03) 3406-5475 ●●● *The 'Cité salad', served in limitless quantities, has made the reputation of this bistro despite the seven other appetizers which are just as mouthwatering. You will thoroughly enjoy the tripe or ratatouille. At lunchtime, the* teishoku *at ¥1,200–1,800 consists of a succulent chicken confit (not on Sundays or public holidays). Closed Mondays.*

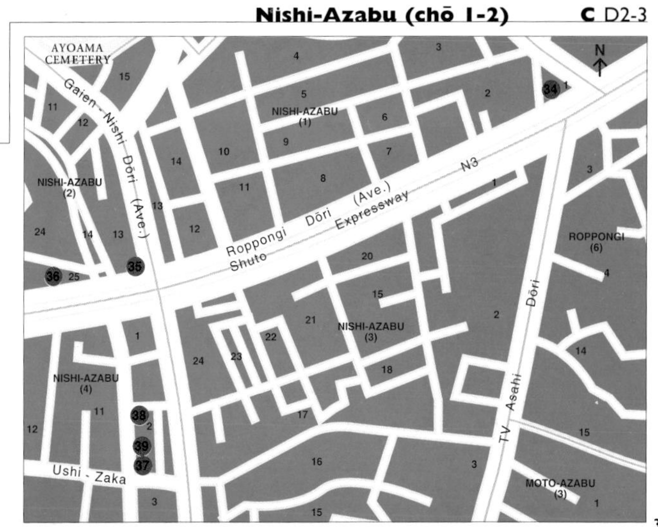

38

39

西麻布 分とく山

38

37

In the area

Where to stay: ➥ 26 ➥ 30
After dark: ➥ 70 ➥ 72 ➥ 74 ➥ 76 ➥ 78
What to see: ➥ 84 ➥ 102
Where to shop: ➥ 130 ➥ 143

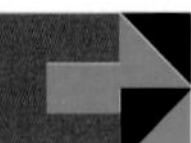

Where to eat

たぬき **Tanuki** (40)

4-5-8 Nishi-Azabu, Minato-ku ☎ (03) 3409-3884

Hiro-o ***Kaiseki-ryori*** ● *Sun.–Fri. 11.30am–1.30pm, 6–10pm*

There is only a big white *aka-chochin* (lantern) to denote this tiny establishment. On passing through the sliding bamboo door, the pleasant aroma of traditionally cooked rice fills the room. If you order the *gohansetto*, you will be served with a *misoshiru* (*miso* soup), rice, vegetables and a grilled fish you will have chosen à la carte, thus putting together your own *teishoku* (menu). Here you have all the ingredients that delight the Japanese on a daily basis.

香港ガーデン **Hong Kong Garden** (41)

4-5-2 Nishi-Azabu, Minato-ku ☎ (03) 3486-3711

Hiro-o ***Chinese cuisine*** ●● *Mon.–Sat. 11am–2.30pm, 5.30–10pm; Sun., public holidays 11.30am–4pm, 5.30–9.30pm* *Lau Ling*

In a city where every square inch is valued like gold dust, Hong Kong Garden is not ashamed to flaunt its delusions of grandeur. A real commercial empire located in a two-story building, it can accommodate over 800 people. On the first floor, the slogan 'all you can eat' for ¥3,000 represents excellent value for money. Give in to your fondness for the *dim sum* and choose, for example, the *ebi-gyōza* or the *shūmai* (pork and vegetable pâté) from the carts that wend their way continuously among the tables. On the upper floor, the restaurant, bar and private dining rooms impose a much more subdued atmosphere.

ダノイ **Da noi** (42)

B1F, 4-6-7 Nishi-Azabu, Minato-ku ☎ (03) 3797-4444

Hiro-o ***Italian cuisine*** ●●● *Tue.–Sun. 11.30am–2pm, 6–11pm*

A buzzing trattoria-style ambience reigns at Da-noi in the evenings. The kitchens opening onto the dining room, the tightly packed tables and the shelves lined with bottles of Tuscan wine contribute to the party spirit. It is so busy that reservations sometimes can't be honored. This solid reputation has been won by the excellence of the Tuscan food, the family atmosphere and the very reasonable prices. The star dishes are spaghetti with cabbage and anchovies, the chicken with potatoes and the tender sides of meat. At lunchtime, meals are served in the little café on the ground floor, where you can feast on a large plate of pasta.

i piselli (43)

5-2-39 Minami-azabu, Minato-ku ☎ (03) 3446-9700

Hiro-o ***Italian cuisine*** ●●● *Mon.–Sat. noon–2.30pm, 6–10.30pm Mon.–Sat. 6pm–2.30am*

I piselli has been one of the most popular Italian restaurants in Tokyo since 1985. The chic, monochrome décor offers a restful setting in which to savor the simple yet refined cuisine. Depending on the season, the chef will prepare for you a salad of peaches with basil, roast duck with balsamic vinegar, or simply the fish of the day. The pasta and caviar or *bottarga* (mullet eggs) is always very good. The lunch menu, at ¥1,500, comprising appetizer, pasta of the day, dessert and coffee, is a real gift.

40

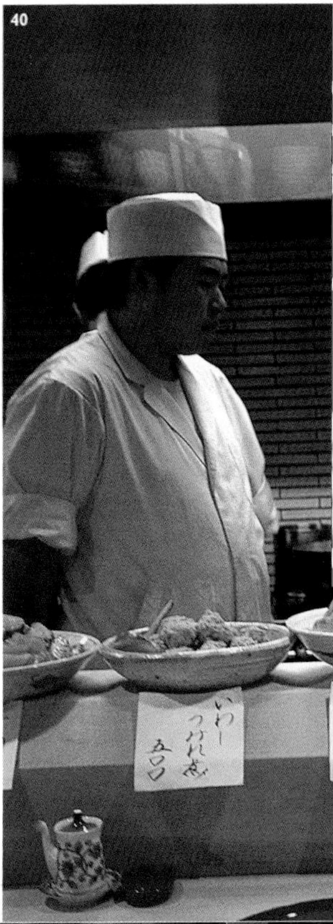
いわし
つみれ煮
五百
厚揚げごぼう
あんかけ
四百
おから
三百

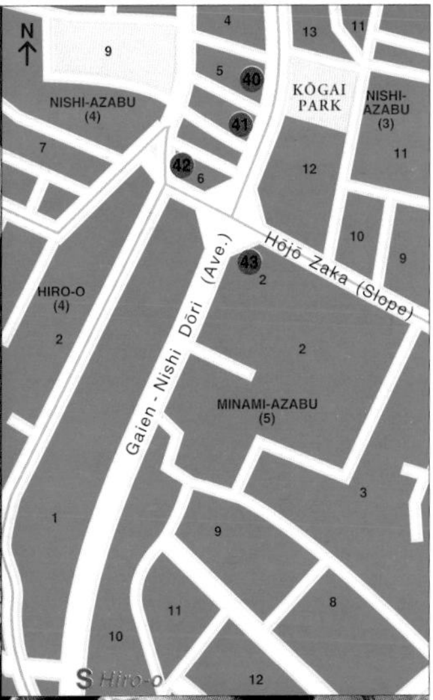
N
NISHI-AZABU (4)
KŌGAI PARK
NISHI-AZABU (3)
HIRO-O (4)
MINAMI-AZABU (5)
Hōjō Zaka (Slope)
Gaien - Nishi Dōri (Ave.)
S Hiro-o
40
41
42
43
1
2
3
4
5
6
7
8
9
10
11
12
13

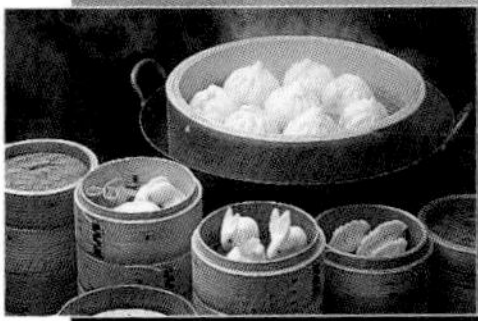

41

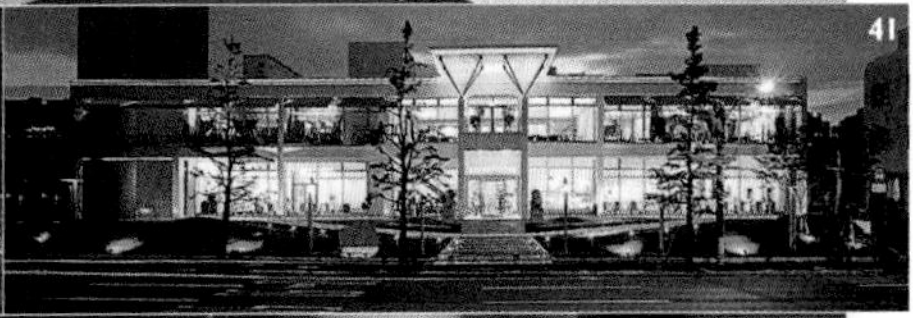

42

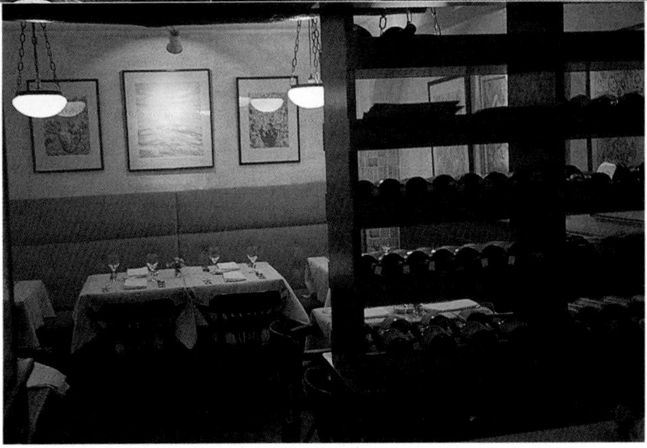

In the area

- Where to stay: ➥ 28
- After dark: ➥ 68 ➥ 74
- What to see: ➥ 94 ➥ 103
- Where to shop: ➥ 126 ➥ 140 ➥ 142

Where to eat

王朝 Dynasty / Ōcho (44)

Tokyo Hilton 2F, 6-6-2 Nishi-Shinjuku, Shinjuku-ku ☎ (03) 3344-5111

Tochōmae **Chinese cuisine** ●●● *daily 11.30am–3pm, 5.30–10pm*

As hotel restaurants go ➥ 28, this one is totally remarkable. As well as the extremely popular dishes, it offers some specialties such as steamed aromatic duck and carp simmered in *shōyu*.

武蔵屋新宿店 Menya Musashi (45)

7-2-6 Nishi-Sinjuku, Shinjuku-ku ☎ (03) 3796-4634

JR Shinjuku **Rāmen** ● *Mon.–Fri. 11.30am–2.30pm, 5.30–9.30pm; Sat., public holidays 11.30am–4pm*

Always packed and buzzing with life, this noodle bar is in every way worthy of its Golden-Gai ➥ 94 neighbors. It's a touch of the movies, Japanese-style. This doesn't stop the cooks serving up simple, natural food with a delicious flavor.

すずや Suzu-Ya (46)

Sugiyama Bldg 2F, 1-23-15, Kabuchiko, Shinjuku-ku ☎ (03) 3209-4480

JR Shinjuku **Tonkatsu** ● *daily 11.30am–10.15pm*

This establishment is well known for its *tonkatsu* served with *chazuké* (rice with green tea). It's a combination of flavors particularly loved by the Japanese. The correct way to eat is to have some *tonkatsu* on its own then enjoy the rest with the rice on which you first pour the green tea.

中村屋 Nakamura-ya (47)

1F, 3-26-13 Shinjuku, Shinjuku-ku ☎ (03) 3352-6161

JR Shinjuku **Yōshoku** ● *daily 11am–9.30pm*

An immense cafeteria where the regulars go for the *kare-raisu*. The Indian-style chicken curry, with the meat left on the bone and served as hot as you like, or the mild *korma* curry (cream and coconut sauce) are well up in the top ten. A wide choice of Chinese dishes.

Not forgetting

■ 割烹新宿中嶋 **Nakajima (48)** Nichihara Bldg B1F, 3-32-5 Shinjuku, Shinjuku-ku ☎ (03) 3356-4534 ●●● *The reputation of this establishment, serving cuisine from the Kyoto and Osaka regions, is founded on the sardine* teishoku, *on offer at lunchtime, whose flavor is really exceptional. Other favorites:* tataki *(fish stew),* tempura *or stew with* shōyu… *You can put together your own menu depending on your appetite. No credit cards; closed Sundays.* 正月屋吉兆 ■**Shougatsu-ya Kichō (49)** Isetan 7F, 3-14-1 Shinjuku, Shinjuku-ku ☎ (03) 3355-6644 ●●●● *This is an establishment that is far above what you expect from a department store cafeteria. Without fuss, and in a peaceful atmosphere, you are served* domburimono *(food in bowls), and the best of* kaiseki *cuisine. Closed Wednesdays.* ■ ニューヨーク・グリル **New York Grill (50)** Park Hyatt Tokyo 52F, 3-7-1-2 Nishi-Shinjuku, Shinjuku-ku ☎ (03) 5323-3458 ●●● *Perched on the top of the Park Hyatt Hotel ➥ 28, this place, where you can enjoy a fine view over Tokyo, is always full. Enjoy a drink at the bar, the meeting place for the Tokyo jet set. American cuisine.*

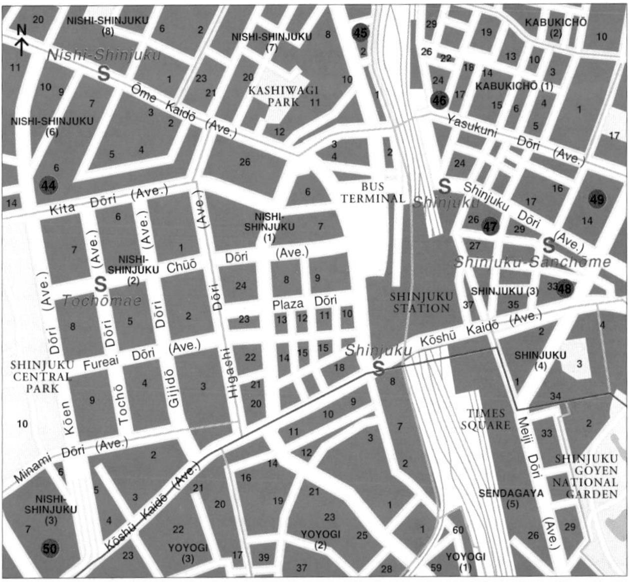

NISHI-SHINJUKU (8)
NISHI-SHINJUKU (7)
KABUKICHŌ (2)
KABUKICHŌ (1)
Nishi-Shinjuku
Ōme Kaidō (Ave.)
KASHIWAGI PARK
NISHI-SHINJUKU (6)
Yasukuni Dōri (Ave.)
BUS TERMINAL
Shinjuku
Shinjuku Dōri (Ave.)
Kita Dōri (Ave.)
NISHI-SHINJUKU (1)
Shinjuku-Sanchōme
NISHI-SHINJUKU (2)
Chūō Dōri (Ave.)
Tochōmae
Plaza Dōri
SHINJUKU STATION
SHINJUKU (3)
Kōshū Kaidō (Ave.)
SHINJUKU (4)
SHINJUKU CENTRAL PARK
Fureai Dōri (Ave.)
Kōen Dōri (Ave.)
Tochō Dōri
Gijidō Dōri
Higashi Dōri
TIMES SQUARE
Meiji Dōri (Ave.)
Minami Dōri (Ave.)
SHINJUKU GOYEN NATIONAL GARDEN
NISHI-SHINJUKU (3)
Kōshū Kaidō (Ave.)
SENDAGAYA (5)
YOYOGI (3)
YOYOGI (2)
YOYOGI (1)

49

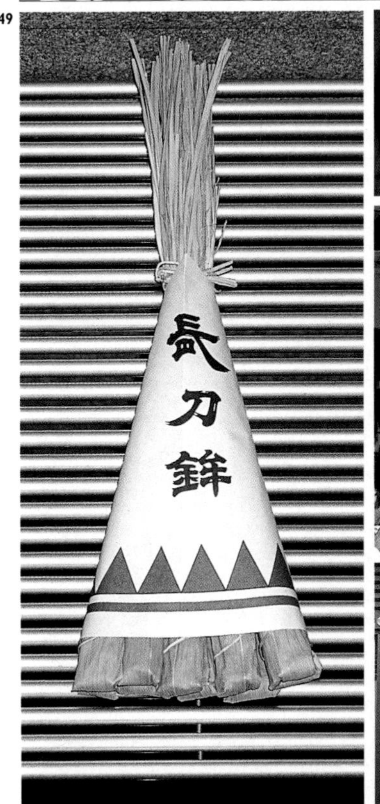

44

45

48

In the area

Where to stay: ➡ 30
After dark : ➡ 68 ➡ 74 ➡ 78
What to see: ➡ 84 ➡ 96 ➡ 98 ➡ 102
Where to shop: ➡ 126 ➡ 134 ➡ 136 ➡ 138 ➡ 142

Where to eat

第一神宮 Dai-ichi jingu (51)

3-41-8 Jingūmae, Shibuya-ku ☎ (03) 3401-9146

M *Gaienmae* ***Korean cuisine*** ●● *daily 5pm–1am; closed Jan. 1*

At nightfall, customers crowd at the door of this pretty establishment on *Killer-dōri*. They come here to stuff themselves with top-quality beef prepared Korean style. The *kalbi* (rib), like the *yukke* (stew), is without compare, and a Californian wine served with it will bring out the delicate flavor. Vegetarians will enjoy the *hiyamugi* just as much, a dish of chilled noodles served with sweet and sour sauce.

ラ・グロッタ La Grotta (52)

Hills Aoyama B1F, 3-39-9 Jingūmae, Shibuya-ku ☎ (03) 3470-7052

M *Gaienmae* ***Italian cuisine*** ●●● *Mon.–Sat. 11.30am–2pm, 6–10pm*

This restaurant is well named since, as with every grotto, you have to search to find the entrance. But the effort will be well worth it. This establishment specializes in dishes such as pork chops or chicken, cooked over charcoal. The wild vegetable salad or the *rigatoni* with Japanese oxtail are delicious.

八竹 Hachiku (53)

6-29-4 Jingūmae, Shibuya-ku ☎ (03) 3407-5858

M *Meiji-jingūmae* ***Sushi*** ● *Mon., Wed.–Sun. 9am–6pm* ➡ *138*

Hachiku sets itself up as an ambassador of the regional cuisine of Osaka, which is characterized by being a little more salty and using slightly less soy sauce. Here you won't be served *nigirizushi* but *hakozushi* (pressed sushi), *futomaki* (with omelet, *shītake*, red pepper...), *chakinzushi* (sushi coated in egg) and excellent *chirashizushi*.

ラ・プラーヤ La Playa (54)

Dai-ni Komatsu Bldg Annex B1, 2-14-4, Shibuya-ku ☎ (03) 5469-9505

M *JR Shibuya* ***Spanish cuisine*** ●●● *Mon.–Sat. 6–11pm*

Cured ham, Spanish omelet, marinated seafood, squid cooked in its own ink – these are only a selection of the appetizing dishes on offer here. Not forgetting, of course, the paella, cooked here with Japanese rice. An excellent wine and sherry list.

Not forgetting

■ オーバカナル **Aux Bacchanales (55)** Palais France 1F, 1-6-1 Jingūmae, Shibuya-ku ☎ (03) 5474-0076 ●●● *Quintessential Paris in the heart of Tokyo. If you feel like a taste of France, make for Aux Bacchanales, where you will be bowled over by the succulent leg of lamb, sliced or cut in steaks. At lunchtime, choose the ¥1,000 set menu, which is good value for money. As well as eating in the restaurant, you can have a fresh baguette and continental breakfast on the terrace, or a glass of wine at the bar....*

■ **Ryū no ko (56)** B1F, 1-8-5 Jingūmae, Shibuya-ku ☎ (03) 3402-9419 ● *Here you will be served Chinese cuisine from Sichuan province. Treat yourself and order the authentic* mabodōfu, *a Chinese meat and pepper tōfu.*

51
53
N
TŌGŌ-JINJA (SHRINE)
JINGŪMAE (1)
(Ave.)
Meiji-Jingūmae
Dōri
Meiji
JINGŪMAE (3)
Killer Dōri
JINGŪMAE (4)
Omote - Sandō (Ave.)
KITA-AOYAMA (3)
JINGŪMAE (6)
Omote-Sandō
JINGŪMAE (5)
KITA-AOYAMA (3)
Road N246
MINAMI-AOYAMA (5)
NAT'L CHILDREN'S CASTLE
Nat'l
Kottō Dōri (Ave.)
SHIBUYA (1)
Aoyama Dōri (Ave.)
SHIBUYA (4)
AOYAMA GAKUIN UNIV.
SHIBUYA (2)
53

In the area

- Where to stay: ➥ 30
- After dark: ➥ 78
- What to see: ➥ 84 ➥ 100
- Where to shop: ➥ 142

Where to eat

久田 Hisada (57)

TTC Bldg B1F, 4-2-48 Hiro-o, Minato-ku ☎ (03) 3444-9130

M *Hiroo* ***Kaiseki-ryori*** ●●●● *Tue.–Fri. noon–1.30pm, 6–9pm; Sat., Sun. 6–9pm*

Discreetly located in a basement, this establishment serves high-quality traditional cuisine. The all-inclusive menu deserves top billing for dinner, while at lunchtime the *teishoku* with fish *tempura* is excellent value for money.

ラ・ビスボッチャ La Bisubocha (58)

2-36-13 Ebisu, Shibuya-ku ☎ (03) 3449-1470

M *Hiroo* ***Italian cuisine*** ●●● *Mon.–Sat. 5.30–10.30pm*

The cheerful 'buona sera!' shouted out by every member of staff whisks you straight to Italy, into the bustling atmosphere of the trattorias of Rome or Milan. The classics of Italian cuisine are served here, but make sure you don't miss the famous risotto with parmesan.

かつ好 Katsuyoshi (59)

Ebisu Garden Place Tower B2F, 4-20-3 Ebisu, Shibuya-ku ☎ (03) 5421-1338

M *JR Ebisu* ***Tonkatsu*** ●● *daily 11.30am–9pm; closed Jan. 1, 2*

Once inside, you soon forget that you're in the basement of the Mitsukoshi ➥ 126 department store. A dark and warm setting, enhanced by light bricks and heavy wood. You can choose between sitting at the bar or on the *tatami*. On the menu are delicate *karomikatsu*, whose paper-thinness brings to mind Austrian Wiener schnitzel, and the *rōsu-hyakumonme-katsu*, thicker but just as tender. Ready-to-cook meat or seafood *tonkatsu* meals, with their sauces and young vegetables, are prepared in store. Menu in English.

Château Restaurant Taillevent-Robuchon (60)

Ebisu Garden Place, 1-13-1 Mita, Meguro-ku ☎ (03) 5421-0080

M *JR Ebisu* ***French cuisine*** ***Restaurant*** *Mon.–Sat. noon–2pm, 6–9.30pm* ●●●●● ***Café Français*** *daily 11.30am–2.30pm, 5.30–9pm* ●●● *2.30– 6pm* ***La Boutique*** *daily 10am–8pm*/***Les Caves Taillevent*** *Tue.–Sun. 11am–7.30pm*

Here's something you won't have seen before! In the center of Ebisu Garden Place there proudly stands an 18th-century-style castle. This unique restaurant is the work of two great Parisian chefs, Taillevent and Robuchon. The whole building is stamped with a refinement worthy of the Age of Enlightenment. Every detail, from the light wood paneling covering the walls to the period furniture and the delicate china, has been thought out to complement the excellent cuisine of these extraordinary chefs. Three times a year, Joël Robuchon brings back new seasonal recipes in his suitcase. Each one, such as the caviar in aspic, the cream of cauliflower soup or the mille-feuilles with crab and tomato, demonstrates a perfect balance between the subtle blending of flavors and the estheticism of gastronomy. On a fine day, lunch or tea on the terrace of the Café Français on the first floor is a privileged experience.

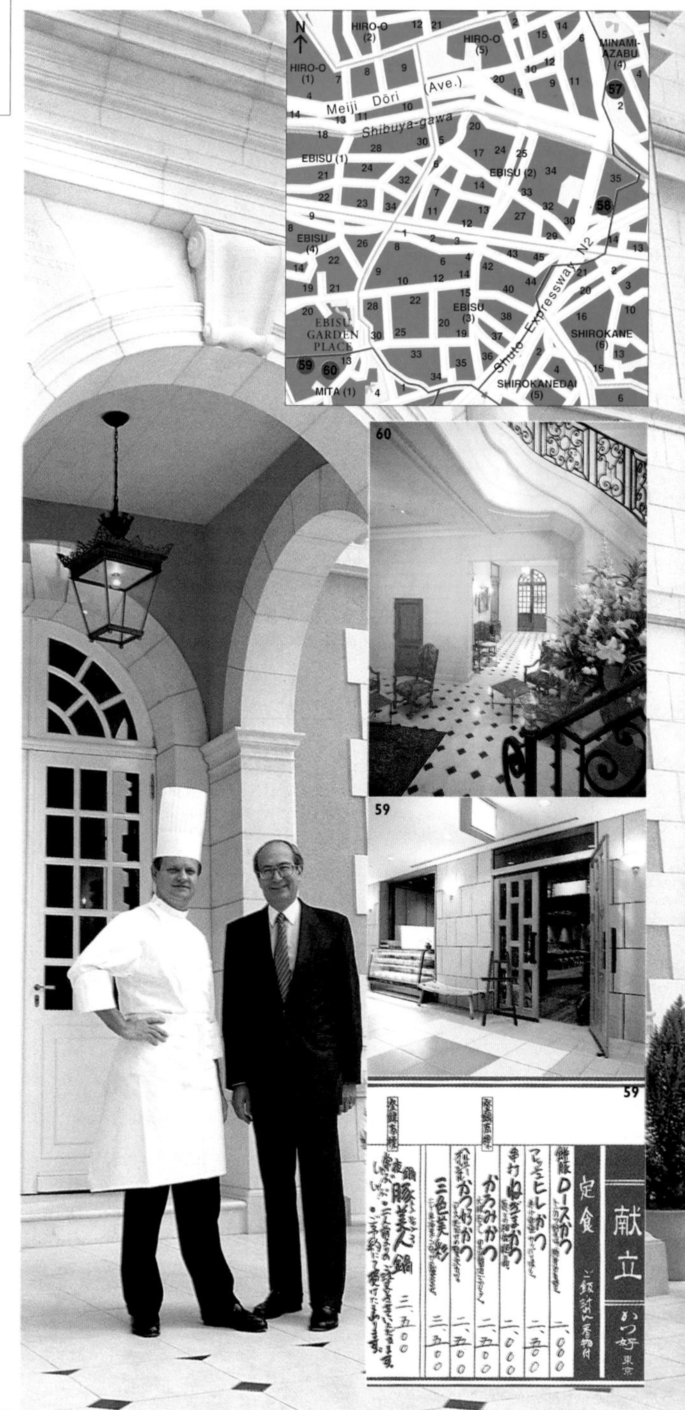
N
HIRO-O (2)
HIRO-O (5)
MINAMI-AZABU (4)
HIRO-O (1)
Meiji Dōri (Ave.)
Shibuya-gawa
EBISU (1)
EBISU (2)
EBISU (4)
EBISU (3)
Shuto Expressway N2
EBISU GARDEN PLACE
SHIROKANE (6)
SHIROKANEDAI (5)
MITA (1)
57
58
59
60
献立
かつ好 東京
定食
ご飯 試ん 香物付
鮮豚ロースかつ
二、000
ヒレかつ
二、五00
ねぎまかつ
二、000
かろみかつ
二、五00
かつ好かつ
二、五00
三色美彩
三、五00
豚美人鍋
三、五00

60

59

59

In the area
- Where to stay: ➡ 19
- After dark: ➡ 70 ➡ 72 ➡ 74
- What to see: ➡ 84, ➡ 102 ➡ 104
- Where to shop: ➡ 143 ➡ 147

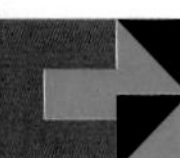

Where to eat

ちんや **Chinya** (61)
1-3-4 Asakusa, Taitō-ku ☎ (03) 3841-0010

Asakusa **Sukiyaki** ●● *Mon., Tue., Thu.–Sun. 11.45am–9.15pm*

Don't be surprised that you have to take your shoes off and put on the *surippa* provided at the door. You're in the *shitamachi* (lower town) of Old Tokyo where even a tourist is expected to follow the everyday customs. A kimono-clad waitress will then lead you to your table in the large traditional dining room where the atmosphere is extremely warm and friendly. Eating here is very informal, and the festive mood eases the conversation between guests. The specialty of the house, *sukiyaki*, is one of the favorite winter dishes of Tokyo residents. Carefully prepared at your table, this dish consists of stir-fried slivers of beef, grilled *tōfu*, *shitake* (mushrooms), *negi* (Japanese leek), *shirataki* (Japanese noodles) and *shungiku* (chrysanthemum leaves) simmered in a sweet-and-sour stock. Dip all the pieces in beaten raw egg, and enjoy.

ラ・シェーブル **La Chèvre** (62)
1-1-12 Nishi-Asakusa, Taitō-ku ☎ (03) 3845-1336

Tawaramachi **French cuisine** ●● *Mon., Tue., Thu.–Sat. 11.30am–2pm, 6–10pm; Sun. 6–10pm; closed Sep. 1–15, Jan. 1*

It is surprising to find a French restaurant in this old and traditional district. However, the Japanese chef conjures up a cuisine that is both simple and sophisticated, subtly marrying classic recipes with produce from the east. Good-value, delicious French food is served, such as tomato soup and oxtail simmered in red wine. The wine list, although far from being exhaustive, offers an excellent selection of Bordeaux and Burgundies. It is advisable to make reservations.

並木薮蕎麦 **Namiki Yabusoba** (63)
2-11-9 Kaminarimon, Taitō-ku ☎ (03) 3841-1340

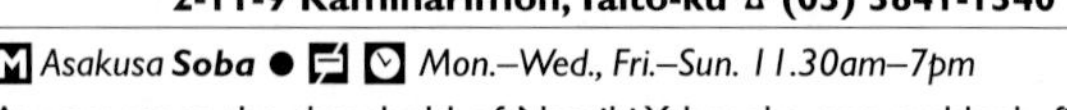

Asakusa **Soba** ● *Mon.–Wed., Fri.–Sun. 11.30am–7pm*

As you cross the threshold of Namiki Yabusoba, you suddenly find yourself transported 100 years back in time. The restaurant retains the décor of bygone shitamachi restaurants and the traditional communal meal. Whether you are sitting at a table or on the raised *tatami*, you will be sharing Edomae *mori* (buckwheat *soba*) with the other guests. These noodles, which you dip lightly in *soba-tsuyu* sauce, are a Tokyo recipe that has been appreciated for generations. As well as *tempura-soba*, in winter you will be offered *kamonaban*, noodles topped with duck and chives.

すぎ田 **Sugita** (64)
3-8-3 Kotobuki, Taitō-ku ☎ (03) 3844-5529

Tarawamachi **Yōshoku** ● *Mon.–Wed., Fri.–Sun. 11.30am–2pm, 5–8.15pm*

If you thought loin of pork was dull, rethink and come to Sugita to try their *tonkatsu*. The menu lists a classic repertoire of *yōshoku*, such as the ever-present *ebi-furai* (shrimp fritters) and the delicious *omuretsu* (omelet).

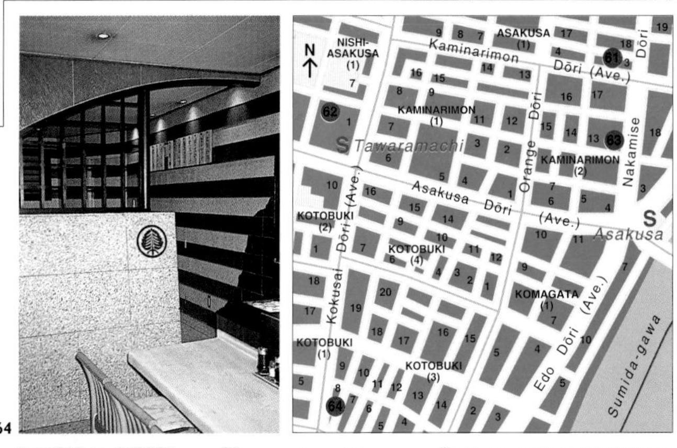
N
NISHI-ASAKUSA (1)
ASAKUSA (1)
Kaminarimon Dōri (Ave.)
KAMINARIMON (1)
Tawaramachi
Orange Dōri
KAMINARIMON (2)
Nakamise Dōri
Asakusa Dōri (Ave.)
Asakusa
KOTOBUKI (2)
Kokusai Dōri (Ave.)
KOTOBUKI (4)
KOMAGATA (1)
Edo Dōri (Ave.)
Sumida-gawa
KOTOBUKI (1)
KOTOBUKI (3)
61
62
63
64

64

62

63

Japanese theater

Arming yourself with a *bentō* (food tray), making comments out loud about the play and the acting during the performance – all this is part and parcel of going to the theater.

Teletourist Comprehensive recorded information about theater and festival events for the week ☎ *(03) 3201-2911*

After dark

Listings...

Magazines

Tōkyō Journal: get hold of the *Cityscope* supplement in bookshops
monthly • *¥600*

Tōkyō Classified newspaper available in kiosks, train stations and some bars
www.tokyoclassified.com
Fri. • *free*

Pia available just about everywhere, but only in Japanese.

Cinema

Films mostly origin[al] with subtitles.
• *¥1,800–2,300*
Tōkyō Film Festival
Shinjuku, in August

Kampai!

A custom to be followed when drinking with Japanese friends: fill up their glasses and they will make sure your glass is topped up in return. *Kampai* (cheers)!

Concerts

Tokyo is one of the most up-to-date cities musically, but attending a concert is a very different experience from what Westerners are used to. Tickets cost at least ¥8,000, at some venues it is forbidden to dance, smoke, eat, take photographs etc. and times are often very odd. Events often start at 7pm to finish at 9pm! The reason: not to miss the last subway train ➡ 10.

44 Nights out

THE INSIDER'S FAVORITES

Japanese style bars

Frequented by 'salarymen' (employees) – very rarely by *gaijin* (foreigners) – *isakaya* (saké houses) and *nomiya* (bars) are nearly always noisy, packed, smoky and friendly. Take note that drinks are always served with *mezze*. In the Shinjuku quarter of Golden Gai (really just a block) you will find over 200 *nomiya*. Tiny, with about four or five places around the bar, they are primarily frequented by regulars. Silence may descend as the door slides open and a *gaijin* enters!

Entrance charge

Discos and clubs apply a cover charge (entrance charge), which often includes two drinks.

Clubs* ● *¥2,500
Discos* ● *¥4,000

INDEX BY AREA AND TYPE

Tokyo can boast a wealth of entertainment: concerts, musical comedies, plays from Japanese and international repertoires, tours by Western companies... The traditional disciplines are not forgotten for all that: almost every day you can see *kabuki* or *nō* theater in the capital, as well as *kyogen*, short satirical plays, and *bunraku*, puppet theater.

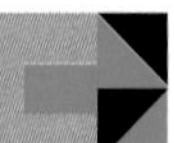

After dark

Kanze Nō Theater - Kanze Nōgaku-dō (1)

1-16-4 Shōtō, Shibuya-ku ☎ (03) 3469-5241

M *Shibuya* ***Nō, kyōgen*** ***Box office*** *daily 10am–6pm* ● *variable*

This theater is the fief of a great *nō* school directed by the Kanze dynasty. The genre's originality lies in its total lack of rehearsal. The spontaneity of the actors gives an innovative appeal to these dark, slow plays, the themes of which invariably derive from religion. The subjects cover five categories: the gods, demons, ghosts, women and insanity. To lighten the gloomy mood, short, satirical comedies, *kyogen*, are interpolated between the acts.

National Theater - Kokuritsu Gekijō (2)

4-1 Hayabusa-chō, Chiyoda-ku ☎ (03) 3265-7411

M *Hanzomon* ***Kabuki, bunraku*** ***Box office*** *daily 10am–6pm* ● *¥1,500–9,500*

Located within the National Diet, the theater successfully evokes those wooden buildings of the 7th century. The Kokuritsu Gekijō actually combines two theaters in one. In its large 1,764-seater auditorium there are performances of *kabuki*, *gagaku* (court music) and traditional dance, while the small 630-seater auditorium presents *bunraku* and *kabuki*. Audio guides.

Kabuki-za (3)

4-12 Ginza, Chūō-ku ☎ (03) 3541-3131

M *Higashi-Ginza* ***Kabuki*** *daily 11am–4pm, 4.30–9pm; closed 26–31 of the month, Dec. 30–June 1* ● *¥ 2,520-16,800* ***Box office*** ☎ *(03) 5565-6000*

Of all Japanese genres, *kabuki* is the most entertaining and popular. Created at the beginning of the Edo period, this theatrical genre is performed solely by men. There are three types of *kabuki*: historical drama, *shosagoto*; operatic plays derived from the puppet theater, *jidaimono*; and scenes from feudal daily life, *sewamono*. The repertoire consists of over 350 plays whose themes mainly focus on the conflict between social obligations (*giri*) and feelings (*ninjo*), or else revenge. There is always a tragic fall. As *kabuki* has not evolved over the centuries, the audience expects no surprises. It is the actors and their incredible stagecraft that continue to fascinate, one example being Tamasaburo Bando, certainly the best-known *onnagata* (female role) actor. Audio guides in English for every performance (4–5 hours approx.); tickets available for a single act.

Not forgetting

■ **National Nō Theater (4)** 4-13-1 Sendagaya, Shibuya-ku ☎ (03) 3423-1331 *Plays performed by companies trained by the two* kyoken *and five* nō *schools.* ■ **Ginza Nō Theater (5)** Ginza Nogaku-do Bldg 8F, 6-5-15 Ginza, Chūō-ku ☎ (03) 3471-0197 *) a small theater in an idyllic setting.*
■ **Tokyo Opera City (6)** 3-20-2 Nishi-shinjuku, Shinjuku-ku ☎ (03) 5353-0788 *Concerts, recitals, ballets.* ■ **The New National Theater (7)** 1-1-1 Honmachi, Shibuya-ku ☎ (03) 5351-3011 *The new entertainment Mecca: operas, ballets, plays and recitals from the Western repertoire.* ■ **Suntory Hall (8)** 1-13-1 Akasaka, Minato-ku ☎ (03) 3505-1001 *The best acoustics in Tokyo.* ■ **Shimbashi Playhouse (9)** 6-18-2 Ginza, Chūō-ku ☎ (03) 3541-2600 *Kabuki in April and May; contemporary Japanese theater the rest of the year.*

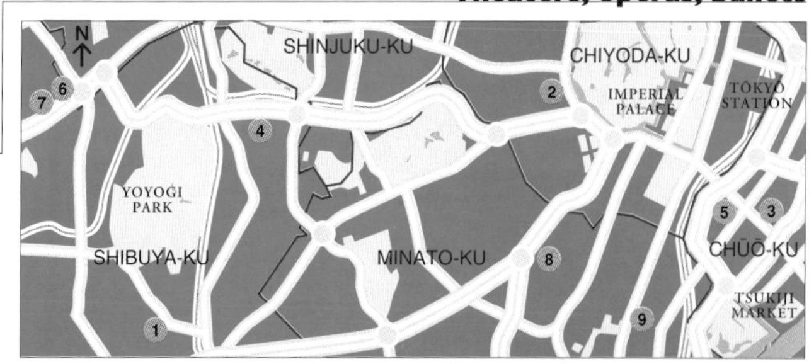
N
SHINJUKU-KU
CHIYODA-KU
IMPERIAL PALACE
TŌKYŌ STATION
YOYOGI PARK
SHIBUYA-KU
MINATO-KU
CHŪŌ-KU
TSUKIJI MARKET
1
2
3
4
5
6
7
8
9

8

4

2

3

8

1

6

In Tokyo, Western-style bars and Japanese establishments compete in the popularity stakes. Irrespective of category, they are more numerous than pebbles on a beach. Greedy for novelty and curious about all things Western, the Japanese are constantly on the lookout for the latest craze...

After dark

Zion (10)

Fuji Bldg 3F, 2-5-7 Ikebukuro, Toshima-ku ☎ (03) 3971-5270

M *Ikebukuro* ***Reggae bar*** *daily 6pm–5am* ● *¥600*

A completely new hip-hop bar, with a cool décor and serving delicious African and Jamaican dishes. No cover charge, and a special dance night on Saturdays.

The Dubliners (11)

Sun Glow Bldg B1F, 1-10-8 Nishi-Ikebukuro, Toshima-ku ☎ (03) 5961-3614

M *Ikebukuro* ***Irish pub*** *Mon.–Fri. 3–11.30pm; Sat. 11.30am–11.30pm; Sun., public holidays 11.30am–10pm* ● *¥850* *1st and 3rd Thu. of the month* *Sun Glow Bldg B1F, 1-10-8 Nishi-Ikebukuro, Toshima-ku ☎ (03) 5951-3614*

At The Dubliners, the 'happy hour' lasts almost all day. You can enjoy a Guinness or an Irish cocktail, served with tasty culinary specialties such as classic beef pie and fish and chips. Only one problem: it closes far too early!

Agave (12)

Clover Bldg B1F, 7-15-10 Roppongi, Minato-ku ☎ (03) 3497-0229

M *Roppongi* ***Tequila bar*** *Mon.–Thu. 6.30pm–2am; Fri., Sat. 6.30pm–4am* ● *¥1,500*

This Mexican bar is the only one to offer more than 400 types of tequila and mescal. Try the Don Diego Margarita or the house specialty, a Margarita spiced with salt, sugar and cayenne pepper. Both are prepared with the tequila of your choice. You must try them with a selection of Mexican tapas and a top-quality cigar.

Kazoo (13)

6-7-17 Roppongi, Minato-ku ☎ (03) 3470-9863

M *Roppongi* ***Wine bar, cigar bar*** *Mon.–Sat. 7pm–5am* ● *¥1,500*

As its proud motto boasts, 'First Things First'. Kazoo cultivates quality before all else, whether it's Cuban cigars, wines or the clientele. The list of available drinks is amazing, and the atmosphere pulsates from sunset to sunrise. Forget your inhibitions (if you have any) and join the dancers in the jungle bar. Private karaoke rooms.

Not forgetting

■ **Salsa Sudada (14)** La Palette Bldg 3F, 7-13-8 Roppongi, Minato-ku ☎ (03) 5474-8806 *This place is without doubt the most popular venue catering for Tokyo's current mad enthusiasm for salsa. There is a ¥1,500 cover charge at the weekend.* ■ **Propaganda (15)** Yua Roppongi Bldg 2F, 3-14-9 Roppongi, Minato-ku ☎ (03) 3423-0988 *On Wednesdays, women drink at half price.* ■ **Club 99 Gaspanic (16)** Gaspanic Bldg B1F, 3-15-24 Roppongi, Minato-ku ☎ (03) 3470-7190 *Open from 9pm through 9am, hence the name: 99. Things really get going here from 3am when the gaijin turn up.* ■ **Kamiya Bar (17)** 1-1-1 Asakusa, Taito-ku ☎ (03) 3841-5400 *) Kamiya was the first Western-style bar to be opened in Tokyo in 1880. You don't come here for the décor, a sort of café with formica tables, but for the atmosphere. Try the electrifying* denki buran, *brandy laced with vermouth, gin, curaçao and wine.*

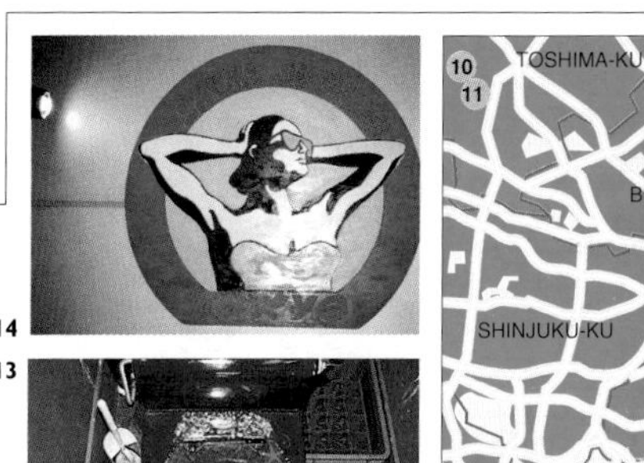

14

13

N
TOSHIMA-KU
TAITŌ-KU
UENO PARK
BUNKYŌ-KU
SHINJUKU-KU
CHIYODA-KU
IMPERIAL PALACE
SUMIDA-KU
SHIBUYA-KU
CHŪŌ-KU
KŌTŌ-KU
MINATO-KU
TSUKIJI MARKET
10
11
17
12
13
14
15
16

13

14

16

In the establishments where you only drink at the bar, drinks are served with appetizers called *chaamu* (charm). A cover charge – allow between ¥200 and ¥1,200 – is usually added to the check, which means that your drink will cost you an exorbitant amount – between $17 and $30. The drinks mentioned below are served without cover charge.

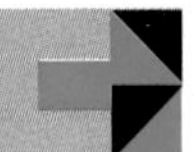

After dark

Wa-on (18)

Nippori Ekimae Bldg 5F, 6-60-9 Higashi-Nippori, Taitō-ku ☎ (03) 5850-8033

M *Nippori* ***Live Japanese music*** *Tue.–Sun. 6pm–11.30pm* ● *¥400*

Unique of its type: you can listen here to live concerts of traditional Japanese music while drinking without ruining yourself. It's also a meeting place for musicians of all origins and musical tendencies, who take part in multicultural jam sessions.

Kuremutsu (19)

2-2-13 Asakusa, Taito-ku ☎ (03) 3842-0906

M *Tōbu-Asakusa* ***Saké bar*** *daily 4–10pm* ● *¥400*

This pub, with its elegant décor, has the feel of a museum of popular art. The Kuremutsu – whose name means something like 'vespers' – is an old establishment full of memories, where the beer and saké are served with traditional accompaniments. A costly but delicious way to experience the 'great Japanese art of convivial drinking and eating'.

Yakitori Luis (20)

Toredo Akasaka Bldg B1F, 5-4-14 Akasaka, Minato-ku ☎ (03) 3585-4197

M *Akasaka* ***Bar, yakitori*** *daily 5pm–11am* ● *¥500-700*

Prices are very reasonable in this establishment that serves 23 sorts of *kushi-yaki* (brochettes). Do order the *ruisu-yaki* of beef served with a *miso* sauce, of grilled chicken soaked in a delicious plum sauce, and of green peppers stuffed with ground meat. It should all be accompanied by a nice chilled beer.

Bois Céleste (21)

2-13-21 Akasaka, Minato-ku ☎ (03) 3588-6292

M *Akasaka, Tameike-sannō* ***Beer bar*** *Mon.–Sat. 6pm–midnight; closed public holidays* ● *¥1 000*

Small and intimate, Bois Céleste is somewhat expensive but its setting is very relaxing. It serves the best selection of traditional, Trappist and abbey-brewed Belgian beers. The owner, a jazz pianist who lived in Brussels for four years, plays the piano most nights of the week. The adjoining restaurant serves Belgian cuisine.

Not forgetting

■ **Fu-Rai (22)** Urban Bldg 1F, 7-13-2 Roppongi, Minato-ku ☎ (03) 3402-2598 *A small bar with a cozy atmosphere. Come early, as there are only thirty places. More than twenty types of* kushi-yaki *are served here, from brochettes of beefsteak to stuffed peppers, a house specialty. Wash them down with beer, saké or* chūhai, *a strong mixture based on fresh fruit juice and* shōchū, *an alcohol that was used in the Edo period as a disinfectant!* ■ **T. H. Harbor Brewery (23)** Bond St, 2-1-3 Higashi-Shinagawa, Shinagawa-ku ☎ (03) 5479-4555 *a microbrewery located in a former warehouse alongside the quay at Bayside. The beers, including Amber Ale, California Pale Ale and Porter, are fine, and the Californian cuisine served in the restaurant, excellent.*

N
18 ARAKAWA-KU
BUNKYŌ-KU
UENO PARK
19
TAITŌ-KU
CHIYODA-KU
IMPERIAL PALACE
20 21
22
CHŪŌ-KU
TSUKIJI MARKET
MINATO-KU
Port of Tokyo
KŌTŌ-KU
23 SHINAGAWA-KU

18

There are perhaps more jazz fanatics in Tokyo than anywhere else in the world. In order to satisfy their fans, bands always include this city in their tours. For this reason it is often easier to hear them here than elsewhere, but this privilege has a price. Most cover charges start at ¥5,000.

After dark

G . H Nine (24)
Uno Bldg 9F, 4-4-6 Ueno, Taitō-ku ☎ (03) 3887-2525

Ueno-Hirokōji, Okachimachi **Live Japanese music** *daily 6pm–midnight/ Show 7pm* ● **Cover charge** *¥500*

A discreetly sophisticated club with affordable prices under the glass pyramid of the Uno Building. A good show in three parts. It is an all-seating venue, but the short sessions spare you a long wait.

Vagabond (25)
1-4-20 Nishi-Shinjuku, Shinjuku-ku ☎ (03) 3348-9109

Shinjuku **Blues** *Mon.–Sat., public holidays 5.30–11pm; Sun. 5.30–10.30pm* ● **Cover charge** *¥500*

The retro and over-elaborate décor is not recommended for claustrophobics, but it contributes to the extraordinary atmosphere of this place where you sip your bourbon to the sound of skat and blues. To get in after 7pm is a real feat. The club serves *yakitori*.

Body & Soul (26)
Anise Minami-Aoyama Bldg B1F, 6-13-9 Minami-Aoyama, Minato-ku ☎ (03) 5466-3348

Omote-Sandō **Jazz** *Mon.–Sat. 6.30pm–midnight/Show 8.30pm, 10.30pm* ● **Cover charge** *¥3,500*

A great little jazz club. The reasonable cover charge doesn't include drinks. On the other hand, you can stay all night. The tiered seats are best for an unrestricted view of the stage.

J (27)
5-1-1 Shinjuku, Shinjuku-ku ☎ (03) 3354-0335

Shinjuku-Sanchōme **Jazz** *Mon.–Sat. 5.30pm–1am/Shows 7pm, 9.30pm; public holidays 6.30pm, 9pm* ● **Cover charge** *¥2,000*

Good music and a laid-back atmosphere for a reasonable price. A stone's throw from the gay bars and the Golden-Gai district.

Tokyo Blue Note (28)
Raika Bldg B1F, 6-3-16 Minami-Aoyama, Minato-ku ☎ (03) 3485-0088

Omote-Sandō **Jazz** *Mon.–Sat. 5.30pm–1am/Shows 7pm, 9.30pm; public holidays 6.30pm, 9pm* ● *¥7,000-13,000;* **cover charge** *variable*

The most prestigious jazz club in Tokyo. Sometimes very expensive depending on the artist, but the price is justified by the appearance of celebrities such as Brandford Marsalis, Tony Bennett and Sarah Vaughan.

Pitt Inn (29)
Shimei Bldg B1F, 3-17-7 Roppongi, Minato-ku ☎ (03) 3585-1063

Roppongi **Jazz** *daily 6.30–10.30pm/Shows 7.30pm, 10pm* ● *¥3,500*
Acord Bldg B1F, 2-12-4 Shinjuku, Shinjuku-ku ☎ (03) 3407-5781

A club for serious fans; it is inadvisable to talk during the sessions. Come early because, despite its huge auditorium, the Pitt Inn soon fills up.

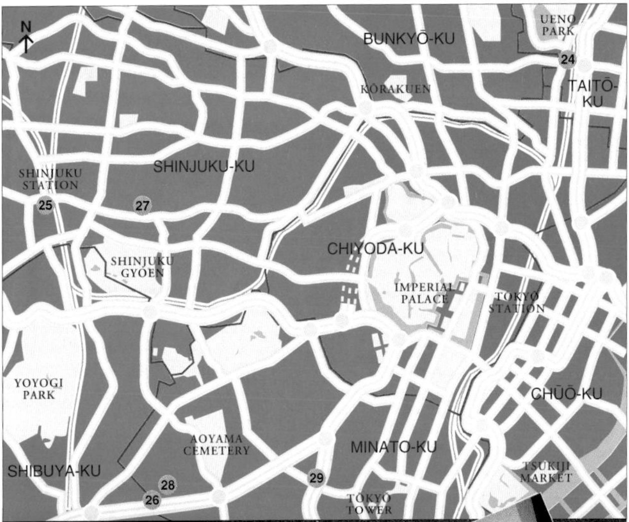

N
BUNKYŌ-KU
UENO PARK
24
TAITŌ-KU
KŌRAKUEN
SHINJUKU STATION
SHINJUKU-KU
25
27
CHIYODA-KU
SHINJUKU GYOEN
IMPERIAL PALACE
TOKYO STATION
YOYOGI PARK
CHŪŌ-KU
AOYAMA CEMETERY
MINATO-KU
SHIBUYA-KU
28
26
29
TSUKIJI MARKET
TOKYO TOWER

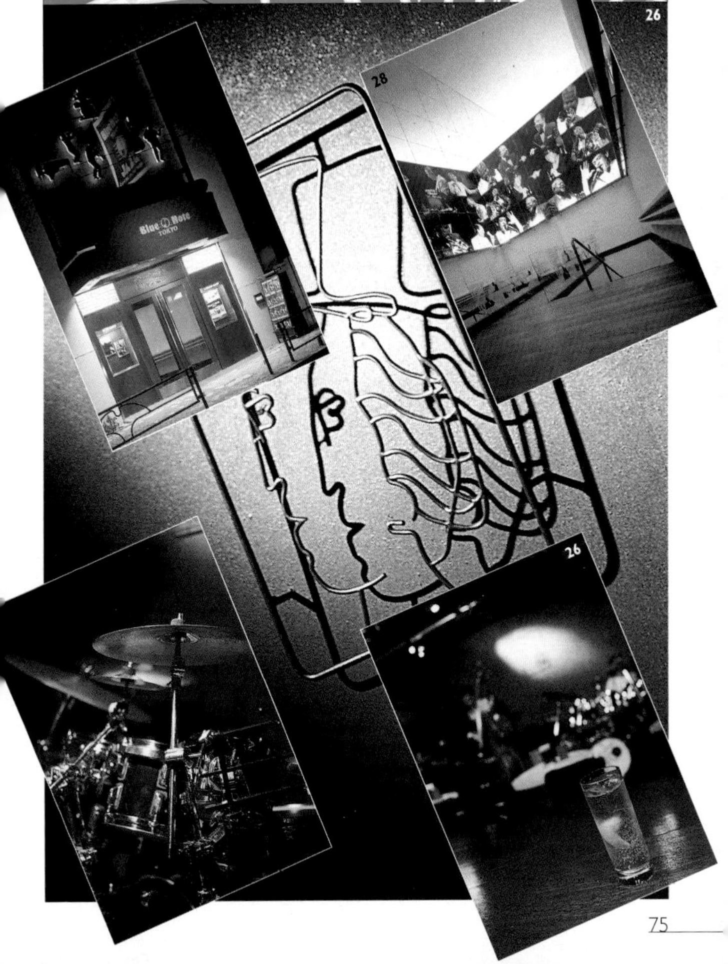

26

28

26

Tokyo's night scene is as changeable as the city itself. Clubs spring up and die with each new musical trend. Consult the *Tokyo Classified* to avoid disappointments. As a general rule, clubs apply a cover charge of about ¥3,000 that includes the first two drinks. Women often get a reduction.

After dark

Paradiso Akasaka (30)

Akasaka Sakae Bldg B1F, 6-6-4 Akasaka, Minato-ku ☎ (03) 3505-0120

M *Akasaka, Tameike-Sannō* ***DJ club*** *Mon.–Sat. 7pm–5am* ● *¥3,000*

One of the biggest and most recently opened clubs in Akasaka presents DJ nights and a different music scene. For some unknown reason models are offered two complimentary drinks!

Fiesta (31)

Taimei Bldg 5F, 3-11-6 Roppongi, Minato-ku ☎ (03) 5410-3008

M *Roppongi* ***Karaoke*** *Mon.–Sat. 7pm–5am* ● *¥3,000*

This karaoke club, one of the most popular, has about 6,000 British and US songs in stock. For just ¥3,000, you can eat, drink and sing away to your favorite hit. A bargain not to be missed for a truly Japanese experience.

Java Jive (32)

Square Bldg B1F & B2F, 3-10-3 Roppongi, Minato-ku ☎ (03) 5466-3348

M *Roppongi* ***Afro-latino club*** *Mon.–Sat. 7pm–midnight* ● *¥3,500*

Open for more than a decade, this club attracts a constant stream of *gaijin*: GIs, expatriates, models... The screening system at the door is draconian: clubbers who look suspect are refused entry. Live reggae starts at 8pm. Between two sets, the in-house DJ mixes house music and Latin hits.

J. Trip End Max (33)

Hara Bldg B1F & B2F, 3-4-18 Higashi-Azabu, Minato-ku ☎ (03) 3586-0369

M *Roppongi, Kamiyachō* ***Rock 'n' roll club*** *Sun.–Thu. 7pm–2am; Fri., Sat. 7pm-5am* ● *¥3,500*

The J. Trip chain is the trendiest in Tokyo, and this club is its flagship. As cool as it is spacious, it's the ideal spot to rock till you drop. Upstairs, the more relaxed atmosphere brings to mind the dark, mysterious mood of a New York nightclub.

Not forgetting

■ **Smash Hits (34)** M2 Bldg B1F, 5-2-26 Hiroo, Shibuya-ku ☎ (03) 3444-0432 *Out of thousands of karaoke clubs in Tokyo, the novelty here is to offer a big stage and a whole pile of accessories that will set you up ready to massacre one of the 10,000 British or US hits in the repertoire for just ¥3,000.* ■ **Lexington Queen (35)** Urban Bldg 1F, 7-13-2 Roppongi, Minato-ku ☎ (03) 3401-1661 *Without doubt Tokyo's club for the jet set. The owner, local celebrity Bill Hersey of* Tokyo Weekender's, *makes it a point of honor to invite the stars of the worlds of music and the movies here when they visit the city and they often accept the invitation. A place to see and be seen.* ■ **Velfarre (36)** 7-14-22 Roppongi, Minato-ku ☎ (03) 3585-1063 Saturday Night Fever: *the sequel. The biggest discotheque in Asia treated itself to a facelift in 1998. With its massive marble staircase, its mirror ball and other extravagances, this disco keeps the look of the 1980s alive.*

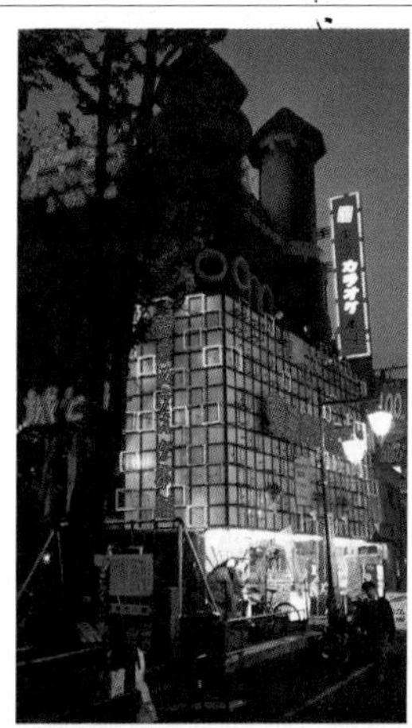

N
Aoyama Dōri S (Ave.)
Aoyama-Itchōme
Akasaka
Tameike-Sannō
S
S
S
30
N3
Gaienmae
Gaien-Higashi Dōri (Ave.)
Nogizaka
S
Gaein-Nishi Dōri
AYOAMA CEMETERY
Shuto Expressway
35
36
32
31
Kamiyachō
S
Sakurada Dōri
Roppongi
S
Roppongi Dōri (Ave.)
Shuto Expressway
MINATO-KU
33
MEGURO-KU
Loop Line
Hiro-o
S
34
MEMORIAL PARK
Shuto Expwy N2

レイク
ディック
オーシーエス
クスリ
TD
カラオケ 747 カラオケ

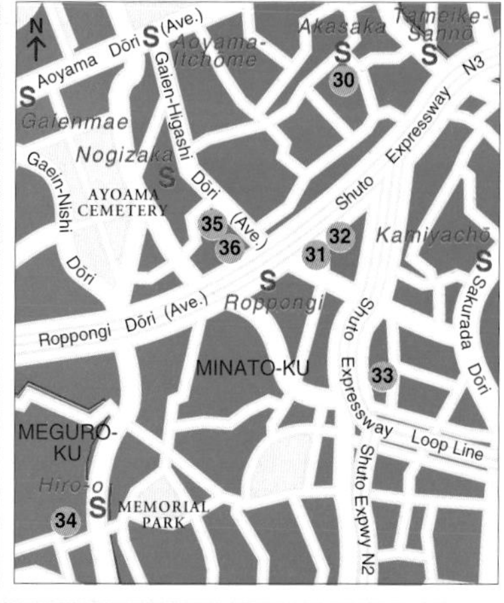

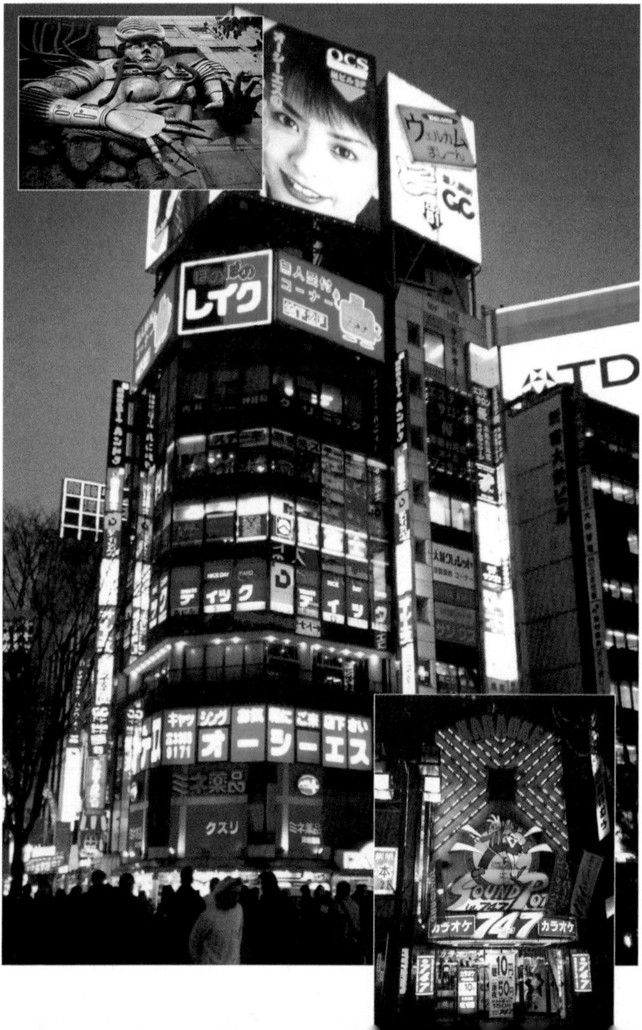

In Tokyo, the dividing line between bar and restaurant is not as clear as in the West. This is due to the fact that the Japanese, food lovers by nature, never drink without accompanying their beer or saké with an appetizer of some kind. Ethnic bars and their exotic cuisine offer them an additional choice that they are quick to appreciate.

After dark

Vahsi At (37)

Palais France Bldg B1F, 1-6-1 Jingūmae, Shibuya-ku ☎ (03) 5474-1136

Meiji-Jingūmae ***Turkish bar*** *daily 11.30am–3pm, 4–11pm* ● *¥600*

With its soothing décor in shades of green, blue and white, Vahsi At takes you straight to the heart of Cappadocia. On the program: marvelously tasty kebabs, delicious Turkish and European wines, your palm read by the chef and belly dancing every Friday evening.

Mandala (38)

DK Sibuya Bldg 3F, 16-9 Sakuragaokachō, Shibuya-ku ☎ (03) 3463-5181

Shibuya ***Nepalese bar*** *Mon.–Sat. 11am–2.30pm, 5pm–1am; Sun., public holidays 5pm–1am* ● *¥700*

The shimmering colors of the fabrics enhanced by the candlelight set the mood in this small Nepalese bar-restaurant. Its vast selection of cocktails will make your mouth water, and you will be able to sample a little-known but excellent cuisine straight from the Himalayas.

Cantina La Fiesta (39)

Roppongi Hanatsubaki Bldg 2F, 3-15-23 Roppongi, Minato-ku ☎ (03) 3475-4412

Roppongi ***Mexican bar*** *Tue.–Thu. 5pm–2am; Fri., Sat. 5pm–4am; Sun., Mon., public holidays 5–10.30pm* ● *¥700*

Without a doubt the best Mexican restaurant in Tokyo. The atmosphere is fantastic and the staff friendly. Begin your gastronomic journey with the delicious *frijoles* and the extraordinary *pollo molé*, while sipping the iced Margaritas.

Phothai (40)

Roppongi Five Plaza Bldg 2F, 5-18-21 Roppongi, Minato-ku ☎ (03) 3505-1504

Roppongi ***Australo-Thai bar*** *Mon.–Thu. 11.30am–2.30pm, 5–11pm; Fri., Sat. 11.30am–2.30pm, 5pm–midnight; Sun. 11.30am–2.30pm* ● *¥700*

Ideal to kick off your evening. You will be able to choose from a vast selection of Australian, Thai and Japanese beers served with a Thai dish such as *sukiyaki*; or those with big appetites can opt for a large steak combined with an Australian wine.

Not forgetting

■ **Belgo 1066 (41)** Shibuya Higashi Ichigōkan B1F, 3-18-7 Shibuya, Shibuya-ku ☎ (03) 3409-4442 *Over 100 varieties of beer served in relaxing, European surroundings.* ■ **Madal (42)** Meguro Business Mansion 5F, 2-15-2 Kami-Osaki, Shinagawa-ku ☎ (03) 3442-3566 *A Nepalese–Tibetan restaurant. Great food, unique décor and low prices. Don't miss it!* ■ **Jamaican Club (43)** Moto Azabu YS Bldg B1F, 2-1-21 Moto-Azabu, Minato-ku ☎ (03) 3473-8998 *Get there after midnight and drink all you can in one hour for just ¥1,500! The menu is no less amazing: alligator, ostrich and piranha. Evenings full of ambiance, with a 'jungle' show.* ■ **Grand Blue (44)** Aoba Roppongi Bldg 1F, 6-13-33 Roppongi, Minato-ku ☎ (03) 5570-1570) *US West Coast atmosphere in the very heart of Roppongi.*

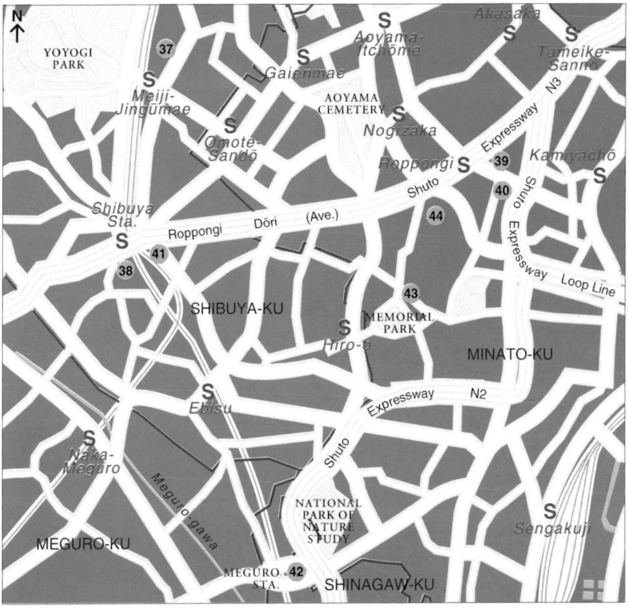

N
YOYOGI PARK
37
Meiji-Jingumae
Gaienmae
Aoyama-itchōme
Akasaka
Tameike-Sannō
AOYAMA CEMETERY
Nogizaka
Omote-Sandō
Roppongi
39
40
Kamiyachō
Shuto Expressway N3
Shibuya Sta.
Roppongi Dōri (Ave.)
41
38
44
Shuto Expressway Loop Line
43
SHIBUYA-KU
MEMORIAL PARK
Hiro-o
MINATO-KU
Ebisu
Shuto Expressway N2
Naka-Meguro
Meguro-gawa
NATIONAL PARK OF NATURE STUDY
Sengakuji
MEGURO-KU
MEGURO STA.
42
SHINAGAW-KU

38

38

Chadō (tea ceremony)

In a room simply adorned with an *ikebana* flower arrangement and a print, the tea master prepares an infusion of *matcha* (powdered green tea). The bowl is passed to each guest who takes it in both hands, gives it a quarter-turn clockwise and empties it in three long mouthfuls. Then he admires the delicacy of the bowl while savoring some pastries ➥ 14

What to see

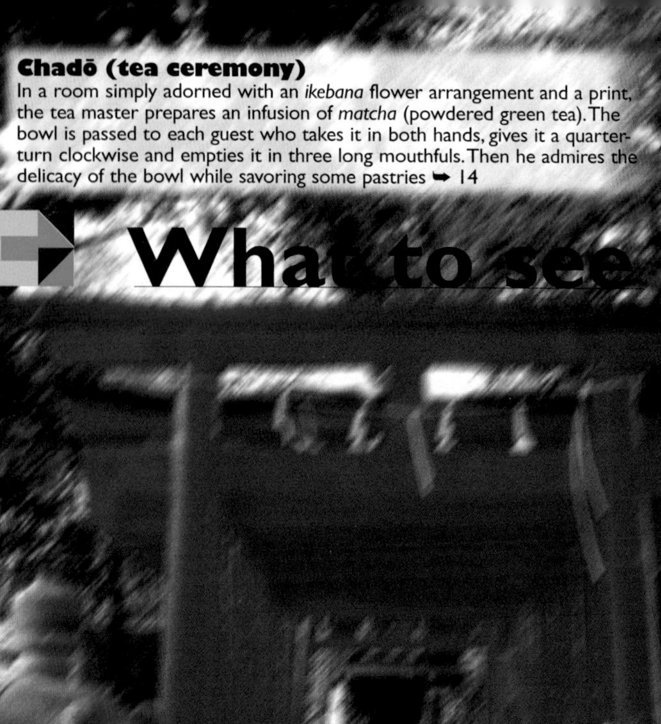

Matsuri

Every month the TIC ➥ 12 publishes a list of the countless *matsuri* (festivals).

January 6 *Denzomeshiki* Firefighters' parade in Edo costume at Chūō-dori Hiroba, Harumi.

February 3 or 4 *Setsubun* Throw beans to ward off evil spirits. At Sensō-ji ➥ 104 and Zōō-ji ➥ 84.

April 8 *Hana matsuri* Buddha's birthday celebrated in all the temples including Sensō-ji ➥104 and Zōjō-ji ➥ 84.

End July *Sumida-gawa Hanabi-taikai* Unmissable festivals of fireworks on the Sumida river. Watch from Kototoi and Shirahige bridges at Asakusa ➥ 104.

September 21 *Nezugongen-matsuri* Another famous Edo festival. Shintō music and dance at Nezu-jinja ➥ 96.

1st weekend October *Furusato* Cultural events and fairs throughout the city, including Sensō-ji ➥ 104 and Ueno Par ➥ 106.

October 30–November 3 *Meiji Reiai-sai* Emperor Meiji's birthday celebrations. Dances and court music, displays of archery performed in costume and martial arts take place at M jingū ➥ 96.

December 14 *Gishi-sai* Commemorative events in honor of the 47 *rōnin* who committed suicide by *seppuku*, at Sengaku-ji ➥ 84.

Ohanami *(flowering)*
One of the great Tokyo traditions is to admire the flowering of trees and plants, an ideal time to organize spontaneous parties. April cherry trees in bloom at Korakuen, Imperial Palace and Yasukini-jinja (for the atmosphere, go to Ueno and Sumida Parks); mid-June irises at Korakuen and Sensō-ji; mid-October–November, chrysanthemums at Korakuen, Hibiya Park and Meiji-jinja.

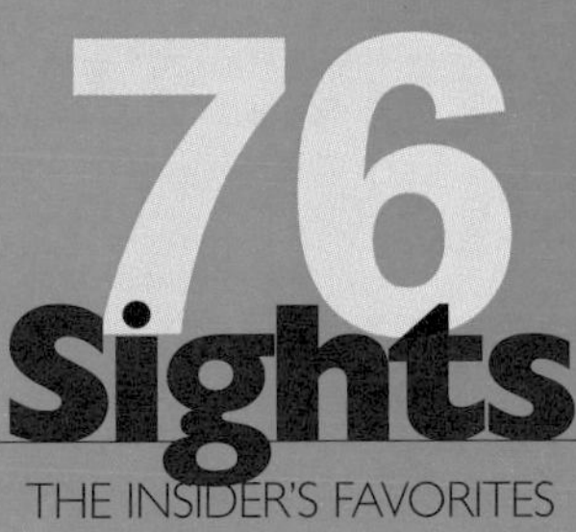

76 Sights

THE INSIDER'S FAVORITES

INDEX BY TYPE

Since 1457, when Dōkan Ōta had his castle raised on the banks of the Sumida-gawa, the formidable expansion of this fishing village has been unstoppable. Successively the shōgunal seat during the Edo period (1600–1868), then the capital of Japan on the restoration of Emperor Meiji, Tokyo retains a rich historic inheritance, despite the vagaries of man and nature.

What to see

(1) ➥ 84

(9) ➥ 86

(18) ➥ 90

(24) ➥ 92

(34) ➥ 96

Gokoku-ji ➥ 84
Founded in 1681 in honor of Keishō-in, mother of the *shōgun* Tsunayoshi Tokugawa, this temple is one of the largest in Tokyo. The Imperial cemetery is located on the hill behind it.

Imperial Palace ➥ 86
Wide drainage canals spanned by bridges, and ramparts dotted with pines, conceal the Emperor's residence.

Tsukiji Market ➥ 90
An impressive display of fish, crustaceans, shellfish and other amazing produce from the sea in the halls of the biggest fish market in the world. About 2,500 tons are sold here every day.

Koishikawa Kōrakuen ➥ 93
This garden's superb landscaped settings are a real incentive to meditation.

Ukiyo-e Ōta Memorial Museum ➥ 96
A remarkable private collection of 1,200 prints, of which 500 are originals. However, none are erotic, as these are not permitted to be displayed.

Tōkyō Metropolitan Museum of Photography ➥ 100
The country of the ever-clicking camera just had to tell the story of photography through displays and monographs by Japanese artists.

Edo-Tōkyō Museum ➥ 102
A trip into the era of the samurai and Tokugawa *shōgun*, Scenes of everyday life and real Edo houses saved from destruction.

Nezu Institute ➥ 103
Japanese painting in all its manifestations: on silk, *washi* and *sōji*, from the Nara period (710–794) to that of Edo (1600–1868).

Sensō-ji ➥ 104
At the very heart of the ebullient Asakusa district stands the oldest temple in the capital (628), dedicated to the goddess Kannon.

Tōkyō National Museum ➥ 106
Unquestionably the most comprehensive and interesting of all the museums in Japan; its collections span Japanese civilization from prehistory to the present time.

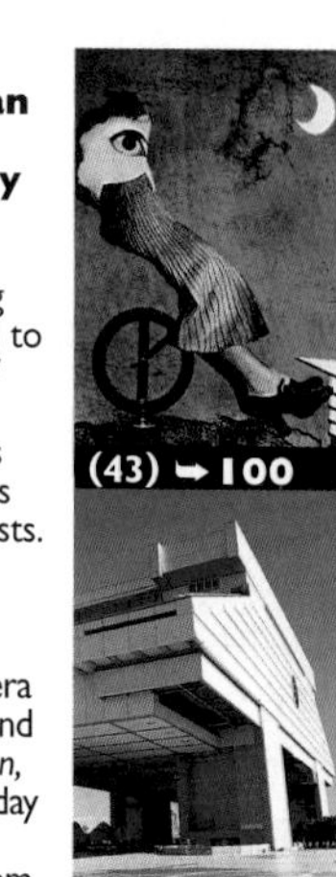

(43) ➥ 100

(48) ➥ 102

(52) ➥ 102

(57) ➥ 104

(61) ➥ 106

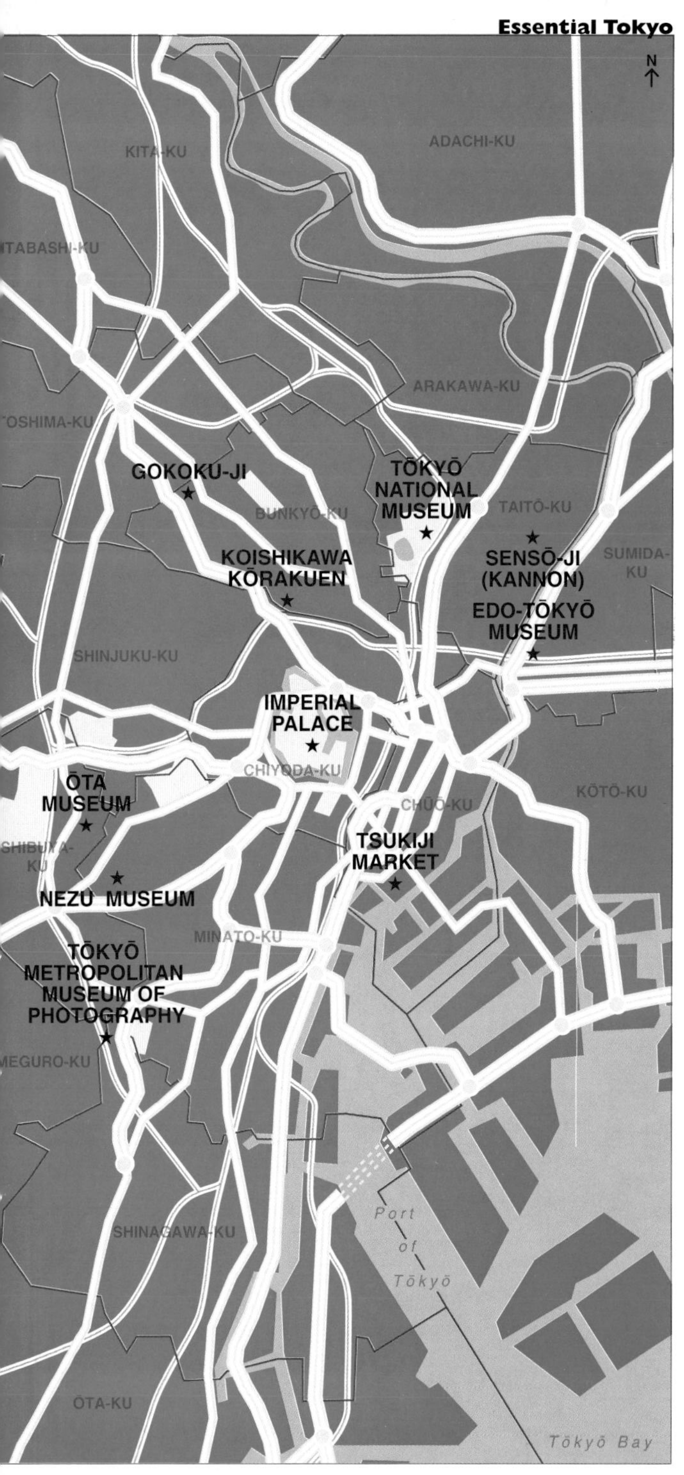
N
KITA-KU
ADACHI-KU
ITABASHI-KU
ARAKAWA-KU
TOSHIMA-KU
GOKOKU-JI
TŌKYŌ NATIONAL MUSEUM
BUNKYŌ-KU
TAITŌ-KU
SUMIDA-KU
SENSŌ-JI (KANNON)
KOISHIKAWA KŌRAKUEN
EDO-TŌKYŌ MUSEUM
SHINJUKU-KU
IMPERIAL PALACE
CHIYODA-KU
ŌTA MUSEUM
CHŪŌ-KU
KŌTŌ-KU
SHIBUYA-KU
TSUKIJI MARKET
NEZU MUSEUM
MINATO-KU
TŌKYŌ METROPOLITAN MUSEUM OF PHOTOGRAPHY
MEGURO-KU
Port of Tōkyō
SHINAGAWA-KU
ŌTA-KU
Tōkyō Bay

Futuristic Tokyo is strewn with vestiges of the past. Visiting its religious heritage – Buddhist temples (*ji* or *tera*), Shintō shrines (*jinja* or *miya*), altars set up by the side of the road, statues of gods, buildings dedicated to the souls of the dead – is to take a walk through Japanese history and architecture.

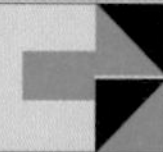

What to see

4

1

1

Gokoku-ji (1)

5-40 Ōtsuka, Bunkyō-ku ☎ (03) 3941-0764

M *Gokokuji* ⏲ *daily 11am–noon, 1–4.30pm* ▦

Strangely underrated, this temple is nevertheless one of the rare survivors from the Edo period. Its main building, magnificently preserved by Tokyo standards, dates from 1681. Ginkgo and *zelkova* (Japanese elms) guide the visitor to the main enclosure, whose Niomon doorway owes its name to the Ni-ō statues on either side, supposed to chase away evil spirits.

Yushima-tenjin (2)

3-30-1 Yushima, Bunkyō-ku ☎ (03) 3836-0753

M *Yushima* ⏲ *daily 9am–7.30pm* ▦ *Festival plum trees in flower mid-Feb.–mid-Mar.*

Sugawara no Michizane, statesman and poet of the 9th century, was deified under the name *Tenjin*, Patron of Learning and the Arts. In the spring examination period, students come in droves to obtain an intercession. They write their petitions on *ema*, wooden votive tablets, that they hang on racks around the main enclosure.

Yasukuni-jinja (3)

3-1-1 Kudan-kita, Chiyoda-ku ☎ (03) 3261-8326

M *Kudanshita* ⏲ ***Sanctuary and museum,*** *daily 9am–4.30pm* ▦
▦ ***Festivals of dance and nō theater July 13–16; Armistice Aug. 15***

This shrine is dedicated to the souls of the 2.5 million Japanese soldiers who have died since its foundation in 1869. It also contains the remains of war criminals from World War II – such as General Tojo – which causes it to be the subject of much debate. The adjacent military museum borders on the morbid, although the atmosphere is lightened by magnificent bronze *tōrl*, the avenue of ginkgo and cherry trees, and the Divine Pond in the center of a graceful Japanese garden.

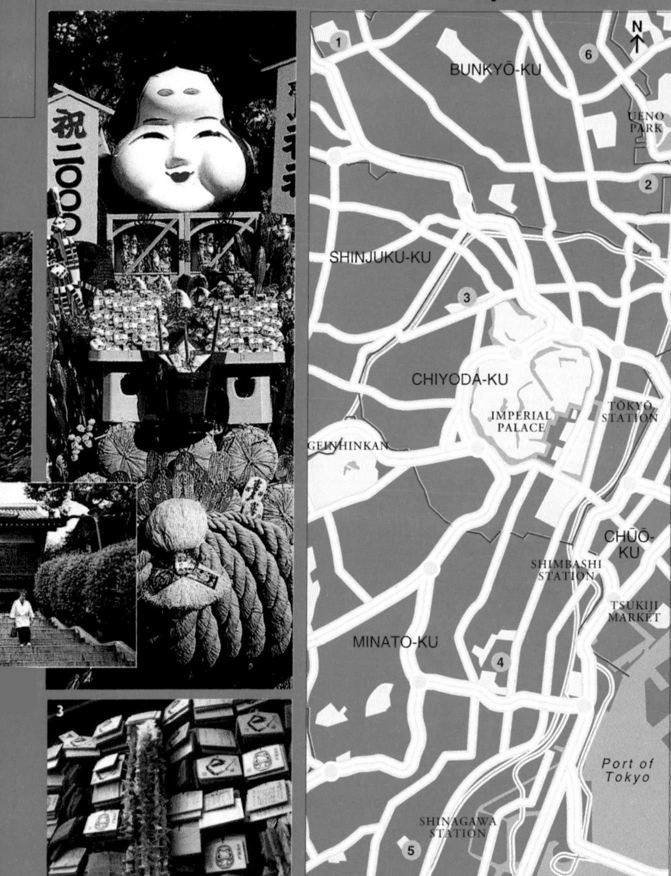

Sengaku-ji (4)

2-11-1 Takanawa, Minato-ku ☎ (03) 3441-2208

Sengakuji *daily 7am–5pm* ***Festivals Apr. 1–7; Nov. 3***

The story of these 47 *rōnin* (masterless samurai) is rooted in the Edo heritage and in the heart of the Japanese, who truly venerate them. Symbols of duty and loyalty, these *rōnin* avenged their murdered master, Asana Naganori (1665–1701), then committed suicide by *seppuku*, ritual disemboweling. Incense burns day after day on their tombs. In a corner of the courtyard, protected by a screen, their master rests side by side with their leader, Oishi Kuranosuke (1659–1703). The temple, rebuilt after World War II, nonetheless retains its gateway dating from 1836, wonderfully carved and decorated with dragons.

Not forgetting

Zōjō-ji (5) 4-7-35 Shiba-Kōen, Minato-Ku ☎ (03) 3432-1431 *The old temple of the Tokugawa samurai clan, founded at the beginning of the 17th century and rebuilt in 1974, retains its massive red-lacquered entrance, the Sanmon (1605), classed as an 'important cultural asset'. It houses numerous sacred objects, including sutras and priceless statues. Festival on April 8.* **Nezu-jinja (6)** 1-23-9 Nezu, Bunkyo-ku ☎ (03) 3822-0753 *This shrine has preserved some interesting curiosities: a Chinese gate (*kara-mon*), a stage for religious dances and a shrine dedicated to the fox Inari. Its row of red torii bears witness to the period when Buddhism and Shintō were closely linked. Restored in 1706 by the fifth* shōgun *Tsunayoshi, the park contains over 3,000 azaleas, flowering at the end of April.*

In the area

- Where to stay: ➥ 20 ➥ 24 ➥ 26
- Where to eat: ➥ 42 ➥ 44 ➥ 46
- After dark: ➥ 68
- Where to shop: ➥ 26 ➥ 128 ➥ 144

What to see

National Museum of Modern Art (7)

3-1 Kitanomaru-kōen, Chiyoda-ku ☎ (03) 3214-2561

Kudanshita *Tue.–Sun. 10am–5pm* ● *¥420; students ¥130; under-18 ¥70*

This museum, built by the architect Yoshiro Taniguchi, presents a panorama of Japanese art from the Meiji period to today. The ground floor is used for temporary exhibitions. The three other levels house permanent collections. The 3,000 or so paintings are shown in rotation and the works on display never number more than 300.

Higashi Gyoen (Imperial Palace East Garden) (8)

1 Chiyoda, Chiyoda-ku ☎ (03) 3213-2050

Otemachi *Tue.– Thu., Sat., Sun. 9am–4pm; closed Dec. 15–Jan. 3* ● *free*

The Edo fortress formerly stood on this site. Nowadays, the old moat surrounds a park which incorporated the Kyū-ninomaru garden, laid out in 1630 by the third *shōgun*, Iemitsu. The main garden houses the Imperial Music Hall, for *bugaku* and *gagaku* court music, as well as traces of the foundations and sections of wall made up of enormous blocks of granite. Priceless pieces from the Imperial collection are exhibited in the museum near the entrance. An uninterrupted view over Nihonbashi from the top of Shiomizaka, 'the slope from which you see the tide'. Of the three gates leading to the garden, Ote-mon is the most visited.

Imperial Palace (9)

JR Tōkyō, Hibiya, Otemachi ***Palace*** *Emperor's birthday (Dec. 23), Jan. 2*

In 1457, the founder of Edo, Ota Dokan, had his residence built on this cliff overlooking Tokyo Bay. Fallen into disuse after his assassination in 1481, it was a century later that Tokugawa Ieyasu installed his military capital here. From this strategic location the *shōgun* dominated Japan until the Meiji restoration in 1868. The present palace, finished in 1968, is a reconstruction of the Imperial Palace destroyed in World War II. Three of the four zones are open to the public, the inner sanctum is only accessible twice a year.

Idemitsu Museum of Art (10)

Imperial Theater 9F, 3-1-1, Marunouchi, Chiyoda-ku ☎ (03) 3272-8600

Hibiya, Yūrakuchō *Tue.–Sun. 10am–5pm*

This museum has a superb collection of Chinese and Japanese ceramics, paintings in gold leaf, screens, *ukiyo-e* (prints), and the works of the great calligraphers. The room containing prehistoric pottery from the Jomon period has a fine view of the Imperial Palace.

Not forgetting

■ **Craft Gallery (11)** 3-1 Kitanomaru-kōen, Chiyoda-ku ☎ (03) 3211-7781 *Installed in the old building of the Imperial Guard, this arts and crafts museum displays pieces of lacquerware, fabrics, dolls and ceramics.* ■ **Hibiya Park (12)** 1-6 Hibiya-kōen, Chiyoda-ku *Set up on the former Meiji tournament arena in 1903, the first European-style park in Tokyo retains its original features: banks of flowers, a fountain in the shape of a stork and trellises covered in wisteria. The old Japanese garden, with its pond and stone lanterns, remains unchanged.*

The palace is the historic and geographic heart of Tokyo. The Imperial family still inhabits this vast, green space, a haven of tranquility only a stone's throw from the Diet (the National Assembly) and the financial districts of Nihonbashi and Marunouchi.

9

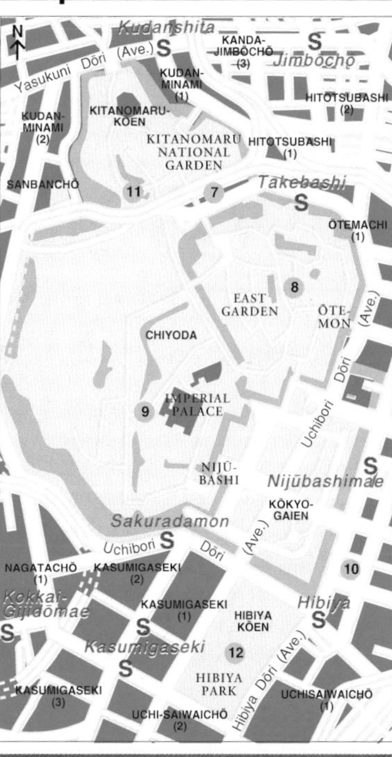

10

10

10

In the area

Where to stay: ➥ 20 ➥ 22 ➥ 24
Where to eat: ➥ 42 ➥ 44 ➥ 46
After dark: ➥ 68
Where to shop: ➥ 126 ➥ 128

What to see

Tokyo Station (13)
1-9-1 Marunouchi, Chūō-ku

JR Tōkyō ***Tokyo Station Museum*** *daily 10am–5pm* ● *¥ 200*

Built by the famous Tatsuno Kingo, the station sports a red-brick English-style façade and draws its inspiration from Amsterdam central station. Finished in 1914, it survived the great *Kanto*, the terrible earthquake of 1923, the bombings of World War II and the insatiable appetite of the property developers. Today, over 3,000 trains pass through daily, constantly transporting commuters to and fro. The west wing is occupied by a European-style hotel ➥ 20 and, right alongside, a small museum tells its story.

Bridgestone Museum (14)
1-10-1 Kyōbashi, Chūō-ku ☎ (03) 3563-0241

Mitsukoshimae *Tue.–Sun. 10am–5.30pm* ● *¥ 700; students ¥ 500*

One of the best private collections in the world of European painting and Western-style Japanese painting from the Meiji period (1868). It gathers together numerous French Impressionists, works by Picasso, Rembrandt, Modigliani and Japanese artists such as Narashige Koide, Shigeru Aoki, Seiki Kuroda and Takeji Fujishima. This museum was created in 1952 as a result of the passion of the industrialist Shōjirō Ishibashi (Ishibashi meaning 'stone bridge') for French Impressionism and his meeting with Shigeru Aoki (1882–1911). This artist's painting, *Une bonne pêche* (1904) marked the beginning of the Japanese Romantic movement. Captivated by Aoki's eventful life, Ishibashi bought most of his paintings from him. Temporary and private exhibitions are also presented.

Tokyo International Forum (15)
3-5-1 Marunouchi, Chiyoda-ku ☎ (03) 5221-9000

JR Yūrakuchō *daily 10am–8pm*

This futuristic masterpiece by the New York architect Raphael Vinoly is traversed by a series of catwalks, with curving walls and a glass atrium reaching 200 ft at its highest point. This cultural complex, long awaited by the inhabitants of Tokyo, brings together conferences, concerts, exhibitions and dance and theatrical events. The elliptical Glass Hall containing the main exhibition hall is amazing at night when the upper floors are lit up. The west building houses six large multi-purpose halls and a superb audio-visual library devoted to Tokyo; the JNTO (Japanese National Tourist Office) has an office on the lower ground floor ➥ 12.

Kabuki-za (16)
4-12 Ginza, Chūō-ku ☎ (03) 3541-3131

Higashi Ginza *daily 10am–6pm; Shows ➥ 68*

Founded in 1899 and rebuilt twice, this white-fronted theater, with its ornamental entrance and Japanese-style roof, dates from 1949 in its current form. It specializes in a dazzling theatrical genre, brimming with panache and highly stylized: *kabuki*, a cocktail of dance, songs, adventure, love and tragedy, whose eclecticism rivals that of Indian movies.

The endless streets of Ginza, lined with cafés and restaurants, form one of the largest shopping centers in Tokyo. Yūrakuchō remains a hub of communication and boasts some beautiful buildings, both ancient and modern.

13

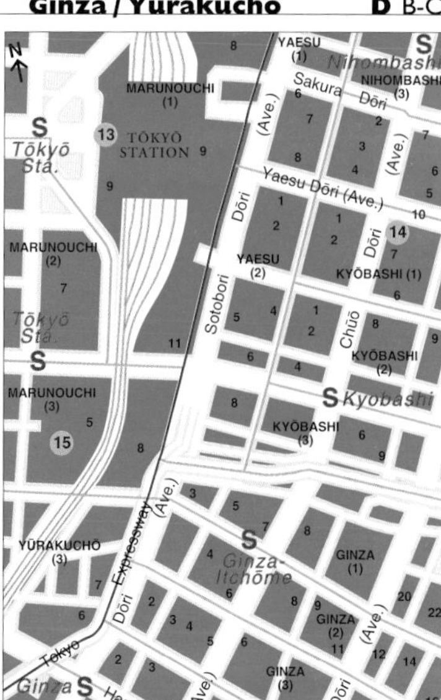

14

In the area
- Where to stay: ➥ 20 ➥ 24
- Where to eat: ➥ 44 ➥ 46
- After dark: ➥ 68
- Where to shop: ➥ 126 ➥ 128

What to see

Tsukiji Hongan-ji (17)
3-15-1 Tsukiji, Chūō-ku ☎ (03) 3541-1131

M Tsukiji ⏲ daily 6am–4pm

This stone temple was built in Asakusa in 1617, then destroyed by fire. In 1935, it was rebuilt on this site by Chuta Ito, a pupil of Tatsuno Kingo, creator of Tokyo central train station ➥ 88. Ito's numerous journeys in Buddhist and Hindu countries inspired these domes and decorative motifs in the form of lotus blossoms. A few opulent touches – a gilded altar and elaborately decorated imposts – bring some warmth to the interior of the main building.

Tsukiji Market (18)
5-2-1 Tsukiji, Chūō-ku ☎ (03) 3542-1111

M Tsukiji ⏲ daily 5am–4pm; closed 2nd and 4th Wed. of the month

Tsukiji, the largest wholesale fish market in the world, occupies ground reclaimed from the sea in the 17th century (Tsukiji simply means 'polder' or 'reclaimed land'). More than 400 varieties of fish pass through here daily. Pluck up your courage and get here at about 5am to attend the tuna auction, the highlight of the day as tuna meat is highly prized by the Japanese. The transactions taking place between 7 and 9.30am are no less picturesque, with buyers from restaurants and stores making their selection among the tons of fish. After this colorful spectacle, make a point of having lunch on the spot. The local bars and restaurants sell at low prices the freshest *sashimi* and sushi in the city.

Hama-Rikyū Onshi-Teien (19)
Chūō-ku ☎ (03) 3541-0200

M Tsukiji, Shimbashi ⏲ daily 9am–5pm ¥300; over-65s free

This piece of land, where the *shōgun* hunted duck, was given to the community in 1945. The island on which it is situated, surrounded by fortified drainage ditches from the Edo period, is accessed by the narrow Nanmon bridge or by the waterbus that travels up the Sumida-gawa to join Asakusa. The 'detached palace garden', as it is called, includes a landscaped garden and a nature reserve. A graceful replica of the pavilion where Emperor Meiji received Ulysses S. Grant in 1879 stands in the center of a tidal lake.

Tsukudashima (20)

M Tsukishima

The first inhabitants of this island at the mouth of the Sumida-gawa were, according to legend, spies for the *shōgun* disguised as fishermen. Up until the 1960s, Tsukudashima was only served by a ferry, which helped preserve it from the Edo disturbances. Today, major construction programs have almost wiped out its past. The last remnants are a network of alleyways lined with potted plants and little fish restaurants, and a few beautiful houses from the Meiji and Taisho periods. Near the replica of an old lighthouse a wide *torii* leads to the main shrine on the island, Sumiyoshi Myojin. Dedicated to sailors and fishermen, it is said that Sharaku is buried here, a mythical painter of *ukeyo-e* from the Edo period, whose true identity and existence remain an enigma.

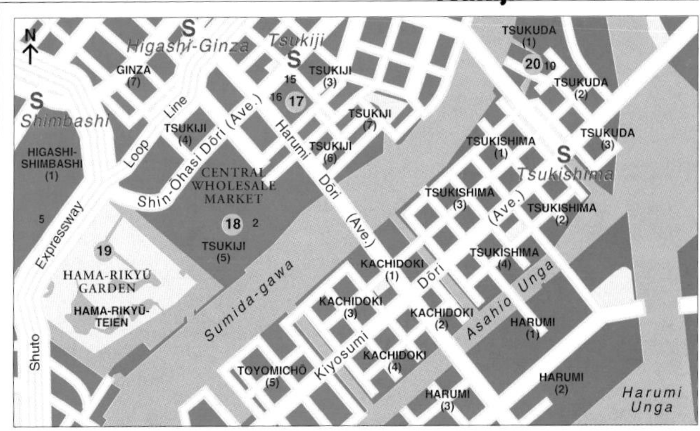

This old coastal district is subject to constant change. Fallen prey to town planners and immense real-estate projects, it has nevertheless managed to preserve some traditional temples and gardens and its huge fish market, remnants of its maritime activity and former prosperity.

17

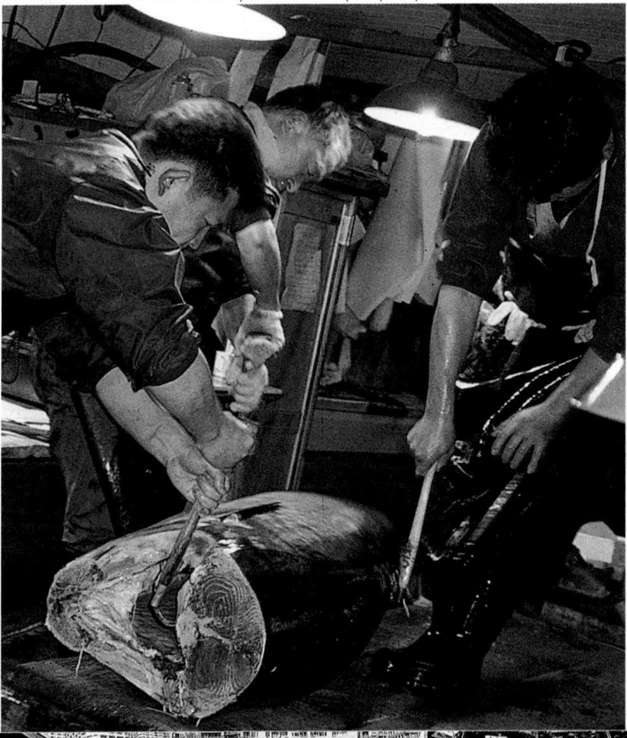

20

20 18

A few parks and gardens live on from the old feudal Edo, for the most part belonging to the lords who ruled over this agricultural province. These green spaces, laid out by them, were designed for their pleasure, whether for games or meditation. Urbanization, rampant since the Meiji period, has only spared 10% of the capital's territory, including these few treasures.

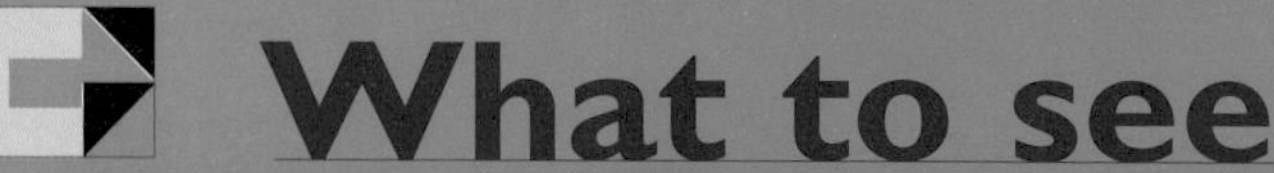

24

Rikugi-en (21)

6-16-3 Hon-Komagome, Bunkyō-ku ☎ (03) 3941-2222

Sugamo, Komagome *daily 9am–5pm* ● *¥300*

Created in the 17th century by the feudal lord Yanagisawa Yoshiyasu, this garden was for many years a place where only the Edo elite could take a stroll. The ponds, hills, streams, flora and arrangements of stones in Rikugi-en (literally 'the garden of the six principles of Chinese poetry, *waka*') represent 88 famous scenes from Chinese and Japanese literature. We'll leave identifying them to the experts! Don't let that stop you appreciating this charming, wooded park that exudes tranquility.

Mukōjima Hyakkaen (22)

3-13-3 Higashi-Mukōjima, Sumida-ku ☎ (03) 3611-8705

Higashi-Mukōjima *Tue.–Sun. 9am–4.30pm* ● *¥200*

The 'garden of a hundred flowers' is one of the most famous yet least visited of the Edo period. Containing species from all over Japan, it dates from 1804 and covers about two acres. Trees, deciduous shrubs, flowering bushes and vigorous plants abound. The most remarkable, a *miyagino-hagi* (wild clover) forms a tunnel about 100 ft long covered in pink flowers in September.

Koishikawa Shokubutsuen (23)

3-7-1 Hakusan, Bunkyō-ku ☎ (03) 3814-0138

Myōgadani *Tue.–Sun. 9am–4.30pm* ● *¥330*

The *shōgun* Tsunayoshi transformed this former feudal property into a medicinal garden devoted to research, then one of his successors had a hospital for the poor built there. In 1877, this verdant botanic garden

21

24

became the property of the University of Tokyo. Today, the botanists continue their studies among the hundred species that grow there. Down below, near the pond, stands the main building of the old school of medicine (1876), a perfectly preserved European-style building with a pink and white façade and a red-lacquered portico.

Koishikawa Kōrakuen (24)

1-6-6 Kōraku, Bunkyō-ku ☎ (03) 3811-3015

M *Suidōbashi, Iidabashi* ◷ *daily 9am–5pm* ● ¥300

This classical Japanese garden, one of the oldest and most beautiful from the Edo period, was begun in 1629 by Yorifusa Tokugawa, founder of the Mito Tokugawa family, and finished 30 years later by his heir. Designed for strolling and contemplation, it is made up of re-creations of picturesque sites in China and Japan, as well as settings inspired by literary scenes. The best known are the Full Moon stone bridge and the small temple dedicated to Benten, the goddess of fortune. Its northern outlook is enlivened by a paddy field, irises and plum trees. The garden also has a vast lotus pond, magnificent in August when in flower, and a smaller pond beside which the Mito devoted themselves to their studies. Its entrance, set back in a small street, can be difficult to find.

Not forgetting

■ **Kiyosumi Teien (25)** 3-3-9 Kiyosumi, Kōtō-ku. ☎ (03) 3641-5892
This beautiful, peaceful 15-acre garden, open daily, owes its current appearance to the baron Yataro Iwasaki, founder of the Mitsubishi group at the end of the 19th century. It has been enhanced by the addition of miscellaneous sculptured rocks from all over Japan, and thousands of carp have come to fill the immense pond. A teahouse stands on an islet accessed by a series of bridges and miniature islands.

In the area

Where to stay: ➥ 28
Where to eat: ➥ 58
After dark: ➥ 75
Where to shop: ➥ 127 ➥ 140 ➥ 142

What to see

Seiji Tōgō Memorial Yasuda Kasai Museum (26)

Yasuda Fire and Marine Insurance Bldg 42F, 1-26-1 Nishi-Sinjuku, Shinjuku-ku ☎ (03) 3349-3081

Shinjuku *Tue.–Sun. 9.30–4.30* ● *¥500; students ¥300*

The painter Seiji Tōgō (1897–1978) is famous for his portraits of young women. A hundred or so of his works are on display in this museum, the highest in the world if you believe its curators! Not surprising, since it is on the 41st floor of a tower with superb views. The public became acquainted with this institution, belonging to an insurance company, in October 1987 when it bought *Sunflowers* by Van Gogh for more than ¥5bn.

Tōkyō Metropolitan Government Building (27)

2-8-1 Nishi-Shinjuku, Shinjuku-ku ☎ (03) 5321-1111

Shinjuku *Tue.–Fri. 9.30am–5pm; Sat., Sun., public holidays 9.30am–7pm; closed Dec. 29–31, Jan. 2–3* ● *free*

Designed by Kenzo Tange, the *Tochō*, as the Japanese call it, dominates the other skyscrapers of Shinjuku. Completed in 1991, it has an immense plaza in front of it, often used for exhibitions and concerts. Each of the two 47-story towers has an observation gallery, on the 44th floor, from which you can enjoy fantastic views over Tokyo and that symbol of Japan, Mount Fuji. The *Tochō* inspires mixed sentiments: architecture worthy of the capital or icy-looking citadel; judge for yourself!

Shinjuku Imperial Gyoen (28)

11 Naitōmachi, Shinjuku-ku ☎ (03) 3350-0151

Shinjuku Gyoenmae ***Park*** *Tue.–Sun. 9am–4.30pm/**Glasshouse** Tue.–Sun. 11am–3.30pm/daily blossoming of cherry trees and chrysanthemums* ● *¥200*

Created in 1906 for the Imperial family, this 185-acre park is the first in Japan to have been designed in a conscious move toward westernization. Numerous non-indigenous species were introduced in the large glasshouse, and English- and French-style gardens were created, without forgetting the traditional Japanese garden. The latter, with its pond, its indispensable stone lanterns, its humpbacked bridges and its gently rounded hillocks, hosts a splendid chrysanthemum festival in the fall.

Bunka Gakuen Costume Museum (29)

Endo Museum Hall 3F, Bunka Gakuen, 3-22-1 Yoyogi, Shibuya-ku ☎ (03) 3299-2387

Shinjuku *Mon.–Fri. 10am–4.30pm; Sat. 10am–3pm* ● *¥300; students ¥200; children ¥100*

Associated with a renowned school for dress design that trained Kenzo, among others, this fashion museum is worth a visit. Costumes dating from the Edo period and rolls of admirably preserved old fabric evoke the laborious work involved in creating the elegance of a not-so-distant past.

Not forgetting

■ **Kabukicho (30)** *Or 'sin city'. The most disreputable area of Tokyo: the debauchery of soaplands (brothels), hostess and girly bars and 'love hotels'. You will also find traditional bars and excellent restaurants.*

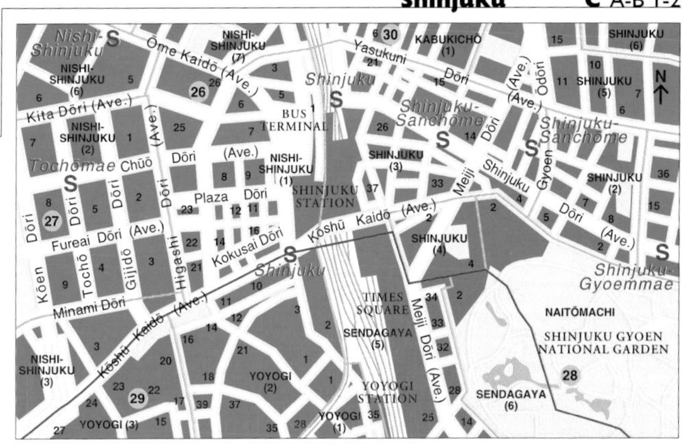

Synonymous with sex, shopping and fun, Shinjuku is also a bastion of fashion and contemporary architecture, a city within a city where everything is within reach.

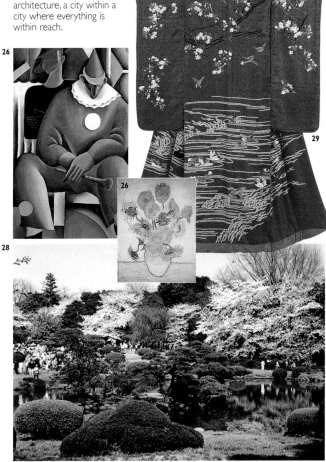

26

29

26

28

In the area

Where to stay: ➥ 28 ➥ 30
Where to eat: ➥ 58 ➥ 60
After dark: ➥ 68 ➥ 74 ➥ 78
Where to shop: ➥ 136 ➥ 138 ➥ 142

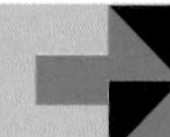

What to see

Meiji Treasure House (31)

Yoyogi-kōen, 1-1 Yoyogi, Kamizonochō, Shibuya-ku ☎ (03) 3261-8326

JR Harajuku *daily: Mar.–Oct. 9am–4.30pm; Nov.–Feb. 9am–4pm* ● *¥200; under-18 ¥120*

Housed in a dreary gray concrete building, this underrated museum houses a collection of Shintoist sacred objects belonging to the Imperial family and the personal possessions of Emperor Meiji and Empress Shoken.

Meiji Shrine (32)

1-1 Yoyogi, Kamizonochō, Shibuya-ku ☎ (03) 3379-5511

JR Harajuku *daily: mid-Mar.–mid-June, mid-Sep.–mid-Dec. 5.40am–5.20pm; mid-June–mid-Sep. 4am–5pm; mid-Dec.–mid-Mar. 6am–5pm*

You enter the immense gardens by a massive *torii* of cypresses. Built in 1920 in memory of Emperor Meiji, this shrine is one of the most popular in Tokyo. Its copper roof, with its simple lines, its unornamented pillars and its white-graveled front courtyard are typically Shintoist. The extremely restful wooded park contains over 125,000 trees, an offering by the Japanese people to their Emperor.

Watari-um Museum (33)

3-7-6 Jingūmae, Shibuya-ku ☎ (03) 3402-3001

Gaienmae *Tue., Thu.–Sun. 11am–7pm; Wed. 11am–9pm* ● *¥800; students ¥600*

Devoted to Japanese and international avant-garde art, this gallery and its studio café partly work on the interactive principle. Expect some surprises. The building, designed by the Swiss architect Mario Botta, also houses the excellent art shop On Sundays ➥ 136.

Ukiyo-e Ōta Memorial Museum (34)

1-10-10 Jingūmae, Shibuya-ku ☎ (03) 3403-0880

Meiji-jingūmae, JR Harajuku *Tue.–Sun. 10.30am–5pm; closed 27–31 of each month, Dec. 19–Jan. 2* ● *¥500; students ¥400*

Hidden away in a little street behind the luxuriant Omotesando-dōri, this delightful museum houses Seizō Ota V's impressive personal collection of *ukiyo-e*. In order to introduce the 12,000 or so prints and scrolls by masters such as Hiroshige (1797–1858), Kunisada (1786–1864) and Utamaro (1753–1806) to the public, the displays are changed every month. As the museum is traditional in conception, you will have to put on *surippa* at the entrance. Try Japanese pastries with green or cherry blossom tea in the graceful décor of the tea room.

Not forgetting

■ **Tōgō-jinja (35)** *Tōgō Temple is an oasis of calm. Dedicated to Admiral Heihachiro Togo, who vanquished the Russian fleet in the Russo-Japanese war, it houses an excellent flea market ➥ 142. Tea ceremonies take place in the gardens.* ■ **Olympic Stadium (36)** 2-1 Jinnan, Shibuya-ku ☎ (03) 3468-1171 *Built by Kenzo Tange for the Tokyo Olympics in 1964, the National Gymnasium hasn't aged a bit. The basketball court and swimming pool are open to the public when not in use for competitions.*

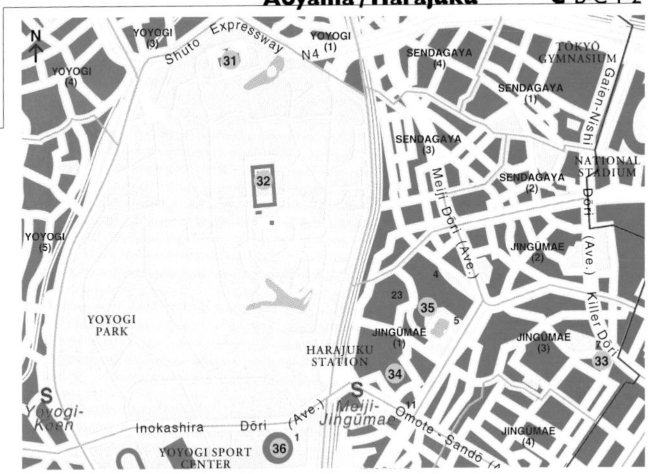

33

Fashion, art and design rub shoulders in this trendy district, also shared by galleries, designer boutiques, fashionable pavement cafés, a wooded park and several important Shintō shrines.

32

34

In the area

- Where to stay: ➥ 30
- Where to eat: ➥ 60
- After dark: ➥ 8 ➥ 74 ➥ 78
- Where to shop: ➥ 134 ➥ 136 ➥ 138

What to see

TEPCO Electric Energy Museum (37)
1-12-10 Jinnan, Shibuya-ku ☎ (03) 3477-1191

JR Shibuya *Thu.–Tue. 10am–6pm* ● *free*

Behind its impressive glass and steel façade, this museum is run by the Tokyo Electric Power Company. Very well organized and highly appreciated by children, its interactive exhibitions and displays look in depth at the mysteries of electricity, from the producer to the consumer. Each of the seven floors presents one particular aspect of electricity in an entertaining and educational way: electronic games (2nd floor), everyday electricity (3rd floor), the energy of tomorrow (5th floor)…

Tobacco & Salt Museum (38)
1-16-8 Jinnan, Shibuya-ku ☎ (03) 347-2041

JR Shibuya *Tue.–Sun. 10am–6pm* ● *¥100; under-18s ¥50*

This museum, nowadays very politically incorrect, won't surprise anyone in a country where nicotine addiction is always on the increase. You will be introduced here to the history of salt and tobacco, as well as production methods in Japan and the rest of the world. Amazing salt sculptures, a collection of ancient pipes, *ukiyo-e* describing the manufacturing process in the old days and scenes showing courtesans smoking, may not be enough, however, to convert fervent anti-smoking campaigners.

Toguri Museum of Art (39)
1-11-3 Shōtō, Shibuya-ku ☎ (03) 3465-0070

JR Shibuya *Tue.–Sun. 9.30–5.30pm* ● *¥1,030, students ¥73; under-18s ¥420*

Housed in a rather unattractive yellow-brick building in the heart of the Shōtō residential district, the Tōguri museum is a must for lovers of ceramics. Over 5,000 wonderful pieces are displayed in rotation, and four annual exhibitions enable you to learn alternately about Japanese, Chinese, Annamite and Korean ceramics. The *Nabeshima* and *Immari* of the Edo period (1615–1867) are especially remarkable.

Shōtō Museum of Art (40)
2-14-14 Shōtō, Shibuya-ku ☎ (03) 3465-9421

JR Shinsen *Tue.–Sun. 9am–5pm* ● *¥300; under-18 ¥100*

This contemporary art gallery, with its cozy atmosphere, presents temporary exhibitions by local or Asian artists, such as the Chinese Fu Pao-shih. One of the galleries houses a tearoom where you can admire the works of art while sipping your tea.

Not forgetting

■ **Bunkamura (41)** Bunkamura B1, 2-24-1, Dōgenzaka, Shibuya-ku. ☎ (03) 3477-3244. *This cleverly named multi-complex (Bunkamura means 'the village of culture') houses, in addition to the Cocoon Theater, shops, cinemas and numerous restaurants, including a subsidiary of the famous Parisian café Les Deux Magots. In the basement there is a small museum for traveling exhibitions. You should be aware that the Orchard Hall is the home of the Tokyo Philharmonic Orchestra.*

Spearheading fashion for the young and trendy, Shibuya is an accumulation of ultra-modern apartment buildings, neon lights, department stores, restaurants, theme bars and also museums and galleries inherited from a rich cultural past.

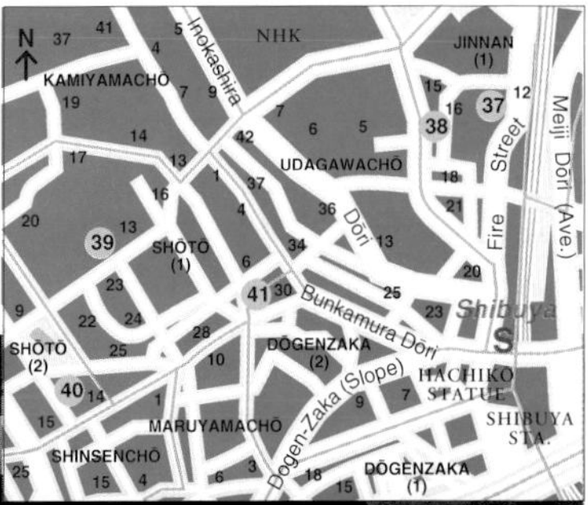

40

38

37

37

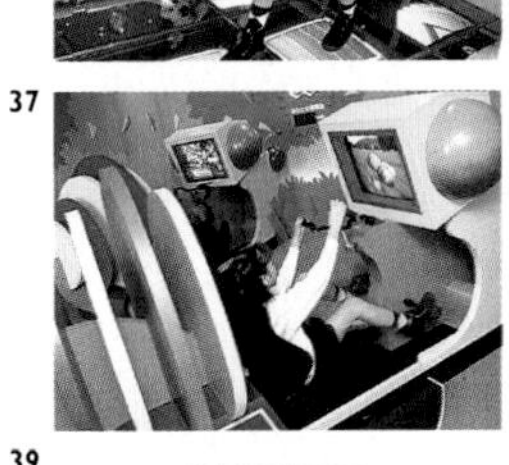

39

41

In the area

Where to stay: ➥ 30
Where to eat: ➥ 62
After dark: ➥ 78
Where to shop: ➥ 142

What to see

Yebisu Beer Museum (42)
Ebisu Garden Place, 4-20-1 Ebisu, Shibuya-ku ☎ (03) 5423-7255

JR Ebisu *Tue.–Sun. 10am–5pm* ● *¥300* *free*

The origins of Yebisu beer go back to 1887 when Nippon Beer Brewery set up its first brewery on the outskirts of the small village of Mita. Today all that remains is this museum celebrating the history, brewing methods and culture of this popular drink. The virtual tour of a brewery may make your mouth water, but you'll have to wait until you get to the bar to try the house recommendations (included in the price).

Tōkyō Metropolitan Museum of Photography (43)
1-13-3 Mita, Meguro-ku ☎ (03) 3280-0031

JR Ebisu *Tue., Wed., Sat. 10am–6pm; Sun. 10am-8pm* ● *¥500; under-18s ¥250*

Four floors of the biggest space in Tokyo dedicated to photography and video house a permanent collection and an Images and Technology Gallery telling the story of film and photography.

National Park for Nature Study (44)
5-21-5 Shiroganedai, Minato-ku ☎ (03) 3441-7176

JR Meguro *Tue.–Sun.: Sep.–Apr. 9am–4pm; May–Aug. 9am–5pm* ● *¥200; under 18 ¥100*

Shizen Kyoikuen, a park for nature study since 1949, is a wonderful surprise in the heart of the metropolis. This last vestige of the old wooded domain of the lord Matsudaira has been left in its original state. It provides a habitat for 500-year-old moss-covered trees and one zone has been managed to preserve indigenous species such as *Benthamidia japonica Hara* and *Erythronium japonicum Decme*, dating from *Musashino*, the pre-Edo period.

Tokyo Metropolitan Teien Art Museum (45)
5-21-9 Shiroganedai, Minato-ku ☎ (03) 3443-0201

JR Meguro *Tue.–Sun. 10am–4pm* ● ***Exhibitions** variable/**Gardens** ¥100; students ¥50*

This museum is housed in the only remaining Art-Deco building in Tokyo. Temporary exhibitions are displayed on the first floor, but the location's main appeal lies in the architecture and the Japanese gardens. After a stay in Paris in the 1920s, Prince Asaka Yasuhiko asked Henri Rapin and René Lalique to build and furnish this house.

Not forgetting

■ **Hatakeyama Memorial Museum (46)** 2-20-12 Shirokanedai, Minato-ku ☎ (03) 3447-5787 *The residence of the tea master Issei Hatakeyama harbors a harmonious ensemble of gardens and teahouses. The main gallery displays objects relating to the tea ceremony – executed by masters Koetsu, Chojiro and Sen no Rikyu – as well as pictorial or calligraphic works by Seisho, Karin and Kezan.*

■ **Meguro Gajoen Museum of Art (47)** 1-8-1 Shimo- Meguro, Meguro-ku ☎ (03) 5434-3821 *The building is a museum in itself. Rikizo Hosokawa, its founder, commissioned artists to decorate all the surfaces of the house. This shrine also holds works of the Meiji, Paisho and Showa periods. Don't miss the garden…or the washrooms!*

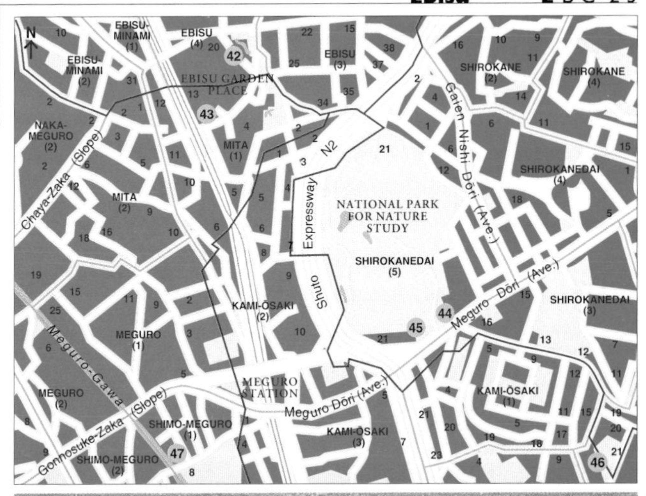

Ebisu, Mita and Shirokanedai are among the smartest residential areas in Tokyo. After having explored their cultural life, their immense parks and their elegant cafés, you can savor the more robust pleasures offered by their various types of bar including beer bars. 44

The Edo period began in 1600 with the *shōgun* Tokugawa Ieyasu, who established his center of domination in Edo. This period saw a new social order in which everything was codified. The Emperor was to remain inaccessible and powerless and the country closed to foreigners until 1868, the beginning of the Meiji period, when Edo was renamed Tokyo.

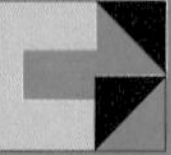

What to see

48

54

Edo-Tōkyō Museum (48)

1-4-1 Yokoami, Sumida-ku ☎ (03) 3626-9974

JR Ryōgoku Tue., Wed., Sat., Sun. 10am–6pm; Thu., Fri. 10am–8pm ● ¥600; under-18s ¥300

Located in an ultra-modern building, this museum presents a lively picture of the life and trading culture of the inhabitants of Edo, from the samurai to the simple city dweller. You will be able to admire reconstructions and models of historic buildings such as the Nihombashi bridge ➥ 23. One section is devoted to the period from 1868 to the postwar reconstruction, demonstrating how natural or human catastrophes have modified the city's topography.

Tabi Museum (49)

1-9-3 Midori, Sumida-ku ☎ (03) 3631-0092

Ryōgoku, Sobu Mon.–Sat. 9am–6pm ● ¥300

The *tabi* have few fans apart from sumotoris and ladies in kimonos. The manufacture of these white, split-toe ankle socks doesn't feature among the fine arts, but their traditional character justifies a visit to this small factory museum.

Fukagawa Edo Museum (50)

1-3-28 Shirakawa, Koto-ku ☎ (03) 3640-8625

Monzen-Nakachō daily 9.30am–5pm; closed 2nd and 4th Mon. of the month ● ¥300; under-18s ¥50

This museum is notable for its eleven original buildings, relating the life of a working district of Fukagawa in the 1840s. Explore the rooms, the vegetable and rice stores, discover the period implements and toys, and marvel at their smallest detail.

52 54 51

Sword Museum (51)

2F, 4-25-10 Yoyogi, Shibuya-ku ☎ (03) 3379-1386

Sangūbashi *Tue.–Sun. 9am–4pm* ● *¥525; students ¥315*

A collection of 6,000 swords and other splendidly tempered blades, including several national treasures. The manufacture of these weapons is considered a true art in Japan. Moreover, the museum is run by the Japanese Society for the Preservation of the Art of the Sword.

Nezu Institute of Fine Arts (52)

6-5-36 Minami-Aoyama, Minato-ku ☎ (03) 3400-2536

Omote-Sandō *Tue.–Sun. 9.30am–4.30pm* ● *¥1,000; students ¥700*

The founder of the Tōbu railroad, Kaichiro Nezu, was a great lover of Chinese art and the tea ceremony. His collection comprises ceramics, paintings, sculptures and valuable lacquerware, as well as extremely rare bronzes of the Shang and Zhou dynasties. Endowed with seven tearooms, the exquisite garden deserves a visit in its own right.

Not forgetting

■ **Drum Museum (53)** Nishi-Akasuka Bldg, 4F, 2-1-1 Nishi-Asakusa, Taitō-ku ☎ (03) 3842-5622 *Traditionally the drum is used in Buddhist festivals. This museum does not only let you find out about them – for example, the enormous taiko, 3 ft in diameter – but also to try them out.* ■ **Kite Museum (54)** Taimeiken 5F, 1-12-10 Nihombashi, Chūō-ku ☎ (03) 3271-2465 *With more than 2,000 types of kite, this museum illustrates a sport deeply rooted in Japanese culture.* ■ **Fire Museum (55)** 3-10 Yotsuya, Shinjuku-ku ☎ (03) 3353-9119 *Ceaselessly fighting fires, poetically called 'flowers of Edo', the fire fighters of Edo have often been depicted in* ukiyo-e. *Scale models, period equipment and interactive games bring them back to life.*

In the area

- Where to stay: ➡ 18
- Where to eat: ➡ 64
- After dark: ➡ 70 ➡ 72
- Where to shop: ➡ 142 ➡ 146

What to see

Kaminari-mon & Nakamise (56)
Kaminarimon dōri, Taitō-ku

Asakusa

The Kaminari-mon or 'Thunder Gate' is the grandest entrance to Sensō-ji temple. This impressive wooden structure is flanked by two statues representing the twin gods of thunder and wind. In the middle, there is a huge red paper lantern. Not far off the Nakamise-dori (the 'inner boutiques') stretches out: a long, narrow street lined with stalls overflowing with a wide selection of traditional articles. There is a festive atmosphere here every day of the week.

Sensō-ji (57)
2-3-1 Asakusa, Taitō-ku ☎ (03) 3842-0181

Asakusa *daily 6am–5pm*

This place became a site of pilgrimage after 1628 when three fishermen raising their nets in the Sumida river found a golden statuette of Kannon, the Buddhist goddess of mercy. The present building, also known as Asakusa Kannon, is a replica of a 1692 edifice, destroyed in World War II. A crowd of worshippers presses up against an immense bronze cauldron containing burning incense, whose healing powers are said to cure any part of the body that touches it. It is placed at the foot of the main building, where you can see a small collection of extremely valuable votive paintings from the 18th and 19th centuries.

Asakusa-jinja (58)
2-3-1 Asakusa, Taitō-ku ☎ (03) 3844-1575

Yushima *daily 6.30am–5pm* ***Festival Sanja matsuri**: May*

The shrine is dedicated to the fishermen who discovered the statuette of Kannon. This is one of the few structures from this group of 17th-century buildings to have survived intact. It is also called Sanja Sanma, the 'shrine of three guardians', a name used by Asakusa's most important festival, the Sanja May Festival. Near the entrance is the Niten-mon gate, built in 1618 and listed as an 'important cultural treasure'.

Dembō-in (59)
2-3-1 Asakusa, Taitō-ku ☎ (03) 3261-8326

Asakusa *daily 9am–4pm; closed Sun., public holidays* ● *free*

This monastic garden, laid out in the 17th century by the Zen landscape gardener Kobori Enshu, is an underestimated treasure. Still owned by the monks who serve Sensō-ji, you can visit it by collecting a ticket at the *shomuka* office on the left of the five-story pagoda.

Not forgetting

■ **Asahi Super Dry (60)** 1-23-1 Azumabashi, Sumida-ku *Built by Phillip Starck for the brewer Asahi, this edifice is one of the most disconcerting ever to have thrust its way up into the sky of the capital. Its surrealist silhouette, topped with a floating structure in the shape of a flame, rests on a massive, black, polished base. It was apparently built in a naval dockyard, using the same methods as for a submarine. There is a fine view from the Asahi Sky Room.*

Situated at the heart of *shitamachi*, one of the most lively districts of the capital, Asakusa (pronounced assak'sa) is a very old religious and craft center and a traditional place of recreation.

56

57

58

In the area

- Where to stay: ➥ 18
- Where to eat: ➥ 50
- After dark: ➥ 70 ➥ 72 ➥ 74
- Where to shop: ➥ 144

What to see

Tōkyō National Museum (61)
13-9 Ueno-kōen, Taitō-ku ☎ (03) 3822-1111

Ueno, JR Ueno, Keisei-Ueno *Tue.–Sun.: Apr.–Sep. 9am–8pm; Oct.–Mar. 9.30am–4.30pm* ● *¥420; under-18s ¥70*

With more than 89,000 works, this museum can boast of having the largest collection of Asian art and archeology in the world. The collection is intelligently dispersed throughout five buildings whose architectural type ranges from the Edo period to that of today, so you can easily organize your visit. Honkan, inaugurated in 1938, exclusively houses Japanese art; Jōmon antiquities are displayed in the Heiseika. The Tokyokan harbors treasures from Central Asia, Korea and China, while the brand new Hōryu-ji Hōmotsukan displays 319 priceless pieces from the grand temple of Hōryu-ji, at Nara.

National Science Museum (62)
7-20 Ueno-kōen, Taitō-ku ☎ (03) 3822-0111

Ueno, JR Ueno, Keisei-Ueno *Tue.–Sun. 9am–4.30pm* ● *¥490; students ¥450; under-18s ¥250*

Crawling with uniformed schoolchildren, cute but very noisy, this museum tells you everything about science, from botany to oceanography, and including ethnology. Two new galleries house video simulations and interactive exhibits.

Tōshō-gū (63)
9-8 Ueno-kōen, Taitō-ku ☎ (03) 3822-3455

Ueno, JR Ueno, Keisei-Ueno ***shrine** daily 9am-4.30pm/**Gardens** daily 9am–sunset* ● *¥200*

This opulent shrine, dedicated to the *shōgun* Tokugawa Ieyasu, is one of the main places of interest in Ueno. Built in 1651, it is also one of the rare monuments in Tokyo to have survived the many ups and downs of history. A fabulous bestiary – birds, monkeys, shells and gilded dragons – decorate its walls, gateways and imposts. Two hundred stone lanterns line the avenue leading to the temple.

Not forgetting

■ **Benten-dō (64)** Shinobazu-dōri, Taitō-ku *The Benzaiten is dedicated to Benten, goddess of beauty and patron of the arts. It stands on a small island on Shinobazu lake, a former arm of the sea comprising the famous lotus pond, a sanctuary for cormorants and migrating birds, as well as a little lake where you can go boating.* ■ **Shitamachi Museum (65)** 2-1 Ueno-kōen, Taitō-ku ☎ (03) 3823-7451 *Edo rediscovered. This museum recounts the history and daily life of the former Edo. Its key exhibits are the dwelling of a merchant and a series of rooms furnished with their implements, tools and toys. Photographs and videos showing the district of Shitamachi up to 1940 complete the scene.* ■ **Asakura Chosokan (66)** 7-1-10 Yanaka, Taitō-ku ☎ (03) 3821-4549 *Gallery of sculptures devoted to the artist Fumio Asakura (1883–1964). Enchanting little water garden and a beautiful view from the observatory on the top floor. Closed on Mondays.* ■ **Yanaka Cemetery (67)** 7 Yanaka, Taitō-ku *This is the final resting place of the last* shōgun *and also of past and present celebrities of Tokyo, including the novelists Soseki Natsume and Ogai Mori. A pleasant walk along the verdant paths, scattered with mossy tombs. Several temples stand within the grounds.*

Time stands still on Ueno hill and in the district of Yanaka, where the trading and artistic past of Edo still survives. It is pleasant to stroll through the narrow streets and gardens where old houses, a host of museums and private temples follow one after the other.

65

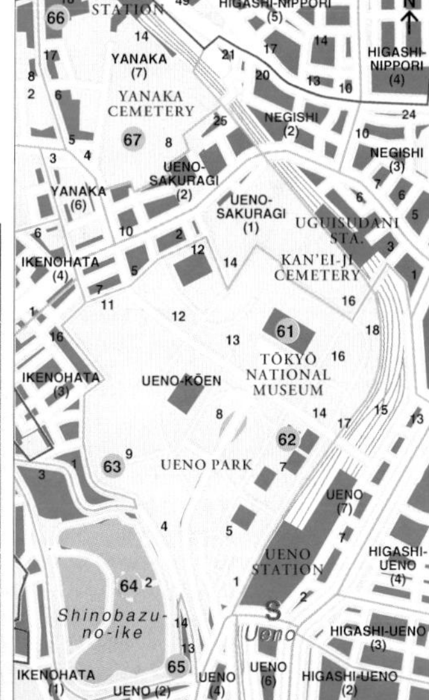

61

64

63

In the area

Where to stay: ➡ 36
Where to eat: ➡ 46
After dark: ➡ 68 ➡ 72
Where to shop: ➡ 128

What to see

Rainbow Bridge (68)

Yurikamome Odaiba Kaihin-Kōen ***pedestrians*** *daily: Apr.–Oct. 10am–9pm; Nov.–Mar. 10am–6pm ● ¥300 Sunset Beach Restaurant Row*

The sea spray that reaches you on the walkway of this 3,012 ft-long bridge will remind you that Tokyo is a port. This is a delightful walk at sunset when the bridge and the big wheel are covered with a thousand lights. Opened in 1993, the bridge joins the city to Odaiba, a district built on reclaimed land during the economic boom of the 1980s. The island is connected to one of the *daiba*, those forts built in the 17th century to protect Edo from invasion. Nearby lies Odaiba Marine Park, an artificial sandy beach with adjoining oases of greenery.

Palette Town (69)

Yurikamome Kokusai-tenjijō Seimon ***Venus Fort*** *Sun.–Thu. 11am–10pm; Fri., Sat. 11am–4am/****Mega Web*** *daily 11am–9pm*

Venus Fort, a vast shopping and leisure zone, is in the new Palette Town complex. Almost 150 shops, restaurants and cafés line its main street, with its surrealist-kitsch décor. An arched roof protects it from the elements, but trompe-l'oeil paintings and cleverly placed lighting create the illusion of a changing sky. A panoramic view of the bay from the giant wheel.

Fuji TV Building (70)

2-4-8 Daiba, Minato-ku ☎ (03) 5500-8888

Yurikamome Odaiba Kaihin-Kōen Tue.–Sun. 10am–8pm ● ¥500

The Fuji-Sankei building, headquarters of Fuji Television and Nippon Broadcasting, stands out from its neighbors as you approach the island. One of the many buildings to the credit of the master architect Kenzo Tange, it comprises two blocks linked by walkways and by a 105-ft-diameter metal sphere remarkably reminiscent of an immense cathode-ray tube, in which the observatory is housed.

Museum of Maritime Science (71)

3-1 Higashi-Yashio, Shinagawa-ku ☎ (03) 5500-1111

Yurikamome Fune-no-Kagakukan daily 10am–5pm; closed Dec. 28–31 ● ¥1,000; under-18 ¥600

This museum is not to be missed: it resembles a liner readying herself to breast the waves. Its exhibits tell the story of navigation and commercial transport. Two authentic floating ships, anchored outside, are open to visitors: the *Soya*, one of the first boats used by the Japanese for Antarctic exploration, and the *Yoteimaru*, one of the ferries serving Honshū and Hokkaidō before the tunnel was opened.

Not forgetting

■ **Tokyo Big Sight (72)** 3-21-1 Ariake, Kōtō-ku ☎ (03) 5530-1111
A monolithic structure made up of upside-down pyramids, the city's new exhibition center houses a conference room and several restaurants, cafés and exhibition halls. Panoramic views from the Observatory Bar Lounge on the 7th floor, with its vast atriums.

The island of Rinkai Fukutoshin is better known as Odaiba. On the way to becoming a chic and ultra-trendy district, it is an urban and architectural testing ground covering an area of 1,107 acres reclaimed from the sea, a godsend to Tokyo.

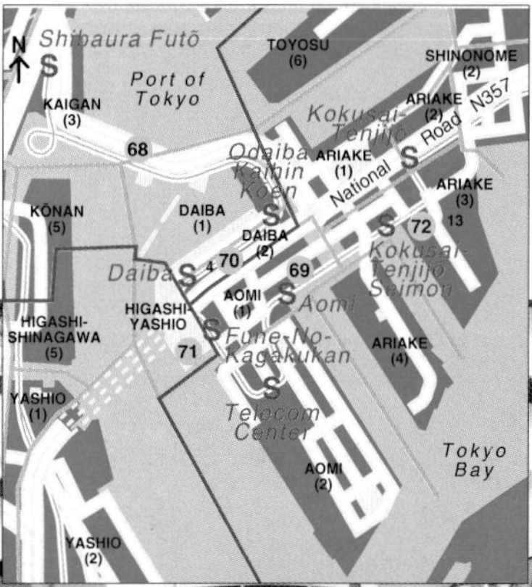

70

72

68

72

Since the Meiji era, which allowed the introduction of western sports, the most popular in Japan have been *sumō* and baseball. Soccer has now caught them up since the creation of the J. League in 1993 and Japan's hosting, with Korea, of the 2002 World Cup. Tokyo will also, however, enable you to discover martial arts that are little known elsewhere.

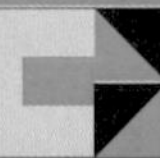

What to see

74

74

73

74

Tōkyō Dome (73)

1-3-61 Kōraku, Bunkyō-ku ☎ (03) 3811-2111

M *Kōrakuen, JR Suidōbashi* ⌚ **museum** *Museum daily 10am–5pm* ● *¥1,200–5,900*

The Tōkyō Dome (1985), better known as the 'Big Egg', hosts baseball matches, baseball being the most popular team game in Japan, where it has been played since 1873. The retractable roof enables games to be played in all weathers. Tokyo is home to three professional clubs: the Nippon Ham Fighters, the Yakult Swallows and the very popular Yomiuri Giants. The Baseball Hall of Fame Museum is adjacent to the building. The Big Egg has capacity for 60,000 people and holds rock concerts (the Rolling Stones have appeared here) and exhibitions as well as matches.

Kokugikan (74)

1-3-28 Yokoami, Sumida-ku ☎ (03) 3623-5111

M *JR Ryōgoku* ⌚ *vary* ● *¥2,100–11,300*

The National Sumo Stadium is the main venue for sumō in the country. Purists prefer to use the term *kokugi*, which means a nationally recognized discipline, to describe this sport, invented 2,000 years ago and whose complex rituals are linked to Shintoism. Three tournaments, each fifteen days long, take place in January, May and September in Tōkyō. The most expensive places – on the *tatami* mats in front of the ring (*dohyo*) – are fiercely coveted. These entitle you to a free snack and souvenir gifts.

72

Nippon Budōkan (75)

2-3 Kitanomaru-kōen, Chiyoda-ku ☎ (03) 3216-5100 ➠ (03) 3216-5118

Ⓜ *Kudanshita* 🕘 *daily 9am–6pm* ● *free*

This temple to the martial arts was built to house judo competitions in the Tokyo Olympic Games in 1964. Since the opening of the Tōkyō Dome it has tended to play second fiddle, but its octagonal structure and its curved roof, recalling the head of a sumō wrestler, have lost none of their impact. The Budokan hosts judo, archery, kendo and Japanese fencing competitions, sporting exhibitions and numerous rock concerts. The Beatles appeared here in 1966.

National Stadium (76)

Kasumigaokamachi, Shinjuku-ku ☎ (03) 3403-1151

Ⓜ *JR Sendagaya* 🕘 ***Variable matches*** ● *¥3,000–5,000/**Museum** 9.30am–4.30pm* ● *¥150; students ¥50*

Soccer now makes a regular appearance at the National Stadium. The first Japanese soccer federation was only set up in 1993, a fact that hasn't stopped the J. League winning many supporters and qualifying for the World Cup in 1998.

Not forgetting

Lalaport Ski Dome SSAWS (77) 2-3-1 Hama-chō, Funabashi-shi, Chiba ☎ (047) 432-7000 Ⓜ Minami-Funabashi (JR Keiyo line) *The longest artificial ski slope in the world, situated in the suburbs of Chiba prefecture, is worth a detour. Built on a polder, it is 262 ft high at the top and measures almost half a mile long by about 328 ft wide. Slopes for all levels, temperature maintained at 41°F. You can rent the necessary clothing and equipment on the spot.*

Further afield

The onsen trail

The volcanic mountains that encircle the plain of Kantō abound in *onsen* ➥ 14 (hot springs). Visiting these thermal spas is one of the favorite pastimes of Tokyo residents. An ideal way to take a break from the bustle of the city. Japanese Hot Springs Complete brochure available at the TIC ➥ 12

Beaches

The coastline of the Bōsō peninsula boasts numerous beaches, the majority being concentrated around Tateyama, Chikura and Katsuura. The most famous is still that of Kujukurihama, a 38-mile-long stretch of sand facing the ocean between Chōshi and Ohara, and always besieged by surfers. Enoshima island, the peninsula and the island of Izu are also less than an hour from Tokyo.

Kyōto
Imperial city and capital of Japan until 1868, Kyōto is still a major center of culture and the arts. With around 2,000 temples and shrines, its dream-like gardens, its hieratic monks and the kimonos that add color to its streets, it presents an image of the old Japan that remains almost intact.
JR Shinkansen Tokyo-Kyōto *3am* • *¥25,000*

22 Days out

Fuji-yama
Mount Fuji, the symbol of Japan, holds a special place in the hearts of the Japanese because of its beauty and its sacred character. Each summer, it is climbed by thousands of pilgrims. Five paths lead to the summit (12,389 ft), the most popular starting at Lake Kawaguchiko and the most traditional at Fuji-Yoshida. Each is divided up into ten stations 10–15 miles apart. Allow about ten hours for the climb, one to go round the crater and six to walk down. Many people choose to begin at the 5th station (*go-gome*) at Kawaguchiko, where the buses from Shinjuku stop. Your aim should be to reach the crater at sunrise. Reserve a bed (¥3,000 approx.) and a meal (¥2,000 approx.) in one of the refuges and plan to take safety equipment: water, torch, batteries, hat and warm, waterproof clothing, as the temperature at the top is 41° F. Japanese proverb: 'the wise man climbs Mount Fuji once, the fool twice.'
Ascent *July 1–Aug. 31*
Fuji-Yoshida Tourist Information Center *daily 9am–5.30pm* ☎ *(0555) 22-7000*
Refuge reservations
☎ *(0555) 22-1948*
Shinjuku bus station; stop Kawaguchiko *2 hrs approx.*
• *¥2,600*
Tokyo Station; change at Tōmei; stop Gotemba *3 hrs 30 mins approx.*
• *¥3,500*

INDEX BY TYPE

Kantō, the widest plain in Japan, extends from the foothills of the Mikuni mountains to the Pacific. Its coastal reaches, punctuated by peninsulas and bays, and its mountains, present landscapes of astonishing beauty: marshland with irises and water lilies, *onsen* tucked away in steep gorges, stretches of fine sand, and the majestic Mount Fuji.

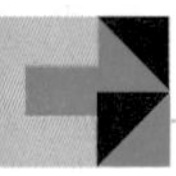

Further afield

Yokohama (6-10)

Shinjuku Station (about 25 mins): take the Odakyu line; station Hakone-Yumoto
every 30 mins
● *one-way about ¥1,820.*

Kamakura (11-15)

Tokyo Station (about 60 mins): take the JR Yokusuka; station Kamakura
every 10–15 mins
● *one-way about ¥890*

Enoshima (16)

Shinjuku Station (about 1hr 10 mins): take the Odakyu line; station Enoshima
every 30 mins
● *one-way about ¥1,030*

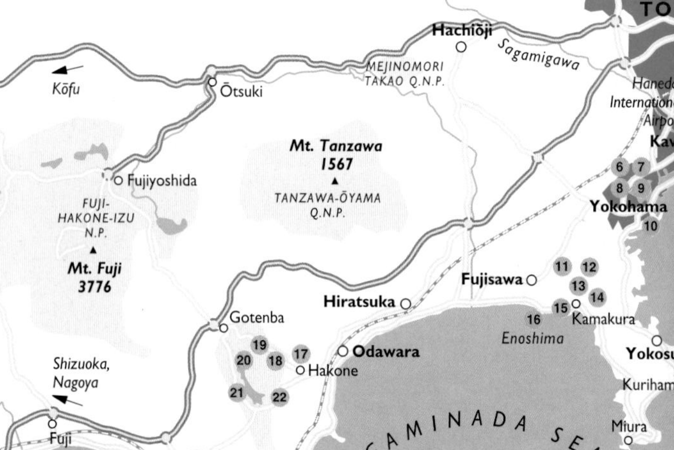

Suruga Bay

IZU-HANTŌ PENINSULA

Itō

FUJI-HAKONE-IZU N.P.

Shimoda

Ōshima Island

Hakone (17-22)

***Shinjuku Station** (about 1hr 35 mins): take the Odakyu line; station Hakone-Yumoto*
every 30 mins
● *one-way about ¥1,820.*

***Tokyo Station** about 45 mins): take the JR Kadoma line, station Odawara; then the Hakone-Tozan train, station Hakone-Yumoto*
every 30mins
● *one-way about ¥3,570.*

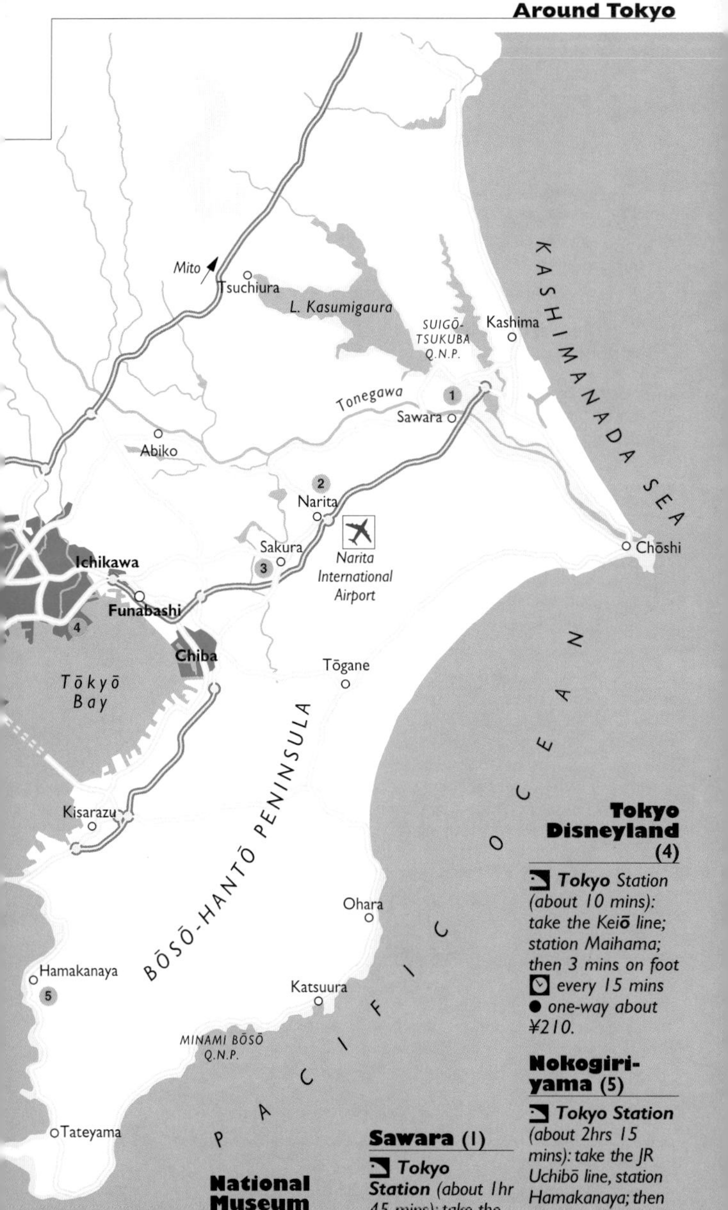

Mito
Tsuchiura
L. Kasumigaura
SUIGŌ-TSUKUBA Q.N.P.
Kashima
KASHIMANADA SEA
Tonegawa
1
Sawara
Abiko
2
Narita
Narita International Airport
Sakura
3
Chōshi
Ichikawa
Funabashi
4
Chiba
Tōkyō Bay
Tōgane
BŌSŌ-HANTŌ PENINSULA
PACIFIC OCEAN
Kisarazu
Ohara
Hamakanaya
5
Katsuura
MINAMI BŌSŌ Q.N.P.
Tateyama

Tokyo Disneyland (4)

Tokyo Station (about 10 mins): take the Keiō line; station Maihama; then 3 mins on foot
every 15 mins
● one-way about ¥210.

Nokogiri-yama (5)

Tokyo Station (about 2hrs 15 mins): take the JR Uchibō line, station Hamakanaya; then the funicular (about 4 mins)
every 15 mins
● one-way about ¥3,480
Tōkyō-wan Ferry (about 30 mins): catch the ferry at Kurihama;
hourly
● one-way about ¥500

Sawara (1)

Tokyo Station (about 1hr 45 mins): take the Suigo line; station Sawara
every 15 mins.
● one-way about ¥3,280
(about 25 mins) station Sawara; stop Aquatic Botanical Garden
● one-way about ¥200

National Museum of Japanese History (3)

Tokyo Station (about 65 mins): take the JR Sōbu line, station Sakura; then 15 mins on foot
every 15 mins
● one-way about ¥950

Narita-san (2)

Tokyo Station (about 1hr 15 mins): take the JR Sōbu line, station Sakura; then 15 mins on foot
every 15 mins
● one-way about ¥1,290

Chiba nestles at the far end of the bay, to the east of Tokyo. This is the old feudal city of Edo, and Disneyland, one of the largest amusement parks in Asia, holds sway on its outskirts. The Boso peninsula, with its 311 miles of coastline, offers a highly varied panorama, with long fine sandy beaches, small fishing ports and *onsen* hidden among wooded hills.

Further afield

Sawara (1)

On the banks of the Tone-gawa, this spot, crisscrossed with canals, is one of the points of departure for visiting Suigō regional park. Two and a half miles to the southwest is Katori-jingū, one of the most venerated shrines in the region, founded in the 3rd century and dedicated to Futsunushi no kami. Not far away lies Suishei shokobutsu-en, a 37-acre garden laid out on marshland. Especially pleasant in the summer months, when its waters are carpeted with lotuses, irises and water lilies, take out a flat-bottomed boat for a fishing trip and a traditional lunch.

Narita-san (2)

Narita, Chiba-ken ☎ (0476) 22-2111

Temple *daily 8.30am–6pm/**Park** Tue.–Sun. 8.30am–4pm* ● *free*
***Festivals**: New Year; Setsubun Apr. 3–4; Gion-E July; Otaki-Age Dec.*

Over twelve million people a year visit Narita-san, also called Shinshō-ji. The gardens and the temple, founded in 940 and dedicated to Fudō Myōō, cover 42 acres. There are several exceptional buildings dating from the Edo period, such as the bell tower (1706) and the three-story pagoda (1803). Once you have passed through the Niō-mon (1831), a flight of steps leads to the Dai Hon-dō (1968), where the famous statue of Fudō, one of the most popular deities of the Buddhist pantheon, stands. Adjoining the gardens, the Naritasan kōen offers the chance of a stroll in the shade of apricot trees, in English- or Japanese-style gardens adorned with boulders and waterfalls.

National Museum of Japanese History (3)

117 Jonai-chō, Sakuri-shi, Chiba-ken ☎ (043) 486-0123

Tue.–Sun. 9.30am–4.30pm ● *¥420; under-18s ¥110*

Established on the former site of Sakura castle, this museum specializes in the history and anthropology of Japan. Offering a wealth of information, it houses 106,000 or so objects presented according to 13 historical and 6 folkloric themes by means of maps, videos, ancient pottery, tools and everyday implements. Its scale models of tumuli, agricultural landscapes, palaces and villages are incredibly detailed.

Tokyo Disneyland (4)

1-1 Maihama, Urayasu-shi, Chiba-ken ☎ (047) 354-0001

P *daily 9am–7pm; variable closing* ● *¥5,200; under-18 ¥4,590; under-12s ¥3,570* *¥600* ***Ticket Center*** *☎ (03) 3595-1777*

The Japanese version of the Magic Kingdom is only 15 short minutes from the center of town. Opened in 1983, it is an exact replica of Disneyland in Los Angeles. It has the same attractions, such as the highly popular Space Mountain and Tomorrowland's Star.

Not forgetting

■ **Nokogiri-yama (5)** *Carved out of the side of Mount Nokogiri, the Daibutusu (1783), at 102 ft high, is the largest effigy of Buddha in Japan. A cable car takes you halfway up the mountain, to a panoramic view over Tokyo bay. The statue of Kannon (108 ft) is not far off, also cut out of the mountain. The group of 1,553 stone effigies of* rakan *(disciples of Buddha), is an equally fascinating sight.*

4

4

PARADE
100 YEARS OF Magic
N
Abiko
Tonegawa
Sawara
Narita
Narita International Airport
TOKYO
Sakura
Funabashi
CHIBA-KEN
Chiba
Tōgane
Tokyo Bay
Kisarazu
BŌSŌ-HANTŌ PENINSULA
Hamakanaya
Katsuura
MINAMI BŌSŌ Q.N.P.
PACIFIC OCEAN
Tateyama

5

2

2

With the opening up of external trade in 1859, the little fishing harbor rapidly became Japan's main international port. Despite its 3.5 million inhabitants, the second largest city in Japan has a feeling of space often missing in Tokyo. Just like San Francisco or Marseilles, Yokohama retains a very cosmopolitan atmosphere.

Further afield

Minato Mirai 21 (6)

2-2-1 Minato-Mirai, Nishi-ku, Yokohama

Sky Garden *daily: Oct.–June Tue.–Sun. 10am–9pm; July–Sep. 10am–10pm* ● *¥1,000; under 18s ¥800; under-12s ¥500 ☎ (045) 222-5030*

Minato Mirai 21, 'the port of the 21st century', is a futuristic complex built on ground won back from the sea. It comprises stores, several hotels and a leisure park where a giant 344-ft wheel has pride of place. The ensemble is dominated by the tallest building in Japan, the Landmark Tower which, at 971 ft high, has become the symbol of the new Yokohama. From the observatory of the Sky Garden (which has nothing of the garden about it!), on the 69th floor, you can see a Lilliputian version of the city and the bay. Yokohama Gulliver Land, a huge wooden dome, houses a captivating exhibition of models that compare the Yokohama of the 1960s with the future Minato Mirai of the year 2010.

Yokohama Maritime Museum (7)

2-2-1 Minato-Mirai, Nishi-ku, Yokohama ☎ (045) 221-0280

Tue.–Sun. 10am–5pm ● *¥600; under-18s ¥200*

This underground, very well designed museum tells the story of the port from the day in 1859 that Commodore Perry claimed the right to trade with the Empire, then fiercely isolationist. You can also admire the *Nippon Maru*, an old three-mast sailing ship built in 1930 that plowed the waves for over 50 years and is used today for training exercises.

Museum of Silk (8)

1 Yamashita-cho, Naka-ku ☎ (045) 641-0841

Tue.–Sun. 9.30am–4.30pm ● *¥300* *Silk market*

This museum pays homage to the past of Yokohama, in times gone by the main silk-exporting port of Japan. The first two floors house exhibitions devoted to the entire manufacturing process, from the breeding of the silkworm to the finished product. A shop in the basement sells articles made of silk, and the tourist office is on the ground floor.

Chinatown (9)

Yamashitachō, Naka-ku, Yokohama

Chinatown, called Chūka-gai here, houses the largest Chinese community in Japan. Its pedestrianized streets take up no more than a couple of blocks, but every square inch is made to pay. Stores, set up shoulder to shoulder, sell every product imaginable – from kitchen utensils to ancestral medicinal herbs, and including silk jackets – as long as they come from China. Take advantage of the opportunity to dine here, practically all the restaurants are excellent.

Not forgetting

■ **Sankei-en Garden (10)** 5-1 Honmoku Sannotani, Naka-ku ☎ (045) 621-0635 *Created in 1906 by a rich silk merchant, this Japanese garden is highly regarded for its cherry and plum trees and its irises. It houses the famous Rinshunkaku pagoda, built by shōgun Tokugawa Yoshinobu, as well as listed buildings from Kyōto and Nara. Open daily except from December 29 to 31.*

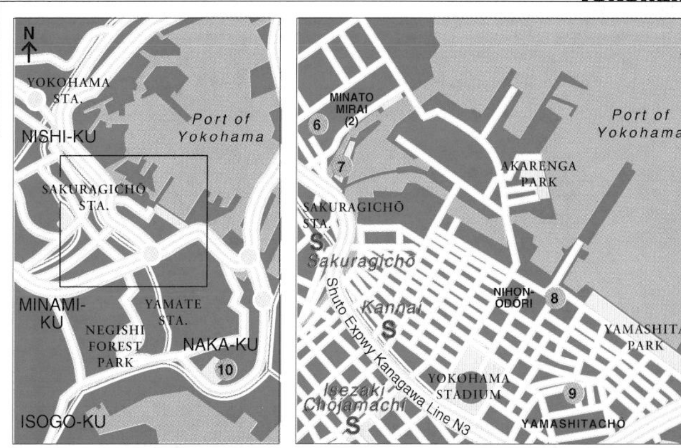
N
YOKOHAMA STA.
Port of Yokohama
NISHI-KU
SAKURAGICHŌ STA.
MINAMI-KU
YAMATE STA.
NEGISHI FOREST PARK
NAKA-KU
10
ISOGO-KU
MINATO MIRAI (2)
6
7
AKARENGA PARK
Sakuragichō
Shuto Expwy Kanagawa Line N3
Kannai
NIHON-ODORI
8
YAMASHITA PARK
YOKOHAMA STADIUM
9
Isezaki Chōjamachi
YAMASHITACHŌ

7

9
7

7

7

Kamakura is pleasantly located by the sea, at the foot of lush, green hills. From 1192 to 1333, it became the capital of Japan when the *shōgun* Minamoto Yorimoto set up his *bakufa* (government) there. This period sees the establishment of a martial, quasi ascetic, ideology derived from Zen that would also be applied to the architecture of temples and gardens.

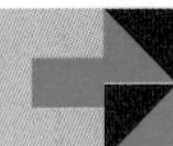

Further afield

Engaku-ji (11)
409 Yama-no-uchi ☎ (0469) 22-0478

M *Kita-Kamakura* ⏲ *daily 8am–4.30pm* ● *free*

The temple of Engaku was founded in 1282. Now shaded by majestic hundred-year-old cedars, the enclosure holds two important national treasures: the Shariden, the room containing sacred Buddha relics, and the bell tower, erected at the top of the hill. The apricot trees and the lake soften the severity of this magnificent Zen temple, the largest in the city.

Tsurugaoka Hachiman-gū (12)
2-131 Yuki-no-shita ☎ (0467) 22-0315

M *Kamakura* ⏲ *daily 8.30am–6pm* ● *free*

Set high on a hill, this beautiful collection of buildings, whose complex history goes back to 1063, was the tutelary shrine of the clan of Minamoto, founder of Kamakura. Despite having been reconstructed, the lesser shrines (Waka iya) and the greater shrines (Kami no miya) are still impressive. Beside the Aka-bashi that crosses the Gempei lake, stands the Mai-den, a dance pavilion that presents nō plays and *kabuki* shows in the spring.

Kamakura Museum of Modern Art (13)
2-131 Yuki-no-shita ☎ (0467) 22-5000

M *Kamakura* ⏲ *Tue.–Sun. 9.30am–4pm; closed public holidays.* ● *¥500*

This museum, designed by Sakakura Junzō, a pupil of Le Corbusier, appears suspended over Gempei lake. It houses an interesting collection of 250 contemporary Japanese and Western works.

Hokuku-ji / Takedera (14)
2 Jomyo-ji ☎ (0467) 22-0762

M *Kamakura* ⏲ *daily 9am–4pm* ● *free*

This Zen temple was built in 1334 for the Rinzai sect and was saved from oblivion by a priest of the region: he restored the gardens and transformed the site into a center devoted to meditation, calligraphy and the tea ceremony. Ask to be served a *matcha*, green tea, in the delightful Takedera pavilion, nestling in the heart of a magnificent bamboo plantation.

Daibutsu - The Great Buddha (15)
4-2-8 Hase ☎ (0467) 22-0703

⏲ *daily 9am–5.30pm* ● *¥200*

Located in the gardens of the temple of Kotoku-in, the Daibutsu (1252), or Great Buddha, is one of the proudest possessions of Kamakura. A symbol of perseverance, it has survived fires, earthquakes and even the tidal wave in 1495 that swept away the wooden building housing it.

Not forgetting

■ **Enoshima Island (16)** *This islet, two and a half miles in circumference, entered into history when fishermen, who had come to pray, founded a shrine on one of its rocks. Later, holy grottos, souvenir traders, cafés and escalators arrived. The whole thing is now amusingly kitsch.*

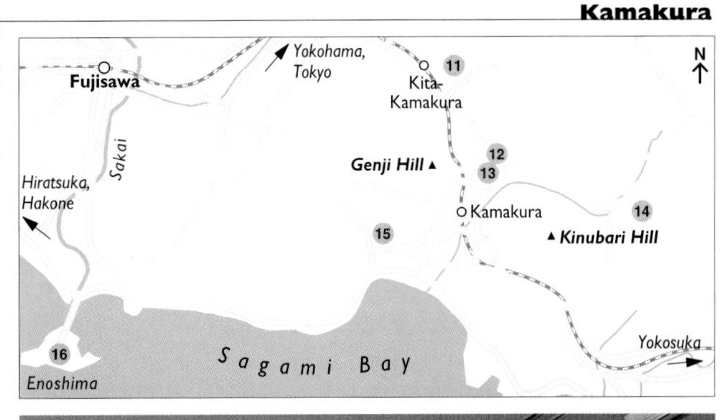
N
Fujisawa
Yokohama, Tokyo
Kita-Kamakura
11
Sakai
Genji Hill
12
13
Hiratsuka, Hakone
Kamakura
14
15
Kinubari Hill
16
Sagami Bay
Yokosuka
Enoshima

13

13

15

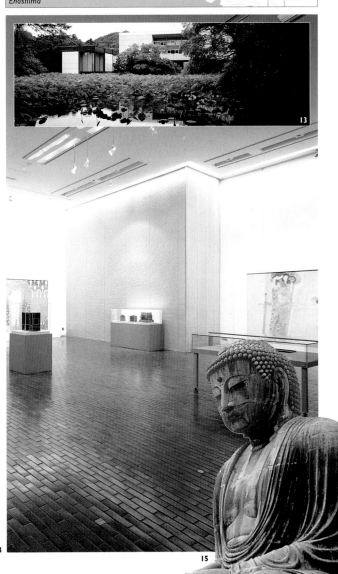

Locked in between Mount Fuji and the sea, the Hakone region is a protected enclave that grew up on the site of an old volcano. Famous for its hot springs, lake, museums and historic places of interest, it was a site of strategic security in the feudal period. At weekends, it is invaded by Tokyo residents who come to relax in the numerous *onsen*.

Further afield

Hakone Yumoto (17)

Despite its crowded streets, its hotels and souvenir stores, Hakone deserves two or three days devoted to it. Its *onsen* (hot springs), located where the Hayakawa and Sukomo-gawa meet, are the most ancient in the region. You will appreciate their properties on immersing yourself in the indoor or outdoor pools located in several excellent hotels and *ryokan*. An introduction to the *onsen* can be had at Tenzan Notemburo, one and a half miles to the south. This public hot spring is equipped with spa facilities, saunas and very good restaurants

Miyanoshita (18)

This enchanting village is set in a valley known for its *onsen*, its antique stores and its panoramic viewpoints. It has been attracting foreign visitors since the 19th century. You must stay, or failing that, drink a cup of tea, at the distinguished Fujiya Hotel, the oldest Western-style establishment in Japan. Its old-fashioned charm and its ornamental garden have hardly changed since it opened.

Hakone Open-Air Museum (19)

1121 Mi-no-taira, Hakone ☎ (0460) 2-1161

daily: Mar.–Oct. 9am–5pm; Nov.–Feb. 9am–4pm ● *¥1,600; under-18s ¥1,200*

Inaugurated in 1969, this museum occupying a 7.4-acre garden designed by the sculptor Bukichi Inoue offers you a delightful way to appreciate the statuary of Rodin, Bourdelle, Giacometti, Calder, Zadkine or Henry Moore, when the weather is good. At the center of the park stands a building that traces the major trends in modern sculpture, and a Picasso pavilion.

Owakudani (20)

***Ōwakudani Natural Science Museum** daily 9am–4.30pm* ● *¥400*

Rightly named 'the valley of boiling hell' in Japanese, this ancient crater of Mount Kami-yama still produces volcanic phenomena: gas- and sulfur-emitting fissures, and springs hot enough to cook an egg. The little educational museum explains the fauna, flora and local climatic and geological features.

Ashi-no-ko (21)

Edged with thick forests, Ashi lake's glassy waters present a perfect reflection of Mount Fuji on a clear day. To enjoy its beauty fully, be sure to take a cruise on the ferry that links Togendai to Hakone-machi. You will glimpse the elegant red torii of the Hakone shrine and the gardens of the Imperial villa, now open to the public.

Not forgetting

■ **Hakone Barrier (22)** *During the Edo period, Hakone-machi, on the south bank of Ashi-no-ko lake, was a checkpoint on the Tokaido road. The town has treated itself to a fine exhibition center tracing the history of this great trading route and a scale model replica of the famous Hakone barrier.*

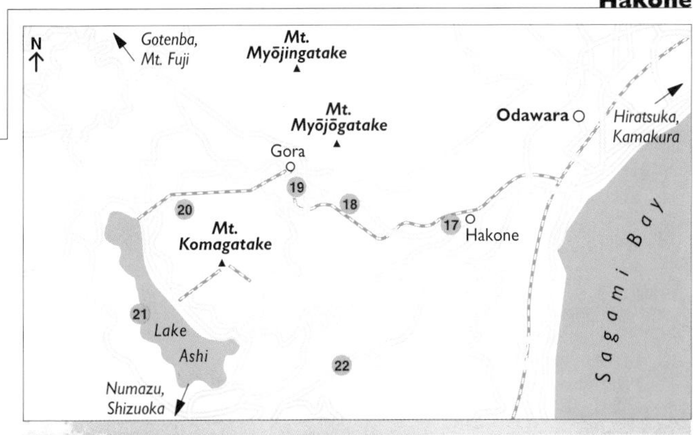
N
Gotenba,
Mt. Fuji
Mt.
Myōjingatake
Mt.
Myōjōgatake
Odawara
Hiratsuka,
Kamakura
Gora
19
20
18
17
Hakone
Mt.
Komagatake
Sagami Bay
21
Lake
Ashi
22
Numazu,
Shizuoka

18

17

21

19

Sales

As a general rule, sales take place in February, August and December.

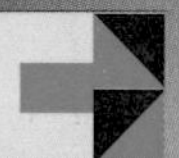

Where to shop

Men's sizes

Shirts

US/UK		Japan
15	=	38
15½	=	40
16½	=	42

Shoes

US	UK	Japan
8½ =	7 =	26½
9½ =	8 =	27
10½ =	9 =	28

Women's sizes

Clothes

US	UK	Japan
12 =	10 =	9
14 =	12 =	11
16 =	14 =	13

Shoes

US	UK	Japan
5½ =	4 =	23
6½ =	5 =	24
7½ =	6 =	26

Quarters

Akihabara *electronics and computer equipment* ***Aoyama*** *Japanese couturiers* ***Asakusa*** *arts and crafts* ***Ginza, Nihombosh*** *international luxury and department stores* ***Harajuku*** *'ready-to-wear' designers* ***Kanda*** *second-hand book stores* ***Kotto-dōri*** *antiques* ***Omote-Sandō*** *Tokyo's Champs-Elysées* ***Shibuya*** *everything for teenagers* ***Shinjuku*** *photography*

Opening times
Stores are generally open 10am–7pm or 8pm and closed one day a week, not necessarily Sunday.
24-hr convenience stores are located around train and subway stations; the best known are Lawson, AM/PM and Seven-Eleven.
Automatic vending machines selling anything from cigarettes to hot and cold drinks, etc. are to be found just about everywhere.

65 Stores

Mingei *(crafts)*

chochin	paper lantern
fude	brush
hasami	scissors
hocho	knife
kansashi	hair accessories
kasa	umbrella
katana	sword
keshohin	cosmetics
ko	incense
kushi	comb
men	mask
sensu	fan
shikki	lacquered articles
sudare	bamboo blind
tabi	socks
tako	kite
tenugi	hand towel
tojiki	ceramics
ukiyo-e	print
washi	paper

INDEX BY TYPE

A unique slogan could be applied to all *depato* (Japanese department stores): 'you'll find everything at…' From clothing to banking services, from home improvement to travel, and including food and furnishings, no form of service provision is forgotten. They have been built near to and inside train stations in order to attract customers.

Where to shop

Isetan (1)

3-14-1 Shinjuku, Shinjuku-ku ☎ (03) 3352-1111

Shinjuku **Department store** *daily 10am–7.30pm; closed some Weds. Tax refund, shipment overseas/Customer service I Club 7F Main Bldg ☎ (03) 3225-2514*

Totally representative of Shinjuku businesses, Isetan appeals to a youngish clientele. For all that, it doesn't forget to cater, with its Clover Town and Super Men's brands, for men and women having difficulty conforming to Japanese sizes. Of course, the floors devoted to food and household equipment are just as well stocked. The restaurants are all to be found in the Isetan Kaikan, one of the store's seven buildings, and the Isetan Museum is on the 7th floor of the Annexe Building.

Takashimaya Times Square (2)

5-24-2 Sendagaya, Shibuya-ku ☎ (03) 5361-1122

Shinjuku **Department store** *Mon., Tue., Thu.–Sun. 10am–7pm Tax refund 2-4-1 Nihombashi, Chūō-ku ☎ (03) 3211-4111*

Takashimaya indulged itself by setting up in the new Times Square. In this vast universe, Kinokuniya Bookstore, Tokyū Hands ➥140 and HMV are found side by side. If you only have limited time to do your shopping, in particular to buy gifts, or simply to gain an insight into what is done in Japan, this store is highly recommended, because it is extremely well laid out and you will not waste any time getting lost. Fashion occupies the first four floors, furnishings are on the 5th floor and kimonos on the 6th. As well as exhibition galleries and restaurants, the store also has an ornamental garden and a recreation area situated on the top-floor terrace. This is an ideal panoramic viewpoint from which to admire Tokyo – and Mount Fuji beyond – from above…

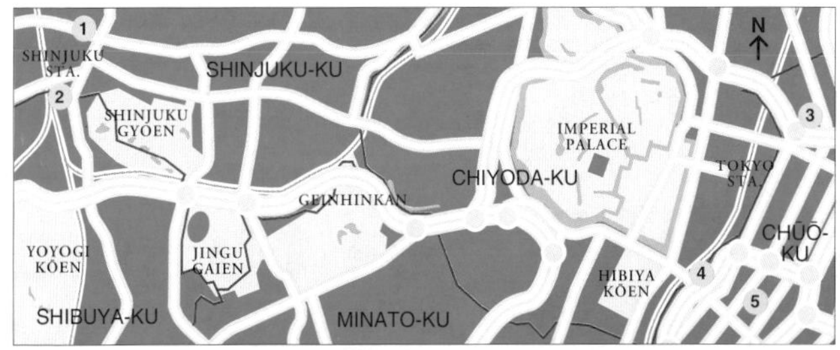

Mitsukoshi (3)

1-4-1 Nihombashi-Muromachi, Chūō-ku ☎ (03) 3241-3311

Mitsukoshimae ***Department store*** *daily 10am–7pm 4-6-16 Ginza, Chūō-ku ☎ (03) 3562-1111; 3-29-1 Shinjuku, Shinjuku-ku ☎ (03) 3354-1111*

At the beginning of the 20th century when it underwent renovation, Mitsukoshi, the oldest store in Japan, took its inspiration from Harrods of London in order to bring a touch of European elegance to its excellent service provision. Customers are greeted by an enormous statue of Kichijouten, the goddess of good fortune, which dominates the lobby. On entering here, you are really stepping into a world of Japanese-style art and décor. Do not miss the food hall in the basement, which has no cause to envy Harrods when it comes to abundance and variety.

Not forgetting

Seibu (4) 21-1 Udagawachō, Shibuya-ku ☎ (03) 3462-0111 *This handy department store is right next to Yūrakuchō train station. It is specially dedicated to women, whose favors it attracts by following the most recent fashions and ever increasing the number of shelves devoted to beauty products and little items of all sorts. A good way of finding out what's 'in' and getting a real overview of Japanese teenage fashion.*

Matsuya (5) 3-6-1 Ginza, Chūō-ku ☎ (03) 3567-1211 *This department store is focused on the concept of light. The articles found here have excellence of design in common, whether they are from Japan or elsewhere. Curios and well-styled furniture, as well as collectable items such as everyday craft objects, are ranged together. Issey Miyake Homme et Femme has its own department on the 3rd floor.*

In the area

- **Where to stay:** ➡ 24
- **Where to eat:** ➡ 44 ➡ 46
- **After dark:** ➡ 68
- **What to see:** ➡ 86 ➡ 88 ➡ 90

Where to shop

Itōya (6)
2-7-15 Ginza, Chūō-ku ☎ (03) 3561-8311

Ginza-Itchōme ***Washi*** *Mon.–Sat. 10am–7pm; Sun., public holidays 10.30am–7pm*

This shop specializes in stationery, office supplies and hobbies. An excellent and affordable selection of material for calligraphy and painting is on offer, ranging from the quill to the high-tech ballpoint pen. *Washi* and souvenirs are to be found in the annex.

Sukiya Camera (7)
5-5 Ginza, Chūō-ku ☎ (03) 3571-5555

Ginza ***Cameras*** *daily 10am–7.30pm; closed Dec.23–Jan.2*

In Japan hobbies are pursued with passion and amateurs are by our standards semi-professionals. Photography is a widespread Japanese hobby which is why medium- (6x6) and large-format (8x4) secondhand cameras are widely available. Even if you aren't a buyer, this shop, specializing in Leica, Kontax, Linhoff and Hasselblad models – with prices reaching astronomical heights, is a real museum.

Shellman (8)
5-5-12 Ginza, Chūō-ku ☎ (03) 5568-1234

Ginza ***Watches*** *Mon., Tue., Thu.–Sun. 11am–8pm*

Old watches by Patek Philippe or Roger Dubuis, complex repeater mechanisms, electronic everlasting calendars…lovers of punctuality owe a visit to this store that also sells its own-brand watches.

Takumi (9)
8-4-2 Ginza, Chūō-ku ☎ (03) 3571-2017

Ginza, Shimbashi ***Articles for the home*** *daily 11am–7pm; closed public holidays*

Traditional Japanese utensils are now finding a contemporary use. This concept, sprung up in the postwar years, is part of the Oak Art movement. For example, here you will find a Japanese-style cocktail-shaker, whether or not such an object forms part of daily life in Japan!

Not forgetting

■ **Kikuhide (10)** 5-14-2 Ginza, Chūō-ku ☎ (03) 3541-8390 *In this store the finest blades await you: fish-filleting knives, carving knives, table knives, wood chisels, etc…* ■ **Mikimoto (11)** 4-5-5 Ginza, Chūō-ku ☎ (03) 3535-4611 *Pearl specialist. This Ali Baba's cave has left its indelible mark on the 20th century.* ■ **Senbikiya (12)** 5-5-1 Ginza, Chūō-ku ☎ (03) 3571-0258 *For more than a century this shop has specialized in seasonal and exotic fruit from all over the world.* ■ **Kyūkyōdō (13)** 5-7-4 Ginza, Chūō-ku ☎ (03) 3571-4429 *There are rows of shelves on the ground floor displaying all types of card (wedding, death, graduation diplomas) and small papier-mâché articles; on the first floor there is a wide variety of Kyōto incense.* ■ **Kunoya (14)** 6-9-8 Ginza, Chūō-ku ☎ (03) 3571-2546*) Founded in 1837, Kunoya specializes in the kimono and all its accessories, such as the* furoshiki, *a piece of fabric with a variety of uses: sometimes a gift-wrap, sometimes a scarf.*

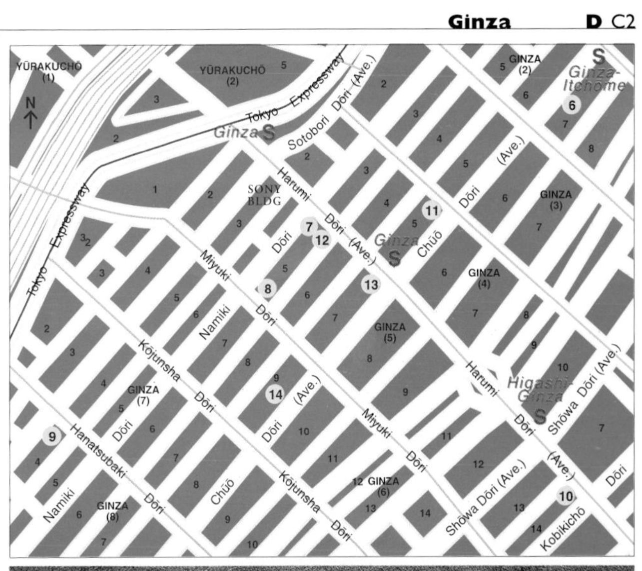
YŪRAKUCHŌ
(1)
YŪRAKUCHŌ
(2)
N
Tokyo Expressway
Ginza
Sotobori Dōri (Ave.)
GINZA
(2)
Ginza-Itchōme
SONY BLDG
Harumi Dōri (Ave.)
Chūō Dōri (Ave.)
GINZA
(3)
Miyuki Dōri
Namiki Dōri
GINZA
(4)
GINZA
(5)
Kōjunsha Dōri
Higashi-Ginza
Shōwa Dōri (Ave.)
GINZA
(7)
Hanatsubaki Dōri
Chūō Dōri (Ave.)
GINZA
(6)
GINZA
(8)
Kobikichō
Namiki
Dōri

13

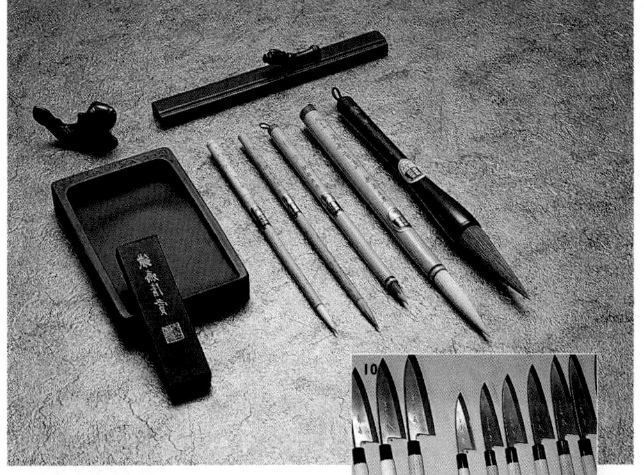

10

13

In the area
- Where to stay: ➥ 26
- Where to eat: ➥ 52 ➥ 56
- After dark: ➥ 68 ➥ 70 ➥ 72 ➥ 74 ➥ 76 ➥ 78
- What to see: ➥ 84

Where to shop

Axis (15)

Axis Bldg, 5-17-1 Roppongi, Minato-ku ☎ (03) 3587-2781

M *Roppongi* ***Articles for the home, toys*** *Mon.–Sat. 11am–7pm; Sun., public holidays 11am–6.30pm*

Prestigious shops and restaurants are arranged around the inner courtyard of the Axis Building. Over Revved sells high-tech office supplies; the Living Motif store is devoted to lifestyle and furnishings, all of Japanese design, and it also houses a bookstore specializing in architecture. As for the Ru Gareeji (The Garage) its specialty is automotive accessories, from care products to Mini Cooper replicas.

Naniwaya (16)

1-8-14 Azabu-Jūban, Minato-ku ☎ (03) 3583-3304

M *Roppongi* ***Patisserie*** *daily 9am–9pm*

Sitting in the tiny back room of this family store, you will taste the best Japanese-style waffles in the whole of Tokyo, bar none. Shaped like sea bream, they are stuffed with *an*, a sweetened purée of *azuki* (red beans). A century of culinary expertise must explain why it is so delicious.

Mamegen (17)

1-8-12 Azabu-Jūban, Minato-ku ☎ (03) 3583-0962

M *Roppongi* ***Patisserie*** *daily 10am–8pm* ***Isetan*** *3-14-1 Shinjuku, Shinjuku-ku*

You will really be amazed by the incredible diversity of home-cooked products: cakes based on red beans, fried or boiled in sugar, *sembei*, small Japanese rice crackers. All these delicacies are the daily delight of the Japanese, who invariably take some home for the weekend or present them as a gift when they make a courtesy call. Tasting them is a simple way of immersing yourself in the local ambience.

Kōgadō (18)

3-3-5 Azabu-Jūban, Minato-ku ☎ (03) 3452-0351

M *Roppongi* ***Articles for the home*** *Mon.–Sat. 10am–7pm*

In Japan, *kō* (incense) is a real way of life, linked to religion. The master of this establishment will be able to explain all the niceties and teach you about *byakudan* (sandalwood) and different varieties of *nerikou* (joss sticks). This is to prepare you for *kō-do*, a game that arrived from China over 1,000 years ago and has become the prerogative of sophisticated minds. A sort of snakes and ladders following strict rules of etiquette and ceremony, it consists of moving samurai forward by recognizing different incense essences with your eyes closed. Your move!

Not forgetting

■ **Hai Fung Hu (19)** 101 Takano Bldg, 2-13-19 Minami-Azabu, Minato-ku ☎ (03) 3455-3588 *A lover of Chinese teas, the proprietor imports, among others, the best* ryokucha *(green tea),* hanhakkou-cha *(semi-fermented tea) and black tea from every province of China and Taiwan. The shop also sells bowls and teapots in crimson china clay from Lishin or purple sand cherry, as well as Chinese antiques. You will be won over by the setting, but especially by the helpfulness of the owner who will get you to taste each tea before you find the one you like best.*

16

18

15

17

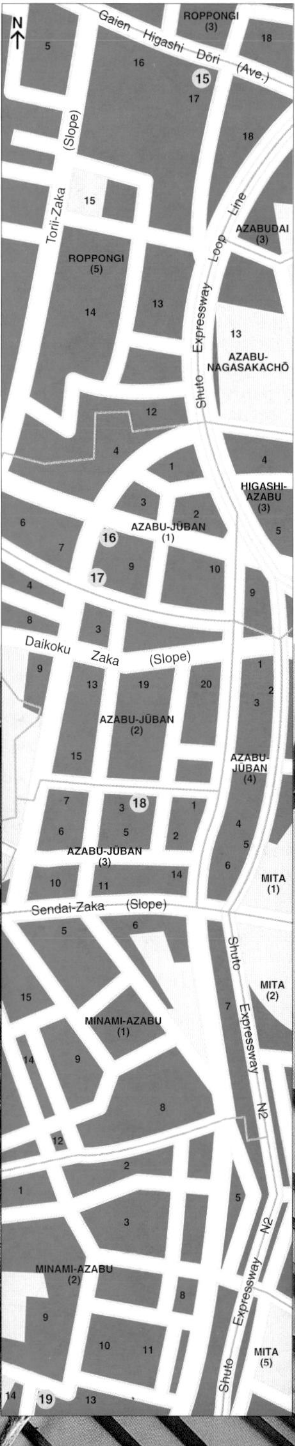

Gaien Higashi Dōri (Ave.)
ROPPONGI (3)
Torii-Zaka (Slope)
ROPPONGI (5)
Shuto Expressway Loop Line
AZABUDAI (3)
AZABU-NAGASAKACHŌ
HIGASHI-AZABU (3)
AZABU-JŪBAN (1)
Daikoku Zaka (Slope)
AZABU-JŪBAN (2)
AZABU-JŪBAN (4)
AZABU-JŪBAN (3)
MITA (1)
Sendai-Zaka (Slope)
Shuto Expressway N2
MITA (2)
MINAMI-AZABU (1)
MINAMI-AZABU (2)
MITA (5)

In the area
Where to stay: ➡ 26 ➡ 30
Where to eat: ➡ 54 ➡ 56
After dark: ➡ 70 ➡ 74 ➡ 76 ➡ 78
What to see: ➡ 102

Where to shop

His Tube (20)

6-4-9 Minami-Aoyama, Minato-ku ☎ (03) 3498-5178

M *Omote-Sandō* ***Men's fashions*** *Mon.–Sat. noon–8pm; Sun., public holidays 11am–8pm; closed 2nd and 3rd Tue. of the month*

The designer Hisao Saito has been imposing his style of men's fashion throughout Japan for about thirty years now. He built his reputation by creating a simple and elegant style, marrying traditional methods of manufacture with contemporary materials for his hand-knitted sweaters.

Billiken Shokai (21)

5-17-6 Minami-Aoyama, Minato-ku ☎ (03) 3400-2214

M *Omote-Sandō* ***Toys*** *Mon.–Sat. noon–8pm*

Japan has supplied the imaginative world of this planet with a good number of cartoon characters born of the manga tradition – kicking off with Godzilla and Goldorak – from which tin toys were derived. Whether mass produced or in limited editions, these androids, intergalactic villains, stellar heroes and androgynous creatures fight over every square inch of this diminutive shop, delighting fans of today... and yesterday.

Daily Catch (22)

Point Bldg B1F, 5-18-5 Minami-Aoyama, Minato-ku ☎ (03) 5469-0468

M *Omote-Sandō* ***Articles for the home, antiques, cigars*** *daily noon–7pm; closed 2nd Tue. of the month*

It's difficult to describe in a few words all the treasures that this Zen shop conceals. Let's just say that here you are invited to view a highly avant-garde lifestyle, a union of the contemporary and traditional. At the back of the shop is the Cuban cigar cabinet, very popular with aficionados such as Arnold Schwarzenegger.

Washi Kōbō (23)

1-8-10 Minami-Aoyama, Minato-ku ☎ (03) 3405-1841

M *Omote-Sandō* ***Articles for the home*** *Mon.–Sat. 10am–6pm; closed public holidays*

Washi is that famous handmade Japanese paper. It is made from the bark of a shrub, either *kozou* or *mitsumata*, which is cut into chips, soaked and boiled, then run under cold water in a square wooden frame. The resultant sheet of paper offers a pleasing variety of grain and texture. This shop has made the paper its specialty and carries *washi* in all forms, from gift-wrap to lampshades, not to mention kites and greeting cards.

Tōkyō (24)

2-25-13 Nishi-Azabu, Minato-ku ☎ (03) 3797-4494

M *Omote-Sandō* ***Articles for the home*** *Mon.–Sat. 10am–6pm; closed public holidays*

The 'Fishermen's Pavilion' presents everyday objects tinged with beauty. The owner, with a keen eye for discovery and an exquisite esthetic sense, has selected the work of designers from every region of Japan: pottery, porcelain and utensils of lacquered wood. He will explain his marvelous collection and the way the items are crafted by hand.

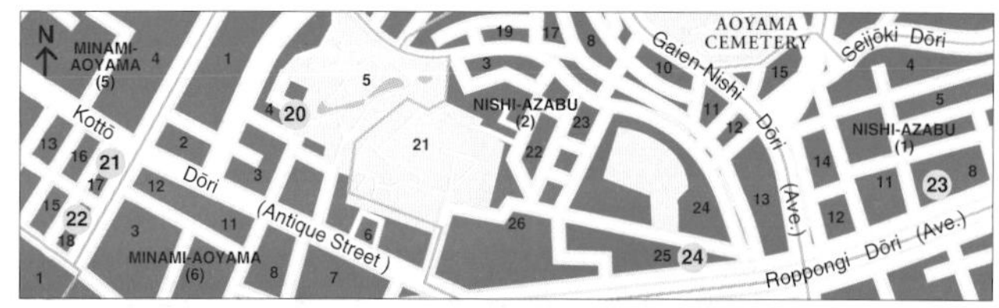

Away from Kottō-dōri, rightly dubbed the street of the antique dealers, numerous designer showrooms and boutiques can be found hidden away in the back streets. Each one specializes in one aspect of the Japanese way of life.

22

24

24

23

22

In the area

Where to stay: ➡ 30
Where to eat: ➡ 60
After dark: ➡ 68 ➡ 78
What to see: ➡ 96 ➡ 98 ➡ 102

Where to shop

Tōrindō (25)

3-6-18 Kita-Aoyama, Minato-ku ☎ (03) 3400-8703

M *Omote-sandō* ***Patisserie, confectionery*** *daily 10am–10pm; closed Dec. 30–Jan. 2*

It is here that you will without doubt find the best *gochika* in town. These Japanese specialties consist of seasonal fruits or edible roots, boiled in non-refined sugar, then dried for use in cakes or sweetmeats. The shop also doubles as a gallery: artists fresh from Tokyo's University of Arts and Crafts display and sell their works at – still – reasonable prices.

Natural House (26)

3-6-18 Kita-Aoyama, Minato-ku ☎ (03) 3498-2277

M *Omote-sandō* ***Organic food*** *daily 10am–10pm; closed Jan. 1*

This supermarket brings together organic produce, foodstuffs and beauty products. The business, whose popularity is continually growing, opened in the 1980s when the Japanese began to turn toward 'natural' food. An unmissable destination for health-food fans.

Comme des Garçons (27)

5-2-1 Minami-Aoyama, Minato-ku ☎ (03) 3406-3951

M *Omote-sandō* ***Men's and women's fashions*** *daily 11am–8pm; closed Dec. 25–Jan. 2* *Comme des Garçons 2, 5-12-3 Minami-Aoyama, Minato-ku ☎ (03) 3498-1400*

Designer Rei Kawakubo's collections have offered a fresh surprise every season since the 1980s. In this pilot shop, whose architecture admirably reflects its innovative spirit, his creations, neatly set out in a white maze, display a mix of minimalism and provocation. Fashion victims in search of 'Tokyo fashion' will no doubt find their Holy Grail here.

Kinokuniya (28)

3-11-18 Kita-Aoyama, Minato-ku ☎ (03) 3409-1231

M *Omote-sandō* ***Food*** *daily 9.30am–8pm; closed Jan. 1*

The supermarket for 'expats'. Do you miss blueberry muffins or mince pies? Head for Kinokuji-ya! All the best products from around the world are assembled here. From Australian beer to the wines of Alsace, not to mention baked beans and muesli, these are luxury solutions to avoid homesickness. For a general survey of Japan, there is an excellent selection of foods and specialties from every prefecture.

Not forgetting

Aoyama Book Center (29) Cosmos Bldg B1F, 5-53-67 Jingūmae, Shibuya-ku ☎ (03) 3479-0479 *The shelves of this bookstore, very probably the finest in all Tokyo, vaunt works in English, as well as art books. The owners also have a store in Roppongi which – and this is worth knowing – remains open until 5am. Here you will find the* Visual Book (MOOK) *magazine, always on the lookout for news relating to Tokyo and Japan, and Japanese arts and crafts, containing numerous unusual photos. One of the rare places to find tourist postcards!*

25

25

25

小鯛焼

Omote-Sandō,the Imperial way leading to the Meiji shrine ➡ 96, has been dubbed the Champs-Elysées of Tokyo. Not only due to its physical similarity but also due to the concentration of major international brands to be found here. However, this chic and highly international meeting point is also home to some major Japanese couturiers.

11

27

In the area

- Where to stay: ➡ 26
- Where to eat: ➡ 60
- After dark: ➡ 70 ➡ 76
- What to see: ➡ 96 ➡ 102

Where to shop

Indenya (30)
2-12-15 Minami-Aoyama, Minato-ku ☎ (03) 3479-3200

M *Gaiemmae* ***Leather goods*** *Mon.–Sun. 10am–6pm*

Inden, to which the store owes its name, is craft work imported from India. This tanned, cured and dyed doeskin, which is then pierced and decorated with lacquer beads, is made into purses or bags. Long ago, samurai also wore it to decorate their armor. This craft has been revived to make not just handbags and wallets but also small, typically Japanese objects. You certainly see very few of these accessories outside Japan, and here is a unique chance to give someone a rare souvenir.

On Sundays (31)
Watari-um Museum, 3-7-6 Jingūmae, Shibuya-ku ☎ (03) 3470-1424

M *Gaiemmae* ***Books, postcards*** *Tue., Thu.–Sat. 11am–8pm; Wed. 11am–9pm*

On Sundays has without a doubt the largest and finest selection of postcards in Tokyo. In the basement, the museum bookstore ➡ 96, the Art Bookstore, displays art books from all over the world, photograph albums, and works on architecture and art and crafts.

Nakamuraen (32)
2-26-38 Minami-Aoyama, Minato-ku ☎ (03) 3401-4188

M *Gaiemmae* ***Teas*** *Mon.–Fri. 9am-7pm; Sat. 10am–6pm; closed public holidays*

Lovers of *cha* (green tea) should get to know this place, as they will find an excellent selection from Shizuoka here. The trays lined up along the counter contain *sencha* (the most common), *genmaicha* (with cereals), *gyokuro* (the best quality) and *matcha* (the famous powdered tea used in the ceremony). Of course, bowls and teapots are also on offer.

Mujirushi Ryōhin (33)
Aoyama Bldg 1F, 2-12-28 Kita-Aoyama, Minato-ku ☎ (03) 3478-5800

M *Gaiemmae* ***Articles for the home, fashions*** *daily 11am–8pm*

Based on a simple concept – 'no name' (the meaning of *mujirushi*) equals low prices – this subsidiary of the Seiyu department stores has won over the entire planet. Customer loyalty was soon established as, over the years, people were delighted to discover an ever-expanding range of high-quality products. Starting in 1981 with a range of underwear and delicacies, it now supplies every type of equipment for the home and for leisure activities, from recycled paper to futons, refrigerators to 100% fruit juices.

Not forgetting

■ **Japan Tradition Craft Center (34)** Plaza 246 Bldg 2F, 3-1-1 Minami-Aoyama, Minato-ku ☎ (03) 3403-2460 *This craft center displays and sells at a very reasonable price almost everything representative of traditional Japan. Items made of bamboo, paper, wood, lacquer, stone, ceramics and metal; clothes and accessories of silk, linen, cotton and other fibers, all gathered together in a single locality. This place was born from a Ministry of Trade and Industry initiative that supports and protects Japan's heritage for educational reasons and to ensure continuity.*

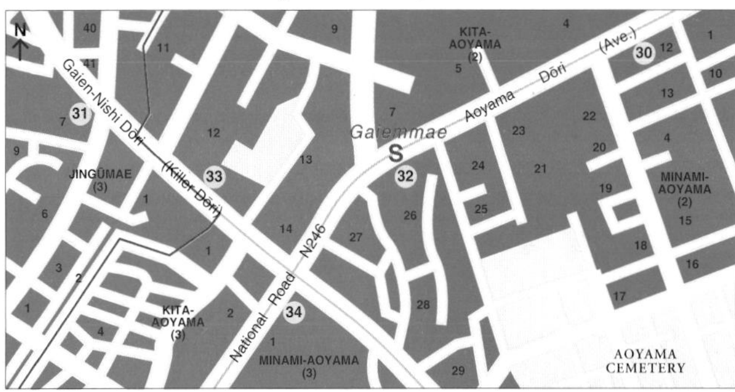

Situated between the National Stadium and the Aoyama cemetery this district, rather more residential than commercial, harbors a selection of diverse and original shops as well as very good European restaurants.

33

31

30

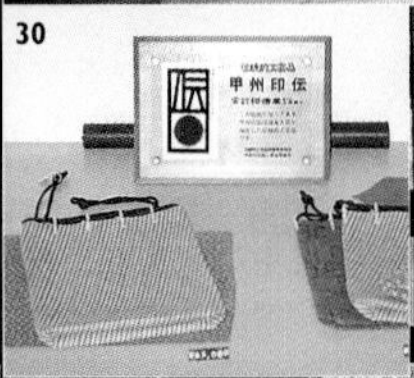

32

30

In the area

Where to stay: ➥ 28 ➥ 30
Where to eat: ➥ 58 ➥ 60
After dark: ➥ 68 ➥ 78
What to see: ➥ 96 ➥ 98

Where to shop

United Arrows (35)
3-28-1 Jingūmae, Shibuya-ku ☎ (03) 3479-8180

M *Meiji-jingūmae* ***Men's fashions*** *Mon.–Fri. noon–8pm; Sat., Sun., public holidays 11am–8pm* *1-20-11 Jinnan, Shibuya-ku ☎ (03) 3496-2703*

Italian suits that hang perfectly, the smartest of shirts from the Neapolitan Luigi Borelli, shoes from John Lobb and fine cashmere… this male boutique contains the last word in fashion in Japan, just for you. But the world of United Arrows doesn't stop there. A whole string of boutiques is to be found in the district, each as attractive as the next, but each specializing in a particular type of clothing and look.

Shiseidō Parlor Garden C (36)
Harajuku Piazza Bldg 1F, 4-26-18 Jingūmae, Shibuya-ku ☎ (03) 5474-1534

M *Meiji-jingūmae* ***Beauty products*** *daily 11am–8pm; closed 2nd Tue. of the month*

Every Shiseido product is on display here, where the key concepts are abundance and variety. Consultants are at your disposal to reply to all questions, despite their hesitant English, and to guide your choice. This salon sells nothing but gives you the addresses relevant to your choice.

Kiddy Land (37)
6-1-9 Jingūmae, Shibuya-ku ☎ (03) 3409-3431

M *Meiji-jingūmae* ***Games, toys*** *daily 10am–8pm; closed 3rd Tue. of the month*

Created in the 1960s, this establishment assiduously follows trends in toys with the aim of satisfying the wildest dreams of both young and old. Models and video games are piled up together and electric trains are mixed in with soft toys, all in a most disconcerting muddle. All this is hidden behind immense stands on which stars of the big screen, such as Godzilla, Furby and Pikachu, are proudly displayed.

Not forgetting

■ **Hiromichi (38)** Kyōcera Bldg 1F, 6-27-8 Jingūmae, Shibuya-ku ☎ (03) 5778-3024 *Who's the king of 'baby doll' fashion? It's Hiromichi Nakano! This is a delightful and very personal collection, in the same category as a Parisian* maison de couture, *through which Hiromichi shows his homage to the beauty of women.* ■ **Obrero (39)** 6-16-23 Jungūmae, Shibuya-ku ☎ (03) 3406-6401 *Take an ethnic base revised and given a new European treatment, add a Japanese touch and this will give you Tokyo fashion. Although the chemistry is very youthful, a rare sensibility will satisfy the soul in search of beauty and quality.* ■ **Mono Comme Ça (40)** 1-14-27 Jingūmae, Shibuya-ku ☎ (03) 3423-8051 *A sort of Muji but not at all Zen. Here, all the articles, gadgets and clothes are as trendy as possible, such as the telephone clips in different materials and colors fought over by Tokyo teenagers.* ■ **Hachiku (41)** 6-29-4 Jingūmae, Shibuya-ku ☎ (03) 3400-1758 *Osaka-style sushi to be eaten on the spot or to go. Osaka sushi is lightly sweetened and contains omelet or conger eel,* shiitake *mushrooms or lobster flakes. An ideal place for a short break from the shopping.* ■ **Uni Clo (42)** 6-10-8 Jingūmae, Shibuya-ku ☎ (03) 5468-7313 *The Uni Clo chain presents American-style clothes, made in Japan, at very low prices. This is the heart of 'cheap chic' Tokyo.*

If Shibuya district belongs to the over-20s, then Harajuku is the district for teenagers. It's the realm of those gizmos that are indispensable for tribal recognition. The pedestrianized alleyway of Kyū Shibuya-gawa (a former watercourse) and the surrounding area teems with the workrooms of young designers inventing or reinterpreting tomorrow's fashions.

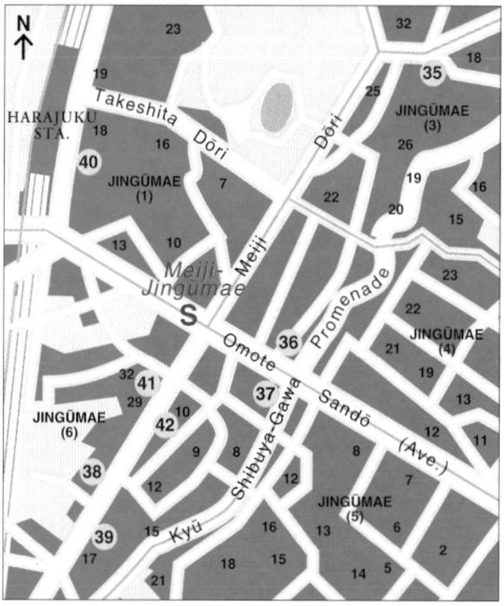

41

41

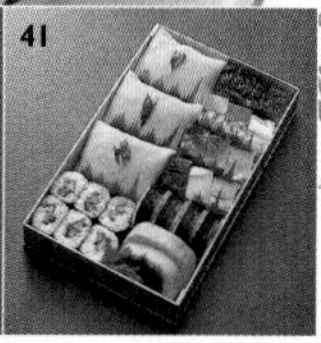

41

38

In the area
Where to stay: ➥ 28
Where to eat: ➥ 58
After dark: ➥ 68 ➥ 74
What to see: ➥ 92 ➥ 102

Where to shop

Beams Japan (43)
3-32-6 Shinjuku, Shinjuku-ku ☎ (03) 5368-7300

M *Shinjuku* ***Articles for the home; men's and women's fashions*** *daily 11am–8pm; closed 3rd Wed. of the month* *3-25 Jingūmae, Shibuya-ku*

This brand name started off with a small boutique in the fashion quarter of Harajuku ➥ 138. Now this flagship store is at the forefront of Japanese fashion. Original suits, bags or shoes specially commissioned from American or European designers, shirts or sweaters, town, sports or formal wear...you will only be offered the very best of its kind. For several years now, the store has been diversifying into articles for the home and has started its own recording company!

Victoria (44)
4-1-11 Shinjuku, Shinjuku-ku ☎ (03) 3354-8811

M *Shinjuku* ***Sporting equipment and sportswear*** *Mon.–Sat. 11am–8pm; Sun., public holidays 10.30am–7.30pm* *3-4 Kanda-Ogawamachi, Chiyoda-ku ☎ (03) 3295-2955 ; 3-10 Udagawachō, Shibuya-ku ☎ (03) 3463-4211*

Victoria is not just one of the rare discount sports stores, it is also the cheapest. If you visit the one in Kanda-Ogawamachi, Tokyo's Latin quarter, you can compare prices, as the sector abounds in establishments of this type. Sportsmen and women from all disciplines are in their element here: ski, snowboarding and other such equipment, articles for outdoor activities, cycling, tennis... An added bonus: each new season brings with it terrific cut-price sales.

Tōkyū Hands (45)
Takashimaya Times Square, 5-24 Sendagaya, Shibuya-ku ☎ (03) 5361-3111

M *Shinjuku* *daily 10am–8pm; closed 2nd and 3rd Mon. of the month* *18 Udagawa-chō, Shibuya-ku ☎ (03) 5489-5111*

Tōkyū Hands is the largest home improvement and leisure store in Tokyo. It carries everything you will need on a daily basis: home-improvement and decorating materials, leisure and garden furniture, tools, kitchen utensils, Japanese paper and office supplies, not forgetting tents and toys. Every floor of the store, brighter and better organized than that of Shibuya, has its own theme. A brochure in English is available at the entrance.

Not forgetting

■ **Yodobashi Camera (46)** 1-11-1 Nishi-Shinjuku, Shinjuku-ku ☎ (03) 3346-1010 *All the major Japanese brands are on display here, from Nikon to Pentax, not forgetting Canon and Minolta, and all at very attractive prices. Products range from cameras, of course, to computer equipment, and from personal stereos to video games. Express photo-developing service.*

■ **Jōshū-ya (47)** 2-10-1 Yoyogi, Shibuya-ku ☎ (03) 5371-4138 *For all lovers of sea or river fishing, this store is a real Aladdin's cave. Lead weights, flies, nets... you'll find a good old reed or bamboo fishing rod, or one of carbon fiber, born of Japanese technology. You'll not fail to land something here!*

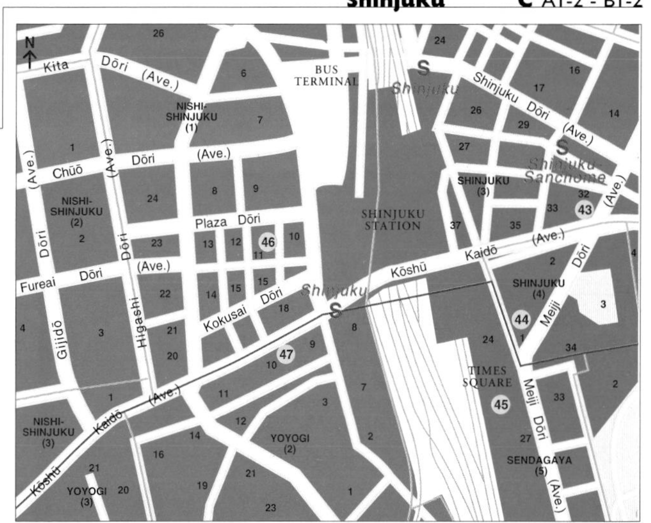
N
Kita Dōri (Ave.)
BUS TERMINAL
Shinjuku
Shinjuku Dōri (Ave.)
NISHI-SHINJUKU (1)
Chūō Dōri (Ave.)
Shinjuku-Sanchōme
NISHI-SHINJUKU (2)
SHINJUKU (3)
Plaza Dōri
SHINJUKU STATION
Fureai Dōri (Ave.)
Kōshū Kaidō (Ave.)
Kokusai Dōri
Shinjuku
SHINJUKU (4)
Meiji Dōri
Gijidō Dōri
Higashi Dōri
TIMES SQUARE
NISHI-SHINJUKU (3)
YOYOGI (2)
Meiji Dōri (Ave.)
SENDAGAYA (5)
YOYOGI (3)
Kōshū Kaidō (Ave.)

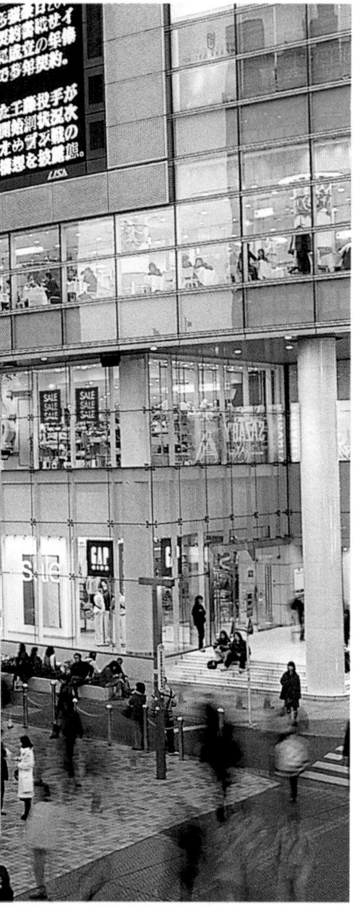

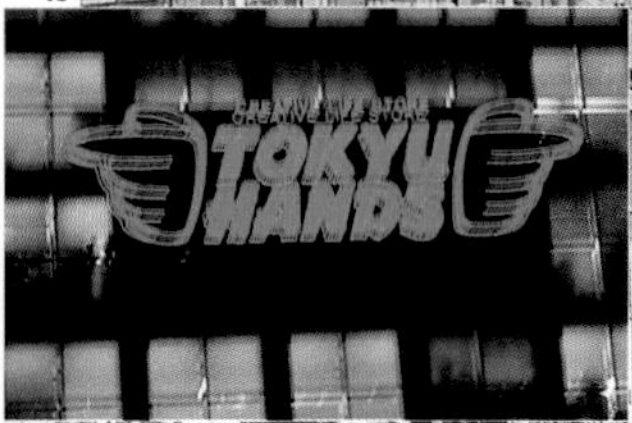

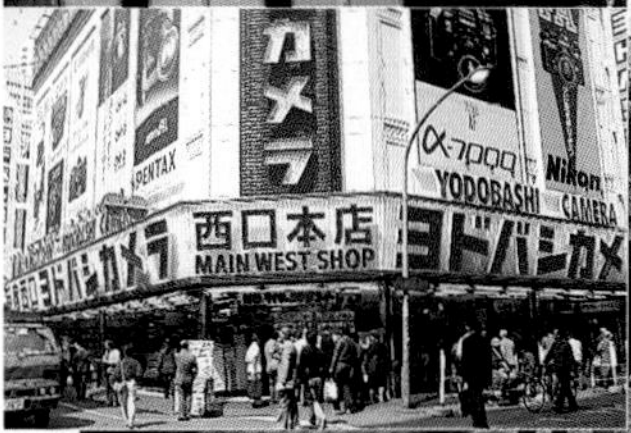

44

45

46

There's no shortage of flea markets in Tokyo. Located for the most part around temples or shrines, these colorful centers for bric-a-brac display wares from both private and trade sources. Among the kimonos, postcards and pieces of pottery, you could perhaps uncover a real antique, such as a *tansu*, for a ridiculous price.

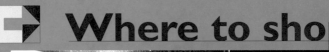

50

Hanazono-jinja Flea Market (48)
5-17 Shinjuku, Shinjuku-ku

M *Shinjuku, Shinjuku-Sanchōme* **Antiques, flea market** *3rd Sun. of the month: sunrise to sunset*

Dealers in secondhand goods and antiques arrive in the courtyard of Hanazono temple not only from Tokyo but also from the prefectures of Kantō and Kyōto to sell rare objects that they have picked up all over Japan. The place is dotted with leafy trees, and it's worth coming for a wander around, if only to immerse yourself in the cool atmosphere. A stroll here has long been a Sunday ritual for the inhabitants of Tokyo.

Tōgō-jinja (49)
1-5-3 Jingūmae, Shibuya-ku

M *Meiji-Jingūmae, Harajuku* **Antiques, flea market** *1st, 4th and 5th Sun. of the month: sunrise to sunset*

Small stalls are spread out all around the courtyard of this temple ➡ 96 devoted to the Japanese victory in the Russo-Japanese war, and even in the avenues leading to Meiji-dōri. You may perhaps get the chance to unearth an old chest of drawers, or a simple or ceremonial kimono among the goods unpacked and roughly displayed on tables, in the trunks of cars or even on the ground. A large selection of articles will be on view for you to choose from, including ceramics from the Meiji or Taishou periods, lacquered utensils, toys or old books. Times are variable depending on the time of year, and the market doesn't take place on rainy days.

Hanae Mori Antique Market (50)

Hanae Mori Bldg, 3-6 Kita-Aoyama, Minato-ku ☎ (03) 3406-1021

Omote-Sandō **Antiques** *daily 11am–7pm*

If you're looking for an antique-dealer district in the heart of Tokyo, try here. You're bound to find what you want in one of the 20 shops located in the basement gallery. Every store specializes in one single type of antique – since the Japanese are truly well-informed amateurs – and offers something to satisfy your craving for the unusual: Japanese glazed earthenware and pottery, traditional indigo fabrics, dolls, and even those famous *katana* (swords)... Beware: you will need authorization to export a sword.

Ameya Yokochō (51)

6-10-7 Ueno, Taitō-ku

Ueno ***Men's and women's fashions, accessories*** *daily 9am–7pm*

You'll need to elbow your way into this alleyway, located under the JR metro line. The arcades are home to dealers selling clothes, shoes and accessories at low prices – come at the end of the day when goods are being sold off – and small booths in the road offer exotic produce and made-up dishes based on fish.

Not forgetting

Nogi-jinja (52) 8-11 Akasaka, minato-ku *Every 3rd Sun. of the month, Nogi temple becomes a low-price market.*

In the area
Where to stay: ➥ 34
Where to eat: ➥ 42 ➥ 44
After dark: ➥ 69
What to see: ➥ 84 ➥ 86 ➥ 102 ➥ 110

Where to shop

T. Zone (53)
4-3 Soto-Kanda, Chiyoda-ku ☎ (03) 3526-7711

M *Akihabara, Suehirochō* ***Computers*** *Mon.–Sat.; 10.30am–8pm; Sun., public holidays 10am–7.30pm* *Tax refund*

Computers, hard disks, screens, programs, peripherals and all types of gadgets! T. Zone lives up to its reputation for quality and offers you here the best selection of products from the Apple range.

Yamagiwa (54)
4-1-1 Soto-Kanda, Chiyoda-ku ☎ (03) 3253-2111

M *Akihabara, Suehirochō* ***Articles for the home, electronics*** *Mon.–Fri. 10.30am–8pm; Sat., Sun. 10am–8pm*

This general department store for electronic and electrical goods puts the emphasis on original lighting. From paper lanterns by the famous sculptor Isamu Noguchi to bamboo standard lamps and anything Japanese, you are likely to find it here.

Laox Duty Free (55)
1-15-3 Soto-Kanda, Chiyoda-ku ☎ (03) 3255-5301

M *Akihabara* ***Computer equipment, electronics, cameras*** *daily 10am–7.30pm* ***Laox Watch & Camera*** *1-15-5 Soto-Kanda ☎ (03) 5297-7194;* ***Laox Main Store*** *1-2-9 Soto-Kanda ☎ (03) 3255-9041 Tax refund, shipping*

You get the impression that in these enormous stores Japan has given access to state-of-the-art electronics to every nation on earth. This mecca is certainly the most practical place to go for those who want to make their purchases duty free and…in English. Computers, hi-fi equipment, digital camcorders and cameras: here you will find a great selection of the very best.

New Shimazu (56)
1-28 Kanda-Sudachō, Chiyoda-ku ☎ (03) 3251-3646

M *Kanda* ***Designer seconds*** *Mon.–Sat. 10.30am–7.30pm; closed public holidays*

All international fashion at very reasonable prices can be found in this little boutique. Tokyo is an expensive city outside the sales period, and when articles labeled Arnys, Prada or Agnona are made affordable, even difficult customers are happy to wait in line at the door. The trend-setters of Tokyo secretly hand this address around, knowing they will find what they want here.

Radio Kaikan (57)
1-15-16 Soto-Kanda, Chiyoda-ku

M *Akihabara* ***Electronics*** *daily 10am–8pm*

A real maze of little aisles lines the ground floor of this building, where small booths follow one after another. Some people may be discouraged by the sheer number of customers, but this is an Ali Baba's cave for anyone who wants to put together his own stereo system. From grandfather's transistor to the chip, and not forgetting the soldering iron and ball bearing, you only have to ask and it will be found for you!

Tokyo residents call this district 'Electric Town' and quite rightly so. Stores, supermarkets and booths follow in quick succession, lit up by a thousand neon lights, over an area of about three-quarters of a square mile. Here a plethora of electrical, electronic and computer products, including the very latest inventions to reach the markets of the West, are stacked up, spread out and displayed – and all at unbeatable prices. The only disadvantage is that voltage and frequency are compatible with the US but not Europe. Take the time to make inquiries in advance, as only a few establishments specialize in multisystems.

56

56

55

In the area

Where to stay: ➡ 18
Where to eat: ➡ 64
After dark: ➡ 70 ➡ 72
What to see: ➡ 102 ➡ 104

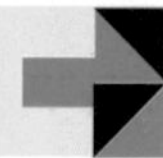

Where to shop

Hanato (58)

2-25-6 Asakusa, Taitō-ku ☎ (03) 3841-6411

M *Asakusa* ***Traditional crafts, lanterns*** *Wed.–Mon. 10am–8.30pm*

Hundreds of lanterns of all sizes hang from the walls and ceiling of this store, waiting for their new owners. The painted-paper lantern, an indispensable accessory for use in festivals or as a sign outside the door, has now found its place in interior design. You can commission one from the craftsman himself, but don't be in too much of a hurry because you sometimes have to wait over three months!

Sukeroku (59)

Nakamise-dori, 2-3-1 Asakusa, Taitō-ku ☎ (03) 3844-0577

M *Asakusa* ***Traditional crafts, toys*** *daily 10am–6pm*

Terracotta statuettes similar to figures placed in the Christmas crib, together with Lilliputian dolls, form well-behaved rows in the display cabinets, or are piled in more anarchic fashion on the counters of this tiny store. Here you will find the revival of an Edo custom – that of hand-modeling figurines of animals and people which enable us to imagine life as it was in Japan in days gone by. There is such a myriad of little people that only by looking carefully will you be able to appreciate the delicacy of the workmanship and the fine detail.

Hyakusuke (60)

2-2-14 Asakusa, Taitō-ku ☎ (03) 3841-7058

M *Asakusa* ***Beauty products*** *Wed.–Mon. 11am–5pm*

This discreet location holds the key to all the beauty secrets of the Japanese woman. The manufacture of totally natural products is carried on here. Get hold of essence of camellia to untangle long hair, of rice for delicate skins or even of loofa, the vegetable sponge. You will also find everything necessary to make yourself up Japanese style.

Not forgetting

■ **Fujiya (61)** 2-2-15 Asakusa, Taitō-ku ☎ (03) 3841-2283 *The* tenugui, *the traditional Japanese towel, was formerly used as a head covering during religious ceremonies. Its use has now become commonplace and Keiji Kawakami, the master-artist of the establishment, will offer you contemporary versions with motifs inspired by kabuki theater, manga characters or simply the seasons* ■ **Yonoya (62)** 1-37-10 Asakusa, Taitō-ku ☎ (03) 3844-1755 *Boxwood combs and hairstyling accessories have been manufactured here since the Edo period, using the same technique. The craftsman cuts, pierces and polishes the pieces of wood under the curious gaze of the visitor.* ■ **The Traditional Craft Museum (63)** 2-22-12 Asakusa, Taitō-ku ☎ (03) 3847-2587 *In the trading gallery of Hisago-dori, this museum showing the handicrafts of Asakusa will give you a fine overview of craft techniques and products, which are also for sale.* ■ **Hōsendo Kyūami (64)** 1-19-6 Askusa, Taitō-ku ☎ (03) 3845-8911 *The fans made by this distinguished establishment consist of a fine layer of paper stretched over a delicately carved bamboo frame. An indispensable accessory for those wearing a kimono or for the odori dancer; hand-painted motifs evoke the seasons, a poem or even a symbolic character.* ■ **Kurodaya (65)** 1-2-11 Asakusa, Taitō-ku ☎ (03) 3844-7511 Washi *notepaper, papier-mâché boxes decorated with Edo-period motifs and a whole host of tiny, sweet, very Japanese objects. You will also find Edo-style antique kites, ready to fly away.*

Asakusa is truly the *shitamachi* or craftsmen's quarter of Edo. Go off in search of an astonishing world, push open the doors of the workshops and uncover riches.

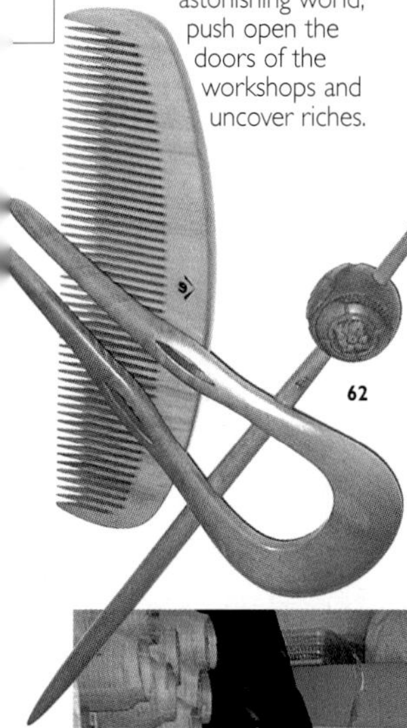

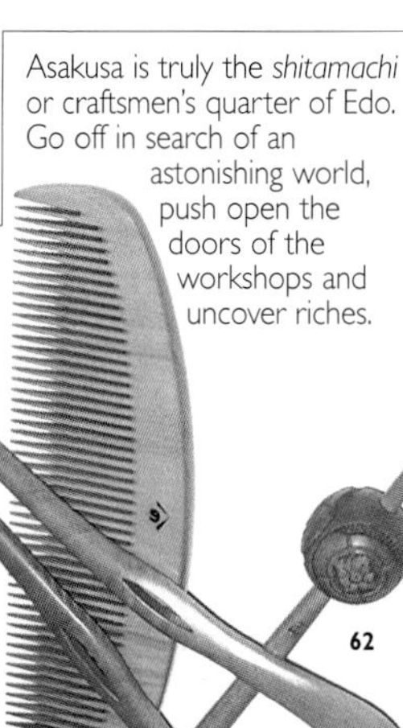

62

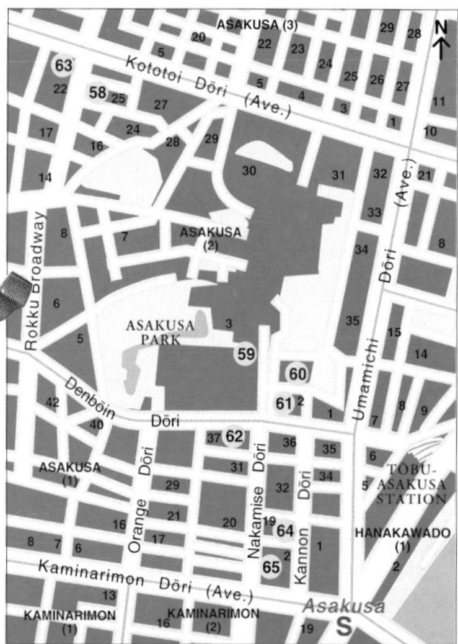

64

64

58

Maps

The TIC ➥ 12 offers a free general map of Tokyo, giving a good overview of the city's major sites: Kodansha publishes the excellent *Tokyo City Atlas: a bilingual guide*, available in large bookstores; the TRTA distributes a brochure with a map in English, *Subways in Tokyo*, which explains how to buy a ticket or SF card ➥ 10.

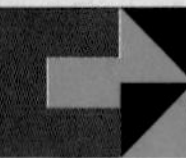

Finding your wa

Short glossary

ken	prefecture
to	metropolis
shi	city
machi	town
ku	administrative quarter
chō	quarter
chōme	minor quarter
dōri	street, avenue
mon	gate
biru	building
eki	station
bashi	bridge
gawa	river
teien	garden
kōen	park
yama	mount
hantō	peninsula
ko	lake
kita	north
minami	south
higashi	east
nishi	west
hidari	left
migi	right

Ku ***(administrative districts)***

Tōkyō has 23 *ku* in total

Adachi-ku
Arakawa-ku
Bunkyō-ku
Chiyoda-ku
Chūō-ku
Edogawa-ku
Itabashi-ku
Katsushika-ku
Kita-ku
Kōtō-ku
Meguro-ku
Minato-ku
Nakano-ku
Nerima-ku
Ōta-ku
Setagawa-ku
Shibuya-ku
Shinagawa-ku
Shinjuku-ku
Suginami-ku
Sumida-ku
Taitō-ku
Toshima-ku

Yamanote and shitamachi

In the Edo period, *yamanote* referred to the 'high city' where the *daimyō* (feudal barons), military aristocrats and other members of Edo's elite lived up on the heights. As for the *shitamachi*, the 'low city', situated on the marshland, it was here that the workers, merchants and artisans lived and carried out their business, as they still do today.

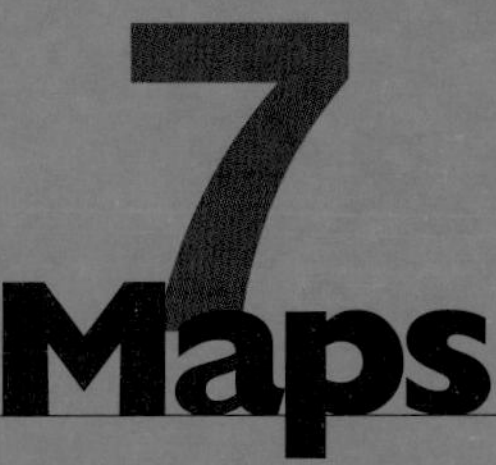

The *chō* and *chōme* of Chiyoda-ku and Shinjuku-ku listed below are shown on the maps by boxed numerals.

Chiyoda-ku A-B-C-D		**Shinjuku-ku** A-C	
Kanda-Neribeichō	1	Higashi-Enokichō	1
Kanda-Aioichō	2	Nakazatochō	2
Kanda-Hanaokachō	3	Akagimotomachi	3
Kanda-Matsunagachō	4	Shimomiyabichō	4
Kanda-Hirakawachō	5	Agebachō	5
Kanda-Sakumagashi	6	Kaguragashi	6
Kanda-Mitoshirochō	7	Ichigaya-Yamabushichō	7
Kanda-Tomiyamachō	8	Kita-Yamabushichō	8
Kanda-Kon'yachō	9	Minami-Yamabushichō	9
K.-Kita-Norimonochō	10	Nijukkimachi	10
Kanda-Konyachō	11	Saikumachi	11
K.-Nishi-Fukudachō	12	Ichigaya-Takajōmachi	12
Kanda-Mikurachō	13	Ichigaya-Chōenjimachi	13

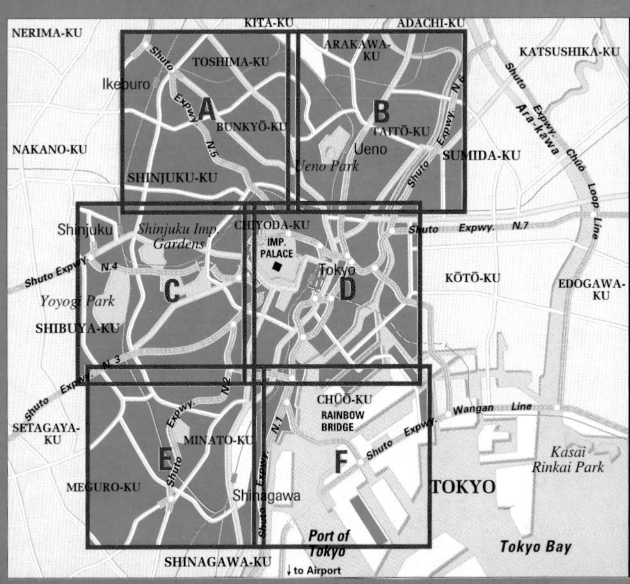

Subway map

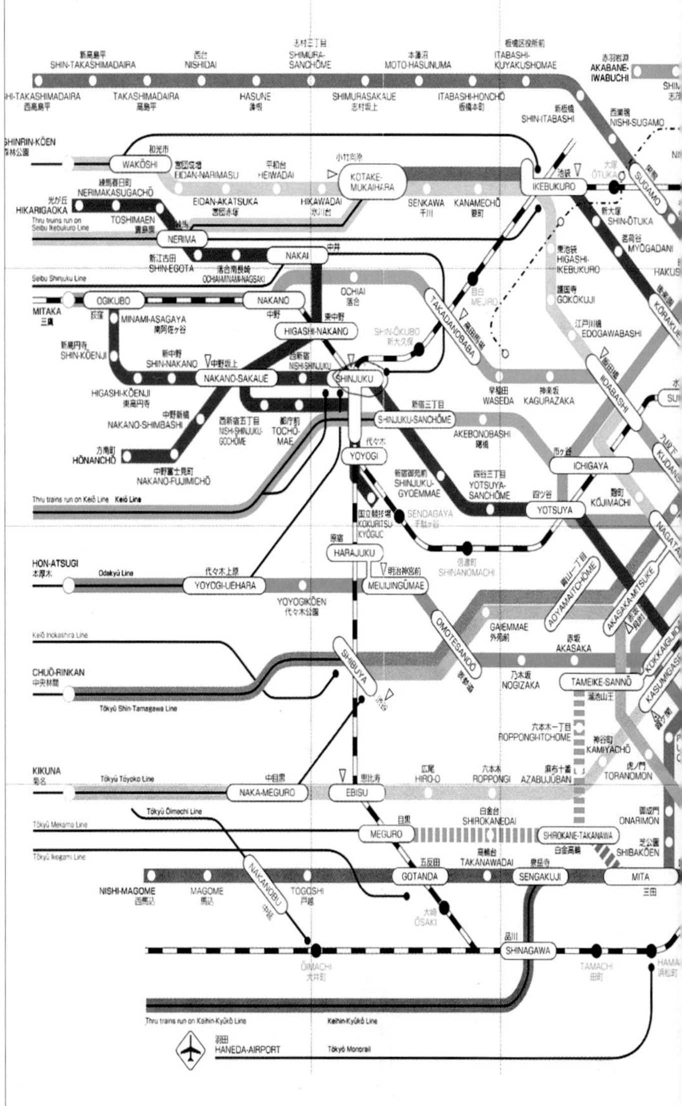

Key and colors of the lines

Ginza Line		Yūrakuchō Line	
Marunouchi Line		Yūrakuchō Line (new line)	
Hibiya Line		Hanzōmon Line	
Tōzai Line		Namboku Line	
Chiyoda Line			

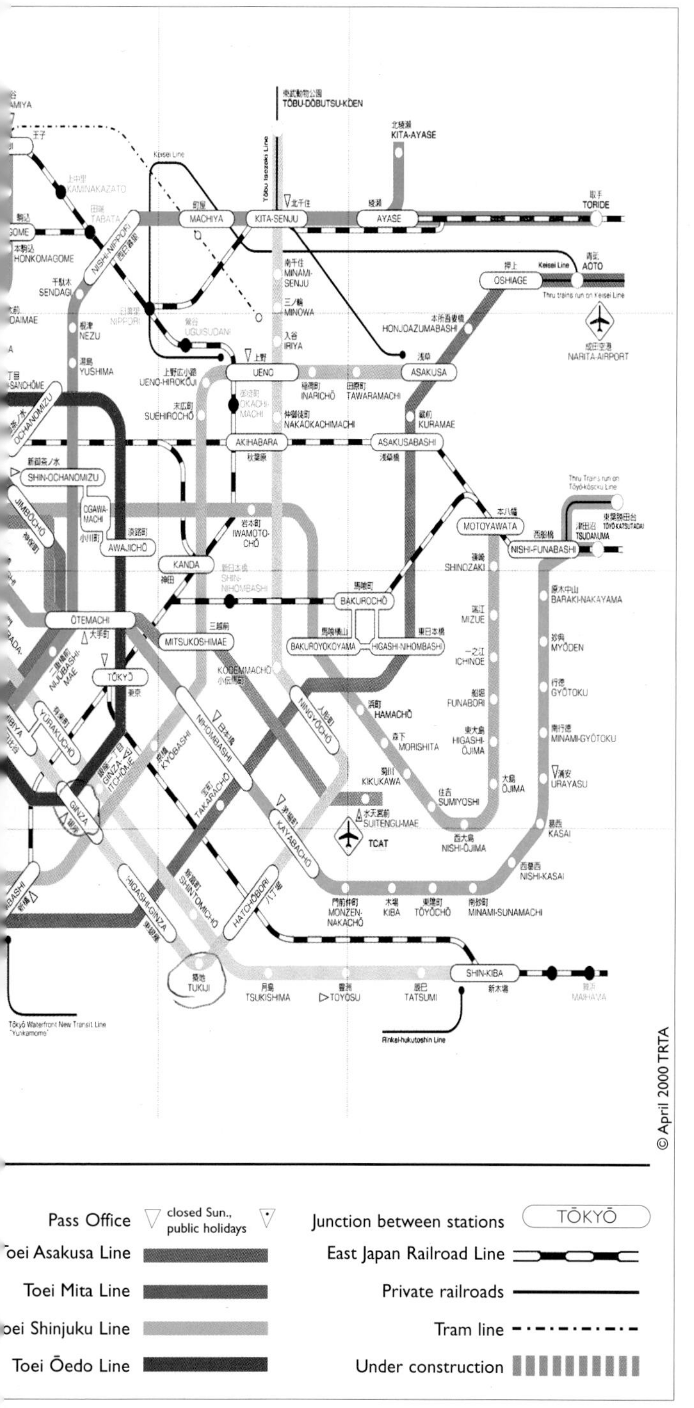

TŌBU-DŌBUTSU-KŌEN
KITA-AYASE
Keisei Line
Tōbu Isezaki Line
KAMINAKAZATO
TABATA
MACHIYA
KITA-SENJU
AYASE
TORIDE
KOMAGOME
HONKOMAGOME
NISHI-NIPPORI
SENDAGI
MINAMI-SENJU
OSHIAGE
Keisei Line
AOTO
MINOWA
NIPPORI
NEZU
UGUISUDANI
HONJOAZUMABASHI
IRIYA
NARITA AIRPORT
YUSHIMA
UENO-HIROKŌJI
UENO
ASAKUSA
INARICHŌ
TAWARAMACHI
SUEHIROCHŌ
OKACHI-MACHI
NAKAOKACHIMACHI
KURAMAE
OCHANOMIZU
AKIHABARA
ASAKUSABASHI
SHIN-OCHANOMIZU
JIMBŌCHŌ
OGAWA-MACHI
AWAJICHŌ
IWAMOTO-CHŌ
MOTOYAWATA
NISHI-FUNABASHI
TSUDANUMA
TŌYŌ KATSUTADAI
KANDA
SHIN-NIHOMBASHI
SHINOZAKI
BAKUROCHŌ
BARAKI-NAKAYAMA
ŌTEMACHI
MITSUKOSHIMAE
BAKUROYOKOYAMA
HIGASHI-NIHOMBASHI
MIZUE
MYŌDEN
ICHINOE
NIJUBASHI-MAE
TŌKYŌ
KODEMMACHŌ
GYŌTOKU
NINGYŌCHŌ
FUNABORI
HAMACHŌ
YURAKUCHŌ
KYŌBASHI
NIHOMBASHI
MORISHITA
HIGASHI-ŌJIMA
MINAMI-GYŌTOKU
GINZA-ITCHŌME
KIKUKAWA
ŌJIMA
URAYASU
TAKARACHŌ
GINZA
SUMIYOSHI
SUITENGU-MAE
KAYABACHŌ
TCAT
KASAI
NISHI-ŌJIMA
NISHI-KASAI
SHINTOMICHŌ
HIGASHI-GINZA
HATCHŌBORI
MONZEN-NAKACHŌ
KIBA
TŌYŌCHŌ
MINAMI-SUNAMACHI
SHIN-KIBA
TSUKIJI
TSUKISHIMA
TOYOSU
TATSUMI
MAIHAMA
Tōkyō Waterfront New Transit Line "Yurikamome"
Rinkai-fukutoshin Line
© April 2000 TRTA
Pass Office
closed Sun., public holidays
Junction between stations
TŌKYŌ
Toei Asakusa Line
East Japan Railroad Line
Toei Mita Line
Private railroads
Toei Shinjuku Line
Tram line
Toei Ōedo Line
Under construction

A
1
2
SHIMO-ITABASHI
ITABASHI
Kumanochō
ITABASHI-KU
Ikebukuro-Honchō
Takinogawa
Nakamaruchō
KITA-IKEBUKURO
Minami-chō
Kawagoe Kaidō
Shuto Expressway N. 5
Saikyō Line
Kami-Ikebukuro
Nishi-Sugan
Taka-matsu
Yamate Dōri
Gekijō Dōri
TOSHIMA CENTRAL HOSP.
Meiji Dōri
Ikebukuro
Kita-Ōtsu
Kasuga Dōri
Higashi-Ikebukuro
ŌTSU
Rikkyō Dōri
RIKKYŌ UNIV.
IKEBUKURO
SUNSHINE CITY
TOSHIMA P.O.
Green Ōdōri
TOSHIMA-KU
(Nat'l Ro
B
Nishi-Ikebukuro
HIGASHI-IKEBUKURO
Minami-Ikebukuro
Zōshigaya Cemetery
Ōtsu
GOKOKU-
Mejiro
MEJIRO
Mejiro Dōri
Zōshigaya
GAKUSHŪIN UNIV.
GOKOKUJI
Shimo-Ochiai
Mejiro-dai
C
Takada
Shin-Mejiro Dōri
ST. MARY'S CATHEDRAL
TAKADANOBABA
Sekiguch
Takadanobaba
Waseda Dōri
Nishi-Waseda
Totsu-kamachi
WASEDA UNIV.
Waseda-Tsurumakichō
Higashi Dōri
Yamanote Saikyō Line
SHINJUKU-KITA P.O.
Toyama Park
WASEDA UNIV.
Baba-Shitachō
Wasedamachi
Toyama
WASEDA
Waseda-Minamichō
Enokic
D
Ōkubo
Kikuichō
INT'L MED. CENTER OF JAPAN
Bentenc
Hyakunin-chō
Meiji Dōri
SHINJUKU-KU
Gaien-
SHIN-ŌKUBO
Ōkubo Dōri
Haramachi
1:27000
0 250 500m
Wakamatsuchō
TOKYO WOMEN'S MED. COLL. HOSP.
Shinjuku
Ichi-Yanagichō
Shokuan Dōri

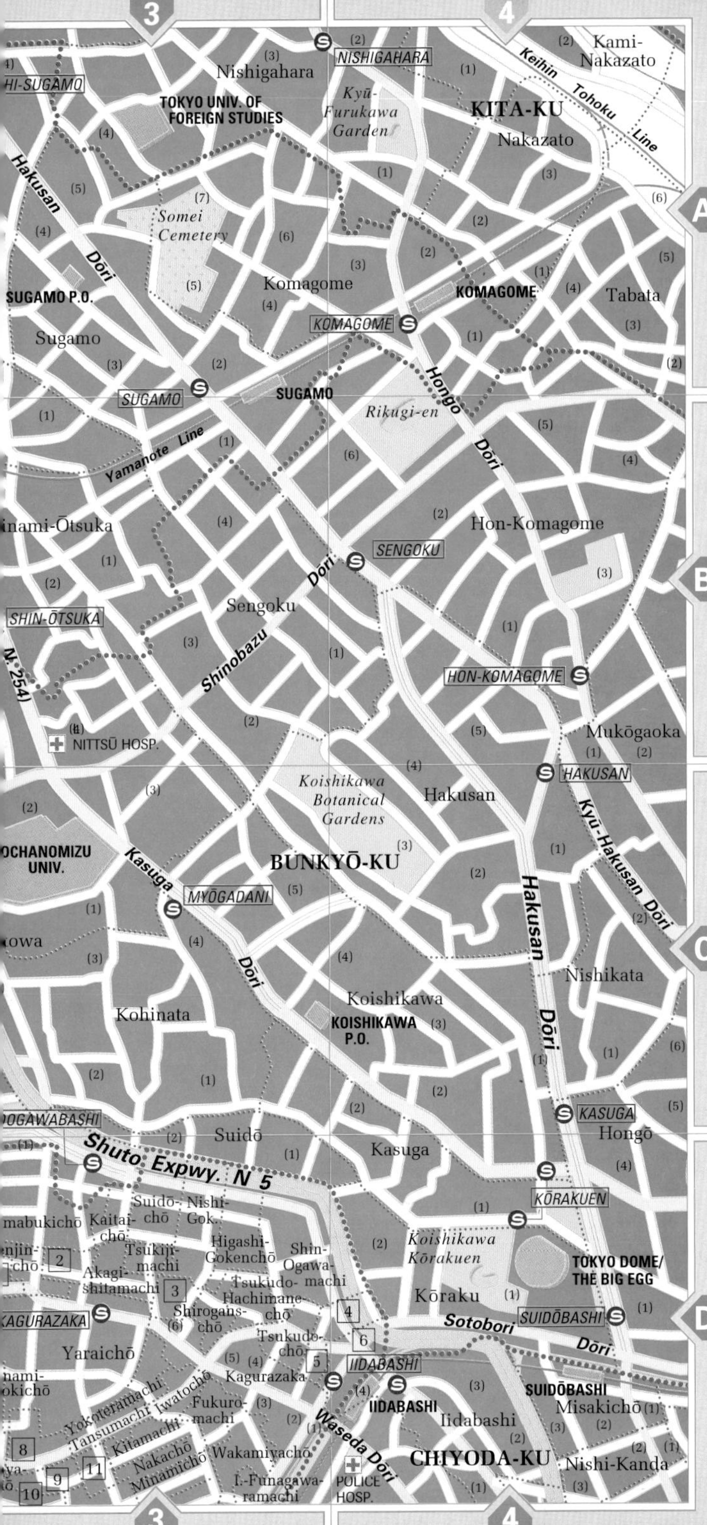

3
4
NISHIGAHARA
Nishigahara
Kami-Nakazato
Keihin Tohoku Line
HI-SUGAMO
TOKYO UNIV. OF FOREIGN STUDIES
Kyū-Furukawa Garden
KITA-KU
Nakazato
Hakusan Dōri
Somei Cemetery
A
Komagome
KOMAGOME
Tabata
SUGAMO P.O.
Sugamo
Hongo Dōri
SUGAMO
Rikugi-en
Yamanote Line
Hon-Komagome
inami-Ōtsuka
SENGOKU
B
Sengoku
SHIN-ŌTSUKA
N. 254
Shinobazu Dōri
HON-KOMAGOME
NITTSŪ HOSP.
Mukōgaoka
HAKUSAN
Koishikawa Botanical Gardens
Hakusan
OCHANOMIZU UNIV.
Kasuga Dōri
BUNKYŌ-KU
Kyū-Hakusan Dōri
MYŌGADANI
Hakusan Dōri
C
Nishikata
Koishikawa
Kohinata
KOISHIKAWA P.O.
KASUGA
OGAWABASHI
Suidō
Hongō
Kasuga
Shuto Expwy. N 5
KŌRAKUEN
Koishikawa Kōrakuen
TOKYO DOME/ THE BIG EGG
Kōraku
KAGURAZAKA
SUIDŌBASHI
D
Sotobori Dōri
Yaraichō
IIDABASHI
Kagurazaka
SUIDŌBASHI
IIDABASHI
Misakichō
Iidabashi
Waseda Dōri
Wakamiyachō
CHIYODA-KU
Nishi-Kanda
POLICE HOSP.

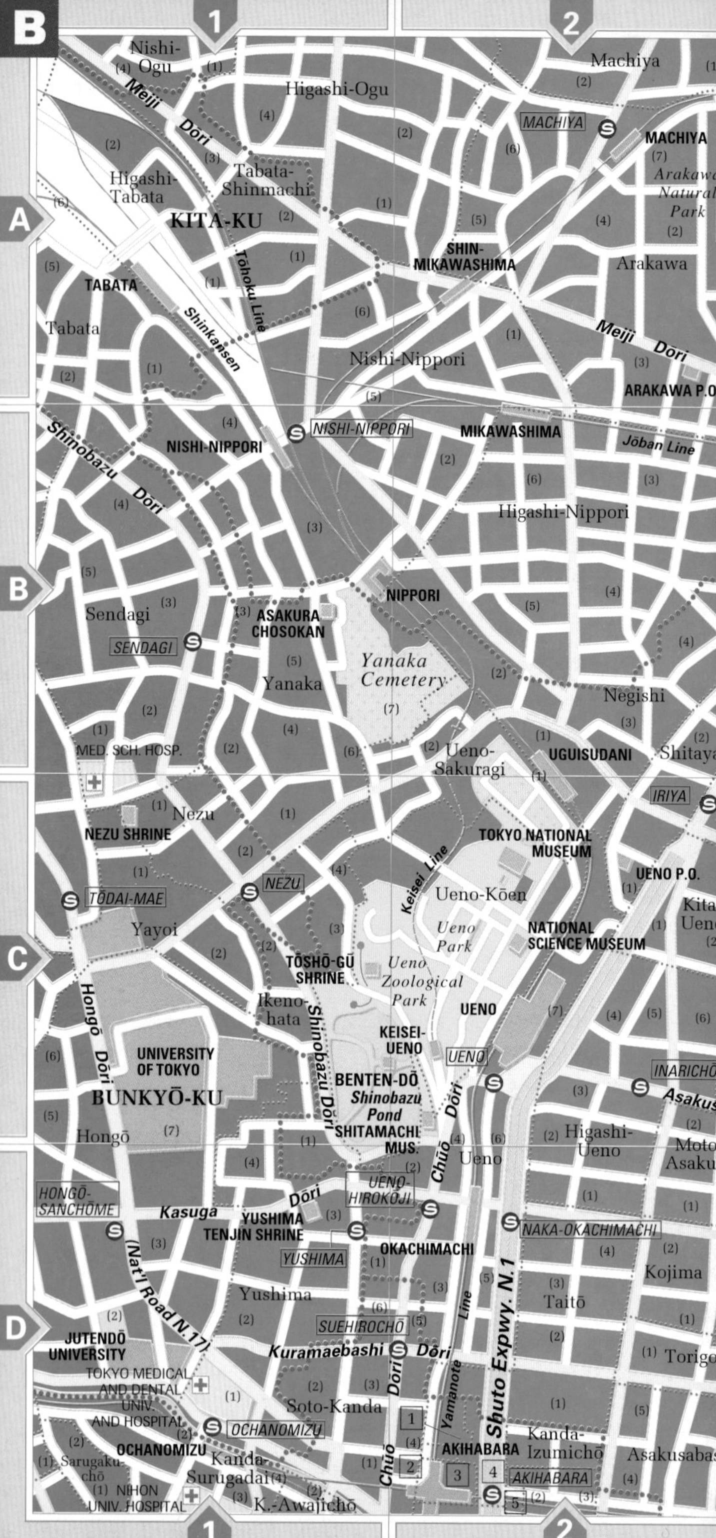
B
1
2
A
B
C
D
Nishi-Ogu
Meiji Dōri
Higashi-Ogu
Machiya
MACHIYA
MACHIYA
Arakawa Natural Park
Higashi-Tabata
Tabata-Shinmachi
KITA-KU
Tōhoku Line
SHIN-MIKAWASHIMA
Arakawa
TABATA
Tabata
Shinkansen
Meiji Dōri
Nishi-Nippori
ARAKAWA P.O.
NISHI-NIPPORI
MIKAWASHIMA
Jōban Line
Shimobazu Dōri
NISHI-NIPPORI
Higashi-Nippori
NIPPORI
Sendagi
ASAKURA CHOSOKAN
SENDAGI
Yanaka Cemetery
Yanaka
Negishi
MED. SCH. HOSP.
Ueno-Sakuragi
UGUISUDANI
Shitaya
IRIYA
Nezu
NEZU SHRINE
TOKYO NATIONAL MUSEUM
UENO P.O.
Keisei Line
NEZU
TŌDAI-MAE
Ueno-Kōen
Kita-Ueno
Yayoi
Ueno Park
NATIONAL SCIENCE MUSEUM
TŌSHŌ-GŪ SHRINE
Ueno Zoological Park
Ikeno-hata
Shinobazu Dōri
UENO
Hongō Dōri
UNIVERSITY OF TOKYO
KEISEI-UENO
UENO
INARICHŌ
BUNKYŌ-KU
BENTEN-DŌ
Shinobazu Pond
Asakusa
Chūō Dōri
SHITAMACHI MUS.
Hongō
Higashi-Ueno
Moto-Asakusa
Ueno
UENO-HIROKŌJI
HONGŌ-SANCHŌME
Kasuga Dōri
YUSHIMA TENJIN SHRINE
NAKA-OKACHIMACHI
OKACHIMACHI
YUSHIMA
(Nat'l Road N.17)
Kojima
Yushima
Taitō
SUEHIROCHŌ
Shuto Expwy. N.1
Yamanote Line
JUTENDŌ UNIVERSITY
Kuramaebashi Dōri
Torigoe
TOKYO MEDICAL AND DENTAL UNIV. AND HOSPITAL
Soto-Kanda
Chūō Dōri
OCHANOMIZU
Kanda-Izumichō
OCHANOMIZU
AKIHABARA
Asakusabashi
Sarugaku-chō
Kanda-Surugadai
AKIHABARA
NIHON UNIV. HOSPITAL
K.-Awajichō

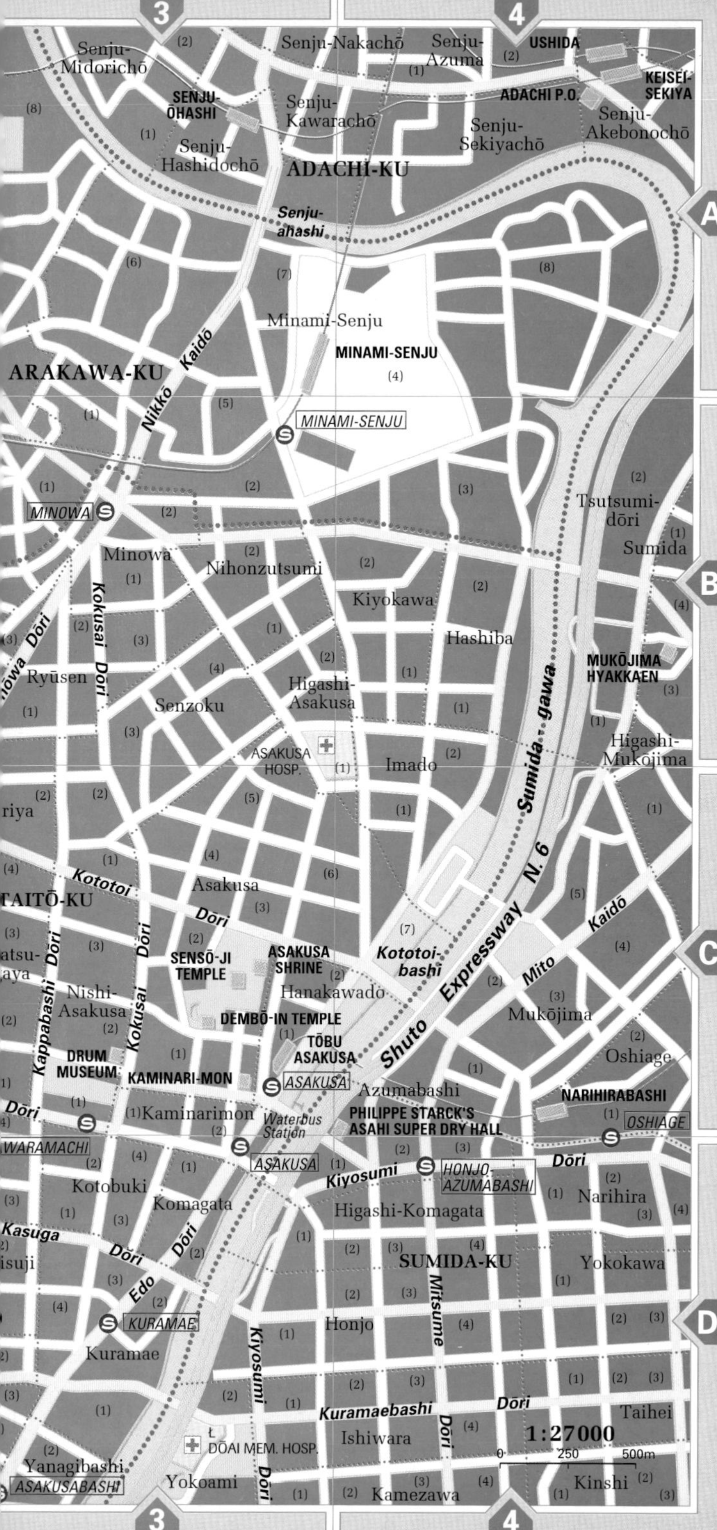

Senju-Midorichō
Senju-Nakachō
Senju-Azuma
USHIDA
KEISEI-SEKIYA
ADACHI P.O.
SENJU-ŌHASHI
Senju-Kawarachō
Senju-Sekiyachō
Senju-Akebonochō
Senju-Hashidochō
ADACHI-KU
Senju-ohashi
Minami-Senju
MINAMI-SENJU
ARAKAWA-KU
Nikkō Kaidō
MINAMI-SENJU
MINOWA
Tsutsumi-dōri
Sumida
Minowa
Nihonzutsumi
Kiyokawa
Kokusai Dōri
Hashiba
Ryūsen
MUKŌJIMA HYAKKAEN
Higashi-Asakusa
Senzoku
ASAKUSA HOSP.
Imado
Higashi-Mukojima
Sumida-gawa
Kototoi
TAITŌ-KU
Asakusa
Dōri
N. 6
Mito Kaidō
Kappabashi Dōri
Kokusai Dōri
SENSŌ-JI TEMPLE
ASAKUSA SHRINE
Kototoi-bashi
Shuto Expressway
Nishi-Asakusa
Hanakawadō
Mukōjima
DEMBŌ-IN TEMPLE
TŌBU ASAKUSA
Oshiage
DRUM MUSEUM
KAMINARI-MON
ASAKUSA
Azumabashi
NARIHIRABASHI
Dōri
Kaminarimon
Waterbus Station
PHILIPPE STARCK'S ASAHI SUPER DRY HALL
OSHIAGE
WARAMACHI
ASAKUSA
Kiyosumi
HONJO-AZUMABASHI
Dōri
Kotobuki
Komagata
Narihira
Higashi-Komagata
Kasuga Dōri
Edo Dōri
SUMIDA-KU
Yokokawa
Mitsume
KURAMAE
Honjo
Kiyosumi
Kuramae
Kuramaebashi
Dōri
Taihei
DŌAI MEM. HOSP.
Ishiwara
1:27000
0
250
500m
Yanagibashi
ASAKUSABASHI
Yokoami
Kamezawa
Kinshi
3
4
A
B
C
D

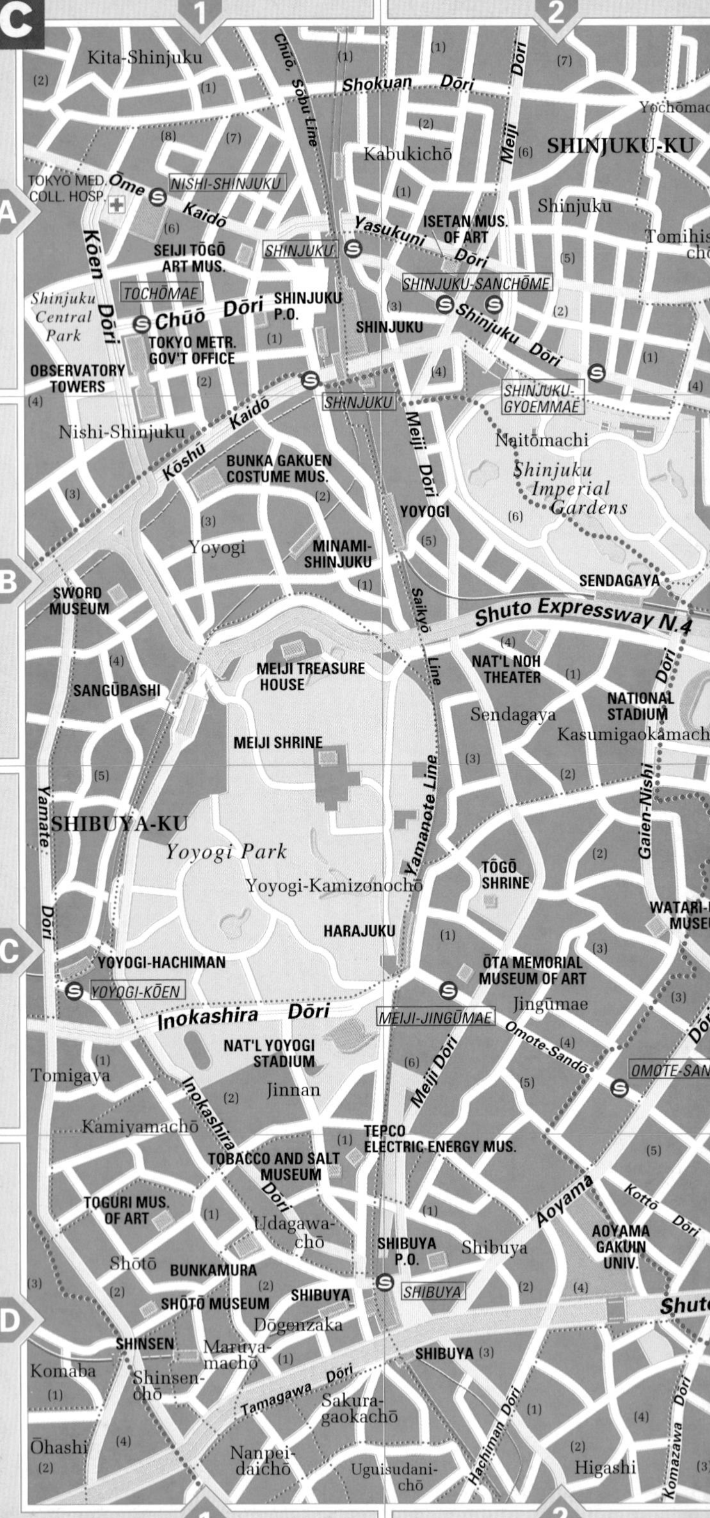
C
SHINJUKU-KU
SHIBUYA-KU
Kita-Shinjuku
Kabukichō
Shinjuku
Nishi-Shinjuku
Yoyogi
Naitōmachi
Shinjuku Imperial Gardens
Shinjuku Central Park
Sendagaya
Kasumigaokamachi
Yoyogi Park
Yoyogi-Kamizonochō
Jingūmae
Tomigaya
Jinnan
Kamiyamachō
Udagawa-chō
Shibuya
Shōtō
Dōgenzaka
Maruya-machō
Komaba
Shinsen-chō
Ōhashi
Sakura-gaokachō
Nanpei-daichō
Uguisudani-chō
Higashi
Yochōmachi
Tomihisa-chō
Shokuan Dōri
Meiji Dōri
Chūō Sobu Line
Ōme Kaidō
Yasukuni Dōri
Shinjuku Dōri
Kōen Dōri
Chūō Dōri
Kōshū Kaidō
Saikyō Line
Shuto Expressway N.4
Yamanote Line
Gaien-Nishi Dōri
Yamate Dōri
Inokashira Dōri
Omote-Sandō
Aoyama Dōri
Kottō Dōri
Tamagawa Dōri
Hachiman Dōri
Komazawa Dōri
Shuto
TOKYO MED. COLL. HOSP.
SEIJI TŌGŌ ART MUS.
ISETAN MUS. OF ART
SHINJUKU P.O.
TOKYO METR. GOV'T OFFICE
OBSERVATORY TOWERS
BUNKA GAKUEN COSTUME MUS.
MINAMI-SHINJUKU
YOYOGI
SENDAGAYA
SWORD MUSEUM
SANGŪBASHI
MEIJI TREASURE HOUSE
NAT'L NOH THEATER
NATIONAL STADIUM
MEIJI SHRINE
TŌGŌ SHRINE
WATARI-UM MUSEUM
HARAJUKU
ŌTA MEMORIAL MUSEUM OF ART
YOYOGI-HACHIMAN
NAT'L YOYOGI STADIUM
TEPCO ELECTRIC ENERGY MUS.
TOBACCO AND SALT MUSEUM
TOGURI MUS. OF ART
AOYAMA GAKUIN UNIV.
SHIBUYA P.O.
BUNKAMURA
SHŌTŌ MUSEUM
SHIBUYA
SHINSEN
SHINJUKU
NISHI-SHINJUKU
TOCHŌMAE
SHINJUKU-SANCHŌME
SHINJUKU-GYOEMMAE
YOYOGI-KŌEN
MEIJI-JINGŪMAE
OMOTE-SANDŌ
A
B
D
1
2

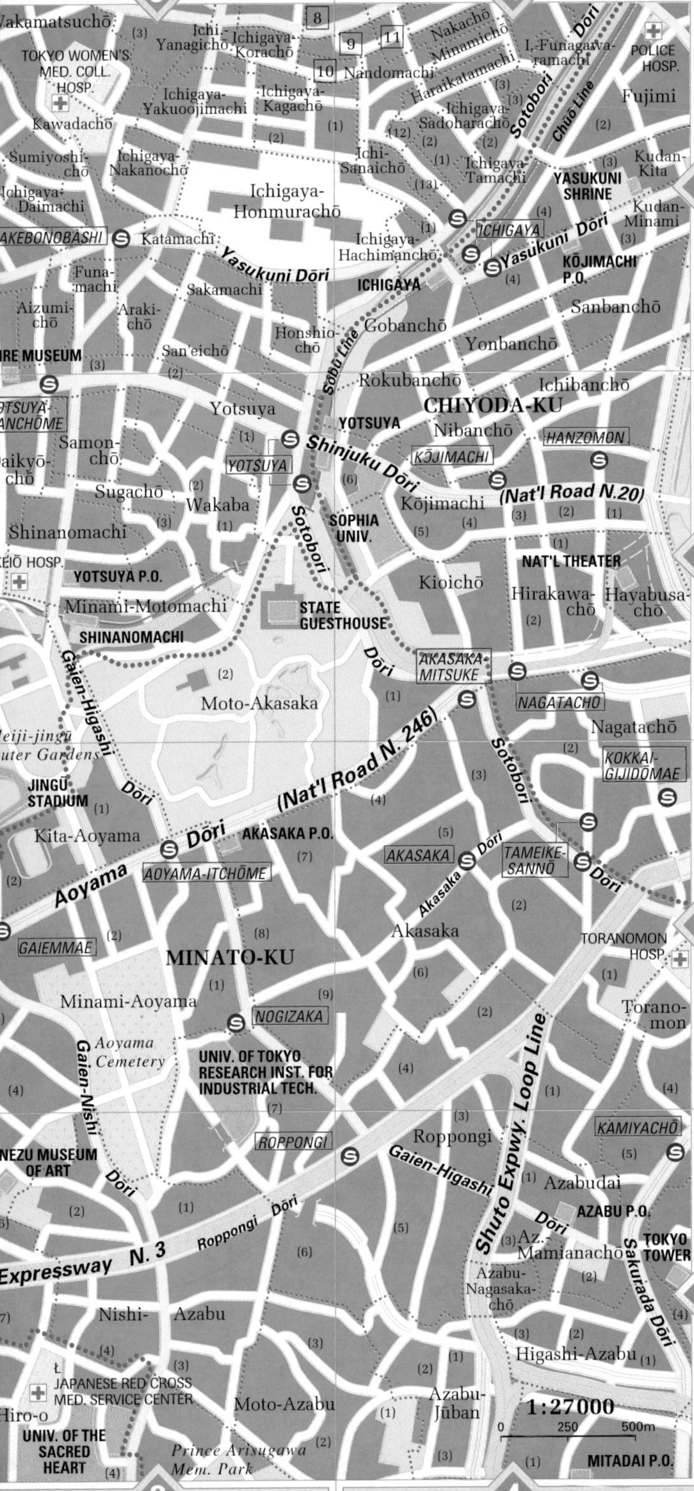
3
4
A
B
C
D
TOKYO WOMEN'S MED. COLL. HOSP.
Ichigaya-Honmurachō
AKEBONOBASHI
Yasukuni Dōri
ICHIGAYA
YASUKUNI SHRINE
POLICE HOSP.
Sotobori Dōri
Chūō Line
Sōbu Line
KŌJIMACHI P.O.
CHIYODA-KU
YOTSUYA
Shinjuku Dōri
(Nat'l Road N.20)
HANZOMON
KŌJIMACHI
SOPHIA UNIV.
NAT'L THEATER
YOTSUYA P.O.
SHINANOMACHI
STATE GUESTHOUSE
AKASAKA-MITSUKE
NAGATACHO
Moto-Akasaka
Meiji-jingū Outer Gardens
Gaien-Higashi Dōri
JINGŪ STADIUM
(Nat'l Road N. 246)
Aoyama Dōri
AKASAKA P.O.
AOYAMA-ITCHŌME
AKASAKA
TAMEIKE-SANNŌ
KOKKAI-GIJIDŌMAE
Akasaka Dōri
GAIEMMAE
MINATO-KU
TORANOMON HOSP.
NOGIZAKA
Aoyama Cemetery
UNIV. OF TOKYO RESEARCH INST. FOR INDUSTRIAL TECH.
Gaien-Nishi Dōri
Shuto Expwy. Loop Line
ROPPONGI
KAMIYACHŌ
NEZU MUSEUM OF ART
AZABU P.O.
TOKYO TOWER
Expressway N. 3
Roppongi Dōri
Sakurada Dōri
Nishi-Azabu
Higashi-Azabu
JAPANESE RED CROSS MED. SERVICE CENTER
Moto-Azabu
Azabu-Jūban
1:27000
0 250 500m
UNIV. OF THE SACRED HEART
Prince Arisugawa Mem. Park
MITADAI P.O.

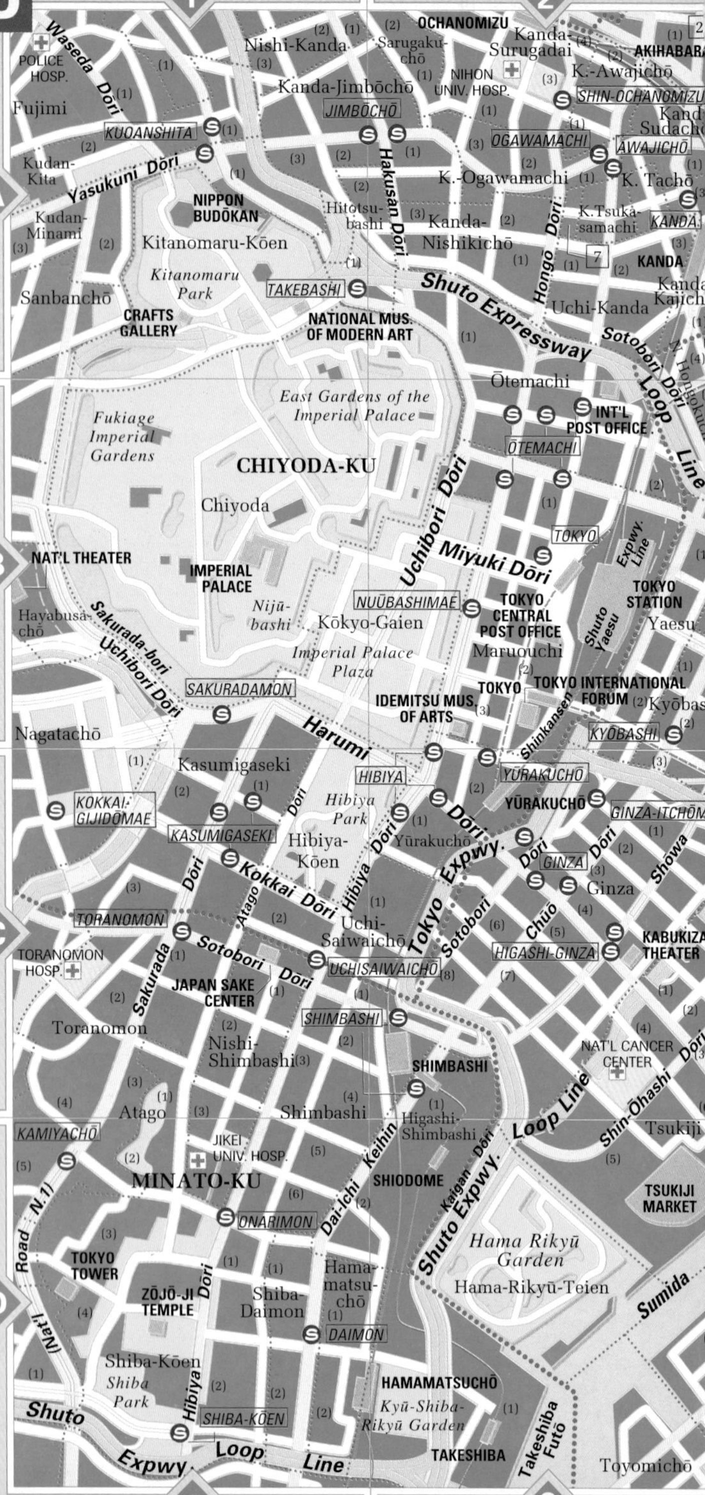

D
1
2
A
B
C
D
OCHANOMIZU
Nishi-Kanda
Sarugaku-chō
Kanda-Surugadai
AKIHABARA
POLICE HOSP.
Waseda Dōri
NIHON UNIV. HOSP.
K.-Awajichō
Kanda-Jimbōchō
JIMBŌCHŌ
SHIN-OCHANOMIZU
Fujimi
KUDANSHITA
OGAWAMACHI
AWAJICHŌ
Kudan-Kita
Yasukuni Dōri
Hakusan Dōri
K.-Ogawamachi
K. Tachō
NIPPON BUDŌKAN
Hitotsu-bashi
Kanda-Nishikichō
K.Tsuka-samachi
KANDA
Kudan-Minami
Kitanomaru-Kōen
Hongo Dōri
Kitanomaru Park
TAKEBASHI
Shuto Expressway
Sanbanchō
Uchi-Kanda
CRAFTS GALLERY
NATIONAL MUS. OF MODERN ART
Sotobori Dōri
Ōtemachi
Loop
East Gardens of the Imperial Palace
INT'L POST OFFICE
Fukiage Imperial Gardens
ŌTEMACHI
Line
CHIYODA-KU
Chiyoda
TOKYO
Uchibori Dōri
Miyuki Dōri
Expwy. Line
NAT'L THEATER
IMPERIAL PALACE
NUŪBASHIMAE
TOKYO CENTRAL POST OFFICE
TOKYO STATION
Hayabusa-chō
Nijū-bashi
Kōkyo-Gaien
Shuto Yaesu
Yaesu
Sakurada-bori
Imperial Palace Plaza
Maruouchi
Uchibori Dōri
TOKYO
TOKYO INTERNATIONAL FORUM
SAKURADAMON
IDEMITSU MUS. OF ARTS
Shinkansen
Kyōbas
Nagatachō
Harumi
KYŌBASHI
Kasumigaseki
YŪRAKUCHŌ
HIBIYA
KOKKAI-GIJIDŌMAE
Hibiya Park
YŪRAKUCHŌ
GINZA-ITCHŌM
Dōri
KASUMIGASEKI
Hibiya-Kōen
Yūrakuchō
GINZA
Kokkai Dōri
Hibiya Dōri
Tokyo Expwy.
Ginza
Shōwa
Atago
Uchi-Saiwaichō
Sotobori
Chūō
TORANOMON
KABUKIZA THEATER
Sotobori Dōri
HIGASHI-GINZA
TORANOMON HOSP.
UCHISAIWAICHŌ
Sakurada
JAPAN SAKE CENTER
SHIMBASHI
Toranomon
Nishi-Shimbashi
NAT'L CANCER CENTER
SHIMBASHI
Atago
Shimbashi
Higashi-Shimbashi
Loop Line
Shin-Ōhashi Dōri
KAMIYACHŌ
JIKEI UNIV. HOSP.
Tsukiji
Keihin
Kaigan Dōri
MINATO-KU
SHIODOME
TSUKIJI MARKET
Dai-Ichi
ONARIMON
Shuto Expwy.
Road N.1
Hama Rikyū Garden
TOKYO TOWER
Hama-matsu-chō
Hama-Rikyū-Teien
ZŌJŌ-JI TEMPLE
Dōri
Shiba-Daimon
Sumida
DAIMON
Shiba-Kōen
Shiba Park
HAMAMATSUCHŌ
(Nat'l
Hibiya
Kyū-Shiba-Rikyū Garden
Shuto
SHIBA-KŌEN
Takeshiba Futō
Expwy
Loop
Line
TAKESHIBA
Toyomichō

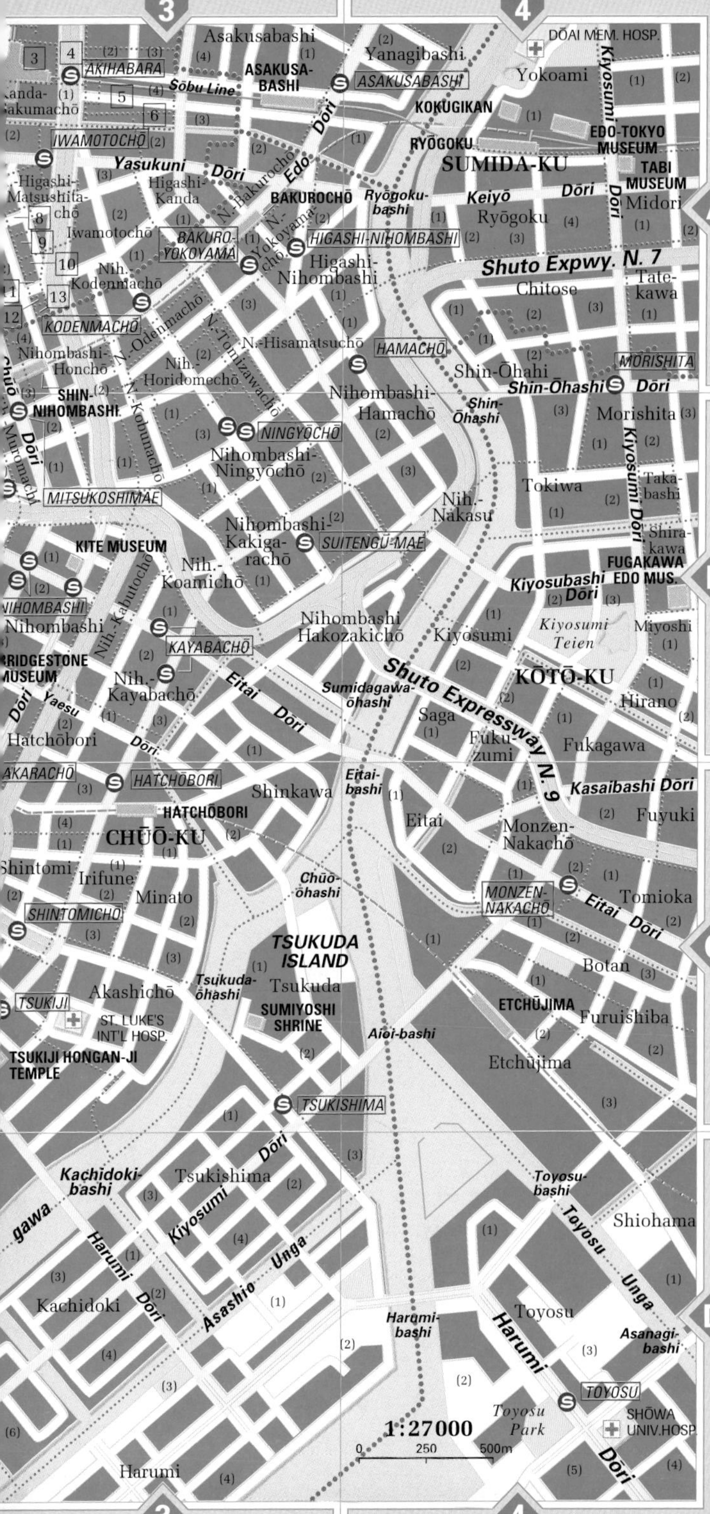

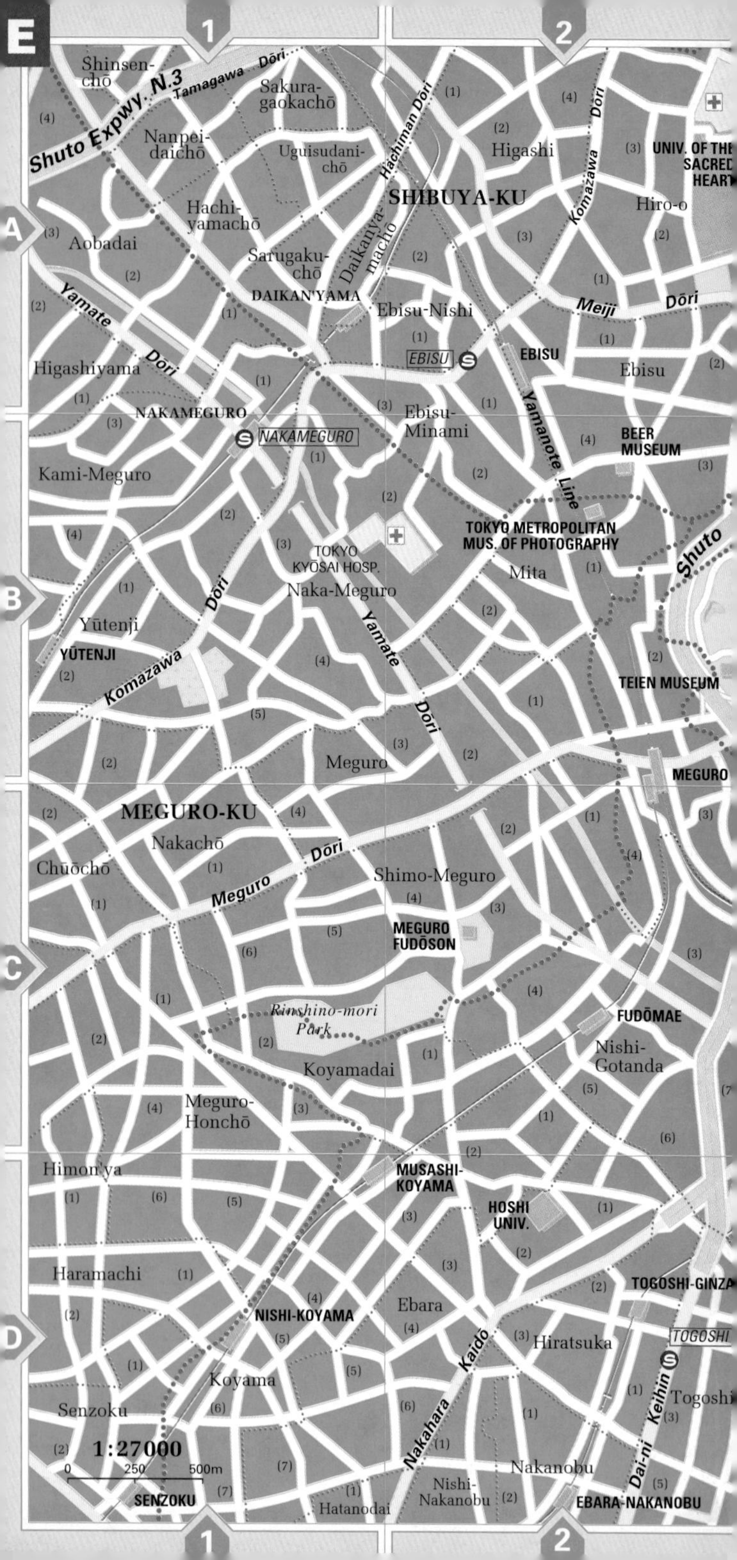

E

1
2

Shinsen-chō
Shuto Expwy. N.3
Tamagawa Dōri
Sakura-gaokachō
Nanpei-daichō
Uguisudani-chō
Hachiman Dōri
Higashi
Komazawa Dōri
UNIV. OF THE SACRED HEART
SHIBUYA-KU
Hiro-o
Hachi-yamachō
Aobadai
Daikanya-machō
Sarugaku-chō
DAIKAN'YAMA
Ebisu-Nishi
Meiji Dōri
Yamate Dōri
EBISU
Ebisu
Higashiyama
NAKAMEGURO
Ebisu-Minami
Yamanote Line
BEER MUSEUM
Kami-Meguro
TOKYO METROPOLITAN MUS. OF PHOTOGRAPHY
TOKYO KYŌSAI HOSP.
Naka-Meguro
Mita
Shuto
Yūtenji
YŪTENJI
Komazawa Dōri
Yamate Dōri
TEIEN MUSEUM
Meguro
MEGURO
MEGURO-KU
Nakachō
Chūōchō
Meguro Dōri
Shimo-Meguro
MEGURO FUDŌSON
Rinshino-mori Park
FUDŌMAE
Nishi-Gotanda
Koyamadai
Meguro-Honchō
Himon'ya
MUSASHI-KOYAMA
HOSHI UNIV.
Haramachi
TOGOSHI-GINZA
NISHI-KOYAMA
Ebara
Hiratsuka
TOGOSHI
Nakahara Kaidō
Koyama
Keihin
Togoshi
Senzoku
1:27000
0 250 500m
Nakanobu
Dai-ni
Nishi-Nakanobu
Hatanodai
SENZOKU
EBARA-NAKANOBU

A
B
C
D

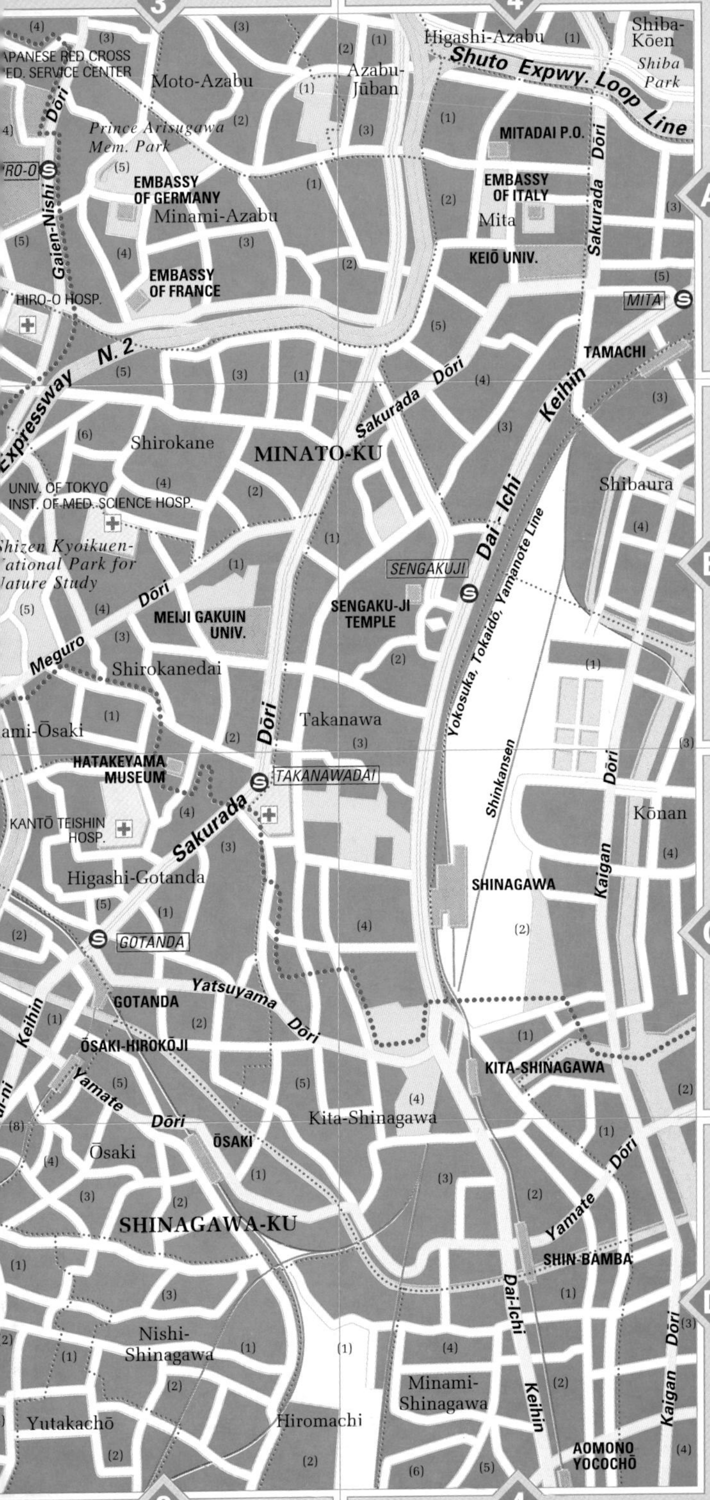

3
4
Moto-Azabu
Azabu-Jūban
Higashi-Azabu
Shiba-Kōen
Shiba Park
Shuto Expwy. Loop Line
Prince Arisugawa Mem. Park
MITADAI P.O.
EMBASSY OF GERMANY
EMBASSY OF ITALY
Minami-Azabu
Mita
Sakurada Dōri
Gaien-Nishi Dōri
EMBASSY OF FRANCE
KEIŌ UNIV.
HIRO-O HOSP.
MITA
A
Expressway N. 2
TAMACHI
Keihin
Sakurada Dōri
Shirokane
MINATO-KU
Shibaura
UNIV. OF TOKYO INST. OF MED. SCIENCE HOSP.
Dai-Ichi
B
SENGAKUJI
Yokosuka, Tokaidō, Yamanote Line
Meguro Dōri
MEIJI GAKUIN UNIV.
SENGAKU-JI TEMPLE
Shirokanedai
Takanawa
HATAKEYAMA MUSEUM
TAKANAWADAI
Shinkansen
Kaigan Dōri
Kōnan
KANTŌ TEISHIN HOSP.
Sakurada
Higashi-Gotanda
SHINAGAWA
C
GOTANDA
GOTANDA
Yatsuyama Dōri
Keihin
ŌSAKI-HIROKŌJI
KITA-SHINAGAWA
Yamate Dōri
Kita-Shinagawa
ŌSAKI
Ōsaki
Yamate Dōri
SHINAGAWA-KU
SHIN-BAMBA
D
Dai-Ichi Keihin
Nishi-Shinagawa
Minami-Shinagawa
Kaigan Dōri
Yutakachō
Hiromachi
AOMONO YOCOCHŌ
3
4

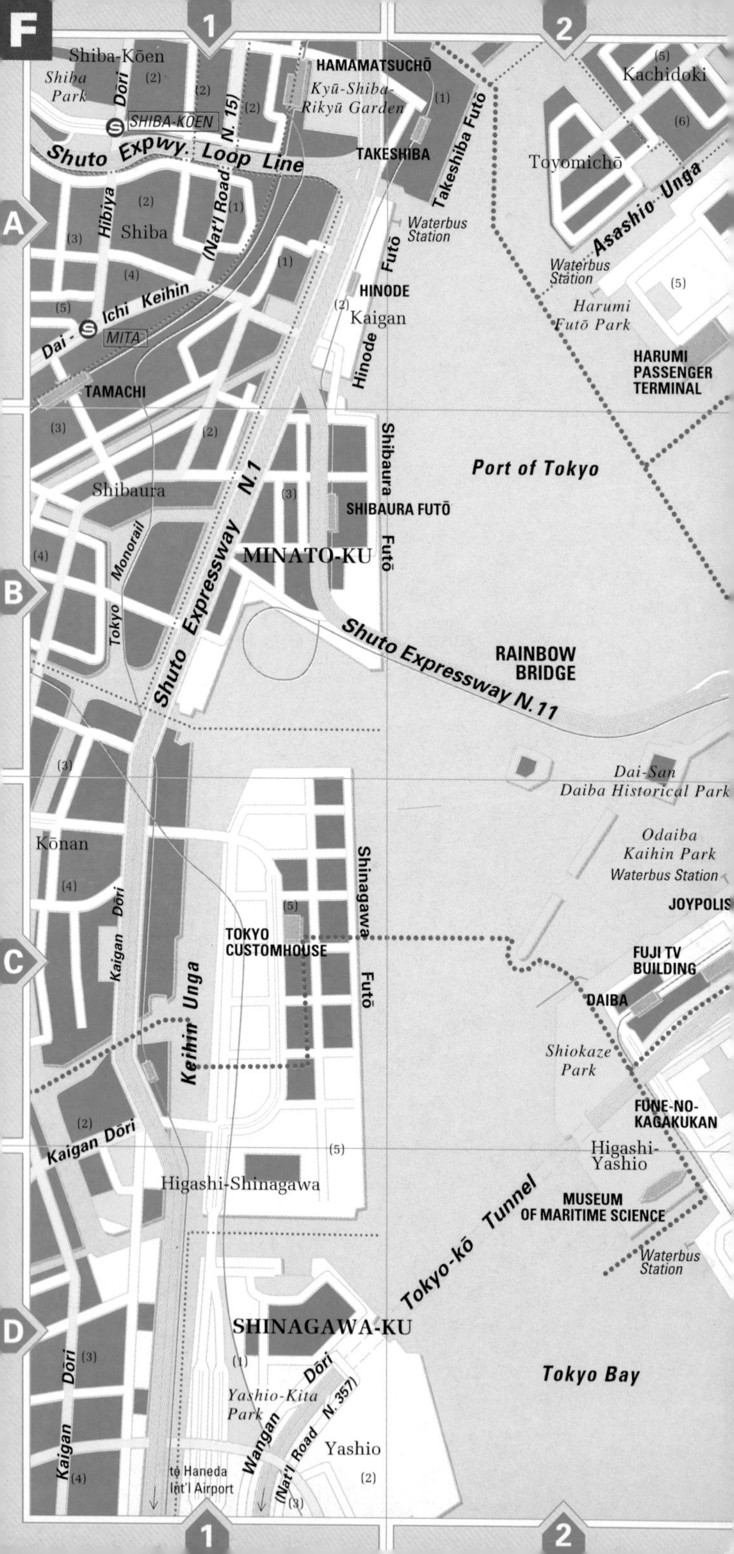

F
Shiba-Kōen
Shiba Park
Dōri
SHIBA-KOEN
HAMAMATSUCHŌ
Kyū-Shiba-Rikyū Garden
TAKESHIBA
Takeshiba Futō
Kachidoki
Toyomichō
Shuto Expwy. Loop Line
(Nat'l Road N. 15)
Hibiya
Shiba
Waterbus Station
Asashio Unga
Dai-Ichi Keihin
MITA
HINODE
Kaigan
Hinode Futō
Harumi Futō Park
HARUMI PASSENGER TERMINAL
TAMACHI
Shibaura Futō
Port of Tokyo
Shibaura
Shuto Expressway N.1
SHIBAURA FUTŌ
MINATO-KU
Tokyo Monorail
Shuto Expressway N.11
RAINBOW BRIDGE
Dai-San Daiba Historical Park
Kōnan
Odaiba Kaihin Park
Shinagawa Futō
JOYPOLIS
Kaigan Dōri
TOKYO CUSTOMHOUSE
FUJI TV BUILDING
DAIBA
Keihin Unga
Shiokaze Park
FUNE-NO-KAGAKUKAN
Higashi-Yashio
Higashi-Shinagawa
Tokyo-kō Tunnel
MUSEUM OF MARITIME SCIENCE
SHINAGAWA-KU
Tokyo Bay
Yashio-Kita Park
Wangan Dōri
(Nat'l Road N. 357)
Yashio
to Haneda Int'l Airport

3
4
A
B
C
D
CHŪŌ-KU
Harumi
TOYOSU
Toyosu Park
SHŌWA UNIV.HOSP.
Harumi Dōri
Shinonome-bashi
Toyosu
Harumi Futō
Harumi Unga
Toyosu Futō
Shinonome
Shinonome Unga
KŌTŌ-KU
SHINONOME
Shuto Expressway Wangan Line (National Road N. 357)
ARIAKE COLOSSEUM
Ariake Tennis-no-mori Park
KOKUSAI-TENJIJŌ
ARIAKE
Ariake
FASHION TOWN
ODAIBA KAIHIN - KŌEN
Wangan Dōri
KOKUSAI-TENJIJŌ-SEIMON
TOKYO BIG SIGHT
TOKYO TELEPORT
Center Promenade
PALETTE TOWN TOKYO
AOMI
Aomi
West Promenade
TELECOM CENTER
TOKYO FERRY TERMINAL
1:27000
0 250 500m

For each *ku*, *chō*, street or subway station, the letter in bold refers to one of the maps (**A–F**), and the letters and numbers mark the grid reference.

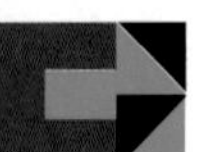

Index
of the *ku*, *chō* and streets

For practical and other information, as well as useful contact numbers concerning travel and life in Tokyo, see the 'Getting there' section on pages 6–15.

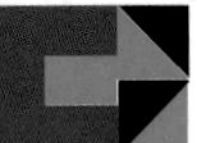

General Index

Thanks to Sophie Paris, to Amicie d'Avout of the Japanese Tourist Office in Paris, and to all the establishments presented in this guide for their cooperation.

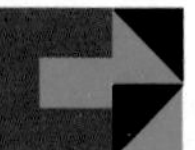

Picture Credits

1 and cover ill. Jean-Marie Guillou
6 Gallimard / Sophie Lenormand
8-9 Gallimard / Sophie Lenormand, JNTO (shinkansen train)
10-11 Gallimard / Sophie Lenormand, JNTO (JR train, vending machines)
12-13 S. Paris (earthquake notice board, telephone), JNTO (kiosk, money), Gall. / S. Lenormand (koban), Gall. / P. Léger (magazines)
14-15 15 Hoaqui / Martel, 16 Diaf / Ben Simmons, 17 and 18 Scope / J. Marthelot,
16 Park Hyatt Hotel
19 1 Kimi Ryokan, 5 Ryokan Asakusa Shigetsu
21 8 Kokusai Kanko Hotel, 9 Tōkyō Station Hotel
23 13 Sumisho Hotel, 14 Royal Park Hotel
25 15 Hotel Seiyo Ginza, 16 Imperial Hotel
27 22 Capitol Tokyū Hotel, 23 Ōkura Hotel, 25 ANA Hotel Tōkyō
29 29 Park Hyatt Hotel, 31 The Century Hyatt, 32 Keio Plaza Inter-Continental Hotel
31 34 Arimax Hotel Shibuya and Gall/Sophie Lenormand (sign), 35 Shibuya Tōbū Hotel
33 39 Takanawa Prince Hotel Sakura Tower, 40 Takanawa Prince Hotel, 44 New Takanawa Prince Hotel
35 46 Hotel Edmont, 47 Tōkyō International Youth Hostel, 48 Hill Top Hotel, 49 Fairmont Hotel, 51 Tōkyō YMCA
37 53 Hotel Nikko Tōkyō
38 Akasaka Rikyū
40-41 1-10 JNTO, except 9 Isehiro (yakitori dish) and 7 Suziya (tonkatsu dish)
43 3 Mikawa, 4 Gall. / S. Lenormand, 5 Isehiro
45 6 Kitcho, 9 Gall. / S. Lenormand, 10 Aux Amis des Vins / Yasui Susumy
47 13 Gall. / Sophie Lenormand, 14 Asyoka / B. Simmons, 16 Gorio, 17 L'Osier, 19 Gall. / S. Lenormand
49 20 Gall. / Sophie Lenormand, 22 Akasaka Rikyū, 23 Sunaba
51 25 Nichōme-Uoshin, 26 Trattoria Valdarno, 29 Gall. / S. Lenormand
53 31 Gall. / Sophie Lenormand, 32 Tempra Uoshin, 33 Nodaiwa
55 37 Gall. / Sophie Lenormand, 38 Waketokuyama, 39 Bistrot de la Cité
57 40 Gall. / Sophie Lenormand, 41 Hong-Kong Garden, 42 Gall. / S. Lenormand
59 44 Dynasty-Ocho / Hilton Tōkyō, 45 Gall. / S. Lenormand, 48 Nakajima, 49 Gall. / S. Lenormand
61 51 Dai-ichi jingu, 52 Sophie Paris, 53 Hachiku
63 59 Katsuyoshi, 60 Château Restaurant Taillevent-Robuchon
65 62 La Chèvre, 63 Namiki Yabusoba, 64 Gall. / S. Lenormand
66 Club 99 Gaspanic
69 1 Kanze Nō Theater, Kanze Nō goku-do, 2 National Theater-Kokuritsu Gekijo / JNTO, 3 Kakubi-za / JNTO, 4 National Nō Theater, 6 Tōkyō Opera City, 8 Suntory Hall
71 13 Kazoo, 14 Salsa Sudada, 16 Club 99 Gaspanic
73 18 Wa-on
75 26 Body and Soul, 28 Tōkyō Blue Note
77 Roppongi, Kabuki-chō, Shinjuku-ku Gall. / S. Lenormand, Kabuki-chō and Shinjuku-ku / Sophie Paris
79 38 Mandala
80 Gallimard / Sophie Lenormand (Hanozono-jinja)
82 1 Sophie Paris, 9 JNTO, 18 Gallimard / Sophie Lenormand, 25 Sophie Paris, 34 Ōta Memorial Museum, 43 Tōkyō Metropolitan Museum of Photography, 48 Sophie Paris, 52 Sophie Paris, 57 JNTO, 61 JNTO
84-85 1 Sophie Paris, 2 JNTO 4 Sophie Paris
87 9 JNTO, 10 Idemitsu Museum of Art
89 13 Sophie Paris, 14 Bridgestone Museum, 15 Tōkyō International Forum, 16 Kabuki-za
91 17 Gall./Sophie Lenormand and Sophie Paris (detail), 20 Gall./Sophie Lenormand
93 Sophie Paris
95 26 Seiji Tōgō Memorial Yasuda Kasai Museum, 28 Shinjuku Imperial Gyoen, 29 Bunka Gakuen Costume Museum
97 32 JNTO and Sophie Paris (int.-ext. view), 33 Watari-um Museum, 34 Ukiyo-e Ōte Memorial Museum
99 37 TEPCO Electric Energy Museum, 38 Tobacco & Salt Museum, 40 Shōtō Museum of Art, 41 Bunkamura
101 42 Yebisu Beer Museum and Gallimard/Sophie Lenormand (statue), 43 Tōkyō Museum of Photography / TMP, 44 Gall. / P. Léger, 45 Tōkyō Metropolitan Teien Art Museum
103 48 Sophie Paris, 51 Sword Museum, 52 Sophie Paris, 54 Kite Museum
105 56 Sophie Paris, 57 JNTO, 58 S. Paris, 59 JNTO
107 61 JNTO, 63 Sophie Paris, 64 Sophie Paris, 65 Gall. / S. Lenormand
109 68 JNTO, 70 Fuji TV , 72 Sophie Paris
110-111 72 Sophie Paris, 73 JNTO, 74 JNTO (sports) and S. Paris (ext.)
117 2 Narita-san, 4 Disneyland / © Disney, 5 Tourist office Chiba
119 7 Yokohama Maritime Museum, 9 DIAF / Ben Simmons 10 Sankei-en
121 13 Kamakura Museum of Modern Art, 15 JNTO
123 17 Hakone Tourist Office, 18 JNTO, 19 Hakone Open-Air Museum, 21 Hakone Tourist Office
126-127 2 Gallimard /P. Léger, 3 Hoaqui/S. Grandadam (int.) and Scope/Jacques Marthelot (ext.), 4 Hoaqui/G. Boutin, 5 Gall./S. Lenormand
129 10 Gallimard / Sophie Lenormand, 12 Sembikiya, 13 Kyukyodo
131 15 Axis, 16 Naniwaya, 17 Mamegen, 18 Kogado
133 22 Daily Catch, 23 Washi Kobo, 24 Tohkyō
135 25 Thorin-do, 27 Comme des garçons, 29 Gallimard / Sophie Lenormand
137 30 Inden-ya and Gallimard / Sophie Lenormand (detail), 31 On Sundays / Watari-um, 32 Gall. / S. Lenormand, 33 Muji
139 37 Kiddy Land, 41 Hachiku
143 49 Gallimard / Sophie Lenormand, 50 Hanae Mori Antique Market, 51 JNTO and Gall. / Sophie Lenormand (stall)
145 55 Gallimard / Sophie Lenormand, 56 New Shimazu,
147 58 Gallimard / Sophie Lenormand, 62 Gall./S. Lenormand, 64 Gall/S. Lenormand
148 Gallimard / Sophie Lenormand